Dr Peter Nockles at Nazarene Theological College graduation, Whitworth Hall, University of Manch

BULLETIN OF THE JOHN RYLANDS LIBRARY

Religion in Britain, 1660–1900: Essays in Honour of Peter B. Nockles

Guest Editors: William Gibson and Geordan Hammond

BULLETIN OF THE JOHN RYLANDS LIBRARY

ISSN 2054-9318 (Print)
ISSN 2054-9326 (Online)

Established in 1903

Members of the Editorial Board 2021

Chair: Andrew Morrison
Editors: Stephen Mossman and Cordelia Warr
Editorial Assistant: Jessica Coatesworth

Editorial Board
Hannah Barker
Joseph Bergin
Paul Fouracre
Roy Gibson
John Hodgson
David Law
Phyllis Mack
David Matthews
John Morgan
Walter Pohl
Lynda Pratt
Julianne Simpson
Carsten Timmermann

Subscriptions

To subscribe please contact: Manchester University Press Journals Subscriptions, J Floor, Renold Building, University of Manchester, Altrincham Street, Manchester, M1 7JA, UK
Tel: +44 (0)161 275 2310
manchesterhive@manchester.ac.uk
https://www.manchesterhive.com/view/journals/bjrl/bjrl-overview.xml

The *Bulletin* is published twice a year. The subscription prices for 2021 are:
Institutions (print and online) £205/$310/€240
Institutions (online only) £169/$249/€195
Individual (print only) £69/$105/€79

The complete archive of the *Bulletin of the John Rylands Library*, from its first issue in 1903 to Volume 80 (1998) is now available to purchase from Manchester University Press. The archive complements the current subscription product (1999 to date), and can be purchased on a one-time basis or as an annual subscription. To obtain pricing information, please contact Shelly Turner at shelly.turner@manchester.ac.uk.

BULLETIN OF THE JOHN RYLANDS LIBRARY

VOLUME 97 NUMBER 1, SPRING 2021

Religion in Britain, 1660–1900: Essays in Honour of Peter B. Nockles

CONTENTS

Introduction *William Gibson and Geordan Hammond*	1

Articles

Engines of Tyranny: The Court Sermons of James II *William Gibson*	11
Engraved Clerical Portraiture in England, c. 1660–1850: An Introductory Survey *Richard Sharp*	25
Thomas Townson and High Church Continuities and Connections in Eighteenth-Century England *Nigel Aston*	53
George Horne, the Hutchinsonian *Derya Gurses Tarbuck*	71
Relational Reading and Imagined Religious Community in Catherine Livingston's Evangelical Spirituality *Rachel Cope*	83
Disappearing Women: The Gendered Politics of Publication of Mary Fletcher's Auto/Biography *Carol Blessing*	97
Seductive Splendour and Caricatured Simplicity: Catholicism and Nonconformity in Nineteenth-Century 'Jewish Conversion' Novels *Andrew Crome*	111
The Spirituality of the Wesleyan Methodists of Brunswick Chapel, Leeds, in the Victorian Era *David Bebbington*	129

Dissolving the 'Sacred Union'? The Disestablishment of the Church in Ireland 145
Stewart J. Brown

Continuity and Development: Looking for Typological Treasure with William Jones of Nayland and E. B. Pusey 161
George Westhaver

Henry Manning's Journey to Roman Catholicism 179
Kenneth Parker

'Am I my brother's keeper?' Cardinal Manning and the Jewish People 195
James Pereiro

Introduction

WILLIAM GIBSON, OXFORD BROOKES UNIVERSITY
GEORDAN HAMMOND, MANCHESTER WESLEY RESEARCH CENTRE
AND NAZARENE THEOLOGICAL COLLEGE

Peter Benedict Nockles was an undergraduate between 1972 and 1975, then graduate student at Worcester College, Oxford, and subsequently at St Cross College, Oxford, between 1976 and 1982, when he was awarded a DPhil for his research.[1] His thesis was supervised by Geoffrey Rowell, chaplain and fellow of Keble College, and later bishop of Gibraltar in Europe. Jeremy Gregory, who in his doctoral studies was researching the Church of England before 1829, writes of this period:

> Peter's thesis confirmed that religious history before that date was much more nuanced and far richer than the conventional labels ('High [and Dry]', 'Low Church', 'Evangelical') allowed, and that George Horne, one of the deans of Canterbury I was studying, was an important (but neglected) figure in Anglican theology. As I completed my thesis, Peter was a source of good advice and we both contributed to a number of what turned out to be seminal publications in the 1990s.

Peter's thesis was admired and widely consulted and, urged on by his examiner John Walsh, he produced a significantly revised and extended version of it as a monograph. Entitled *The Oxford Movement in Context: Anglican High Churchmanship, 1760–1857*, it was published by Cambridge University Press in 1994. It was a book that was widely anticipated; numerous books and articles had cited the thesis before it was published. *The Oxford Movement in Context* is one of those groundbreaking books that it is difficult to imagine being without. Bringing to life such little-known figures as Edward Churton, Hugh James Rose and William Palmer of Worcester College, it shows how High Churchmanship did not disappear between the Nonjurors in the eighteenth century and the Tractarians in the nineteenth, nor was it asleep. It was alive and well; scholars had simply overlooked it. This revisionist rehabilitation of Anglican High Churchmanship provides the context for Peter's thematic analysis of the historical and theological continuities and discontinuities between it and the Oxford Movement. Peter's landmark study won deserved praise from reviewers. What especially stands out in the reviews is the consensus that the book is impressively detailed, along with similar descriptions about it being meticulous, thorough and methodical. Reviewers also often commended it as being convincing and persuasive.[2]

In 1975, Peter spent a year at the Bodleian as an archival trainee. In 1979, he was appointed as an assistant librarian at the John Rylands University Library of Manchester, responsible initially for cataloguing. He was also the English and History subject librarian. In 1987, he moved to be the assistant librarian in Special Collections at the John Rylands Library in Deansgate and in 1990, became the librarian in charge of the Methodist Church Archives at the Rylands. Jeremy Gregory recalls:

> I got to know Peter well when I moved to the University of Manchester in 2000 and I remember his generosity in showing me round the John Rylands Library, Deansgate, on the morning before my interview. A key rationale for my post was to make the early Methodist collections at the Rylands better used and I was extraordinarily fortunate to be able to have Peter on the supervisory teams for several of the outstanding doctoral students who came to work on these sources in the 2000s. Peter, Gareth Lloyd, and I collaborated on the conference celebrating the tercentenary of John Wesley's birth in 2003.

From 2010 to 2016 Peter was librarian in Rare Books and Maps in Special Collections, with responsibility for all theological book collections. He retired from the Rylands in 2016. In his retirement he has retained his strong and long-standing connection with the University of Manchester's Religions and Theology Department, where he is an Honorary Research Fellow, and also with Nazarene Theological College in Didsbury, Manchester. Peter's professional life has been one of dedication and service to the scholarly community. There can be few Methodist scholars, or indeed scholars of religious history more generally, who have used the collections at the Rylands, who do not owe a considerable debt to Peter's quiet and unassuming support and encouragement. His frequent offers of 'have you seen this?' and suggestions of 'we also have this, which you might wish to see' have brought material to numerous researchers that they would not otherwise have found. This is why his name appears in so many of the acknowledgements pages of books on Methodist and religious history. Jeremy Gregory notes:

> There was always something slightly ironic, if not faintly amusing, that Peter, one of the leading scholars of the High Church Anglican establishment, was the custodian of the Methodist Church Archives, though in truth, as Peter's own publications demonstrate, there was more overlap and influence between these, and particularly in early Methodism, than has often been recognised.

Peter's long-time librarian colleague and friend Bill Simpson worked in the John Rylands University Library of Manchester from the time Peter first arrived there up to the mid-1980s, returning as University Librarian and Director of the John Rylands Library from 2002 to 2007. Regarding his early interactions with Peter, Bill commented that he found him a pleasant and unassuming colleague who wore his great learning and scholarship lightly in his everyday dealings with readers and fellow members of staff. He writes: 'I suspect that most of his colleagues were, in fact, largely unaware of the scholarly reputation that he was already building even at that early stage in his career. My recollection is really of a quiet young man who went about his daily tasks helpfully and with diligence and commitment in the role that had been assigned to him and which did not, at least initially, allow him a great deal of scope for the use of his academic expertise in his working life.'

By the time he returned to the Rylands, Bill noted that

> Peter had become well established and hugely respected both as a scholar and as a research librarian based in the historic John Rylands Library. He was, and still is, a man of great integrity and generosity, a devout Christian who has given freely of his time and expertise to both established scholars and young researchers alike, who has done a vast amount to enhance the reputation of the Rylands as a centre for research into the history of Methodism and who has been a valued colleague and friend to a large number of people in the Library, in the University of Manchester, and in the wider world of academic life.

Jeremy Gregory regards Peter as one of the increasingly rare breed of scholar-librarians:

> Peter's career and publications stand firmly in the tradition of the 'scholar-librarian', a post which sometimes sits uneasily with modern university librarians being at the forefront of Information Services, Digital Technology, and Public Engagement. But, as in Peter's case, the scholar-librarian can be crucial in making the riches of the collections of which they are guardians well known, both to academics and the wider public, and can be a seamless link between the sources they curate and the scholars who study them.

In addition to his professional role as a librarian, Peter, himself a Roman Catholic, has been a dedicated scholar of the Oxford Movement and the religious history of the eighteenth and nineteenth centuries, including Anglicanism, Catholicism, Methodism and Nonconformity. He has held visiting fellowships at Oriel College, Oxford; the University of Lund; and the University of Notre Dame. Alongside this Peter developed strong library and scholarly links with the Bridwell Library at Perkins School of Theology, Southern Methodist University; Point Loma Nazarene University; and Asbury Theological Seminary and Asbury University. These relationships and Peter's academic research – he has given papers in a number of countries including Sweden, Italy, France, Germany, the Netherlands and the United States – have connected his library and scholarly lives with his love for travel. Peter's standing as a scholar of John Henry Newman has meant that he has been asked to speak at conferences and seminars all over the world. He has sat on around a dozen doctoral and master's supervision panels and has served as an external examiner over a dozen times at several different universities. Besides contributing sixteen articles to the *Oxford Dictionary of National Biography*, and reviewing manuscripts for an enormously wide range of journals, he has undertaken some of the more abstruse tasks of academic life, such as question-setting for the BBC Radio 4 programme *Mastermind* in 1999. He has also been an indefatigable book reviewer, whose judgement is always sure-footed.

Peter has been a voluminous contributor to collections of essays. He contributed two essays to the history of Oriel College and one to the history of Worcester College.[3] He has also edited and co-edited a number of collections of essays.[4] Most recently he has been one of the co-editors of the *Oxford Handbook of the Oxford Movement*.[5]

In 2020, Peter was awarded the prestigious Gailliot Award by the National Institute for Newman Studies in the United States in recognition of a lifetime achievement in promoting and advancing the study of the life, writings and influence of Newman.

Peter is known for his extraordinary generosity with his time given to supporting scholarly and academic organisations. He has been a conference organiser and council member of the Catholic Record Society; a trustee of the Andrew Duncan Trust and the Catholic National Library. He has served on the committees and advisory boards of a wide range of organisations including the Church of England Record Society, the Historic Libraries Forum, Religious Archives Group, the Methodist Church Archives and History Committee, the Manchester Wesley Research Centre, and the Oxford Centre for Methodism and Church History, and has long been a valued member of the Ecclesiastical History Society.

This volume is an expression of thanks for the scholarly generosity and friendship extended by Peter for over three decades to researchers at the John Rylands Library and in his many professional and personal connections with scholars of early modern and modern religious history. A one-volume *Festschrift* cannot do justice to the range of Peter's scholarly specialisms, nor can it provide space for articles from many of his friends who would want to honour him with an article in a volume dedicated to him. Despite these limitations, we trust that this *Festschrift* is a fitting tribute to Peter's scholarship and friendship. With articles on a range of topics relating to the Church of England (particularly High Churchmanship and the Oxford Movement), Catholicism, Methodism, and even Church–state conflict relating to the Church of Ireland, this issue of the *Bulletin* can be considered broadly representative of Peter's scholarship and scholarly networks.

In honour of Peter's prodigious scholarly contributions, a select bibliography of his published work is provided in the following section.

The Principal Published Writings of Peter B. Nockles[6]

'Saint John Henry Newman: Anglican and Catholic', *International Journal for the Study of the Christian Church*, 20:2 (2020), pp. 98–109.

'The Current State of Newman Scholarship', *British Catholic History*, 35:1 (2020), 105–27.

'The Oxford Movement', in Frederick D. Aquino and Benjamin J. King (eds), *The Oxford Handbook of John Henry Newman* (Oxford: Oxford University Press, 2018), pp. 7–27.

'Pre-Tractarian Oxford: Oriel and the Noetics', 'Conflicts in Oxford: Subscription and Admission of Dissenters, Hampden Controversy, University Reform', 'Histories and Anti-Histories', in Stewart J. Brown, Peter B. Nockles and James Pereiro (eds), *The Oxford Handbook of the Oxford Movement* (Oxford: Oxford University Press, 2017), pp. 79–93, 123–36, 605–21.

'Newman's Tractarian Receptions', in Frederick D. Aquino and Benjamin J. King (eds), *Receptions of Newman* (Oxford: Oxford University Press, 2015), pp. 137–55.

'The Oxford Movement and Evangelicalism: Parallels and Contrasts in Two Nineteenth-Century Movements of Religious Revival', in Robert Webster (ed.), *Perfecting Perfection: Essays in Honor of Henry D. Rack* (Eugene, OR: Pickwick Publications, 2015), pp. 233–59.

'The Reformation Revised? The Contested Reception of the English Reformation in Nineteenth-Century Protestantism', in Peter B. Nockles and Vivienne Westbrook (eds), *Reinventing the Reformation in the Nineteenth Century: A Cultural History*, Bulletin of the John Rylands Library, 90:1 (2014), 231–56.

'Worcester College and the Oxford Movement', in Jonathan Bate and Jessica Goodman (eds), *Worcester: Portrait of an Oxford College* (London: Third Millennium Publications, 2014), pp. 58–67.

'Oriel and Religion, 1800–1833' and 'A House Divided: Oriel in the Era of the Oxford Movement, 1833–1860', in Jeremy Catto (ed.), *Oriel College: A History* (Oxford: Oxford University Press, 2013), pp. 291–327 and 328–70.

'Introduction', 'The Oxford Movement in an Oxford College: Oriel as the Cradle of Tractarianism', 'The Oxford Movement and the United States', in Peter B. Nockles and Stewart J. Brown (eds), *The Oxford Movement: Europe and the Wider World, 1830–1930* (Cambridge: Cambridge University Press, 2012), pp. 1–8, 11–33, 133–50.

'Oriel College and the Making of John Henry Newman', in *Newman et la civilisation britannique: Actes du colloque international de l'ICES, avec le participation de l'Association Française des Amis de Newman, La Roche-sur-Yon, 24 Novembre, 2011*, Etudes Newmaniennes 28 (Paris: Ad Solem, 2012), pp. 15–40.

'Reactions to Robert Southey's *Life of John Wesley* (1820) Reconsidered', *Journal of Ecclesiastical History*, 63:1 (2012), 61–80.

The Oxford Movement and the United States of America (London: Anglo-Catholic History Society, 2012), 16 pp.

'The Making of a Convert: John Henry Newman's Oriel and Littlemore Experience', *Recusant History*, 30:3 (2011), 461–83.

'The Nineteenth Century Reception', *The Acts and Monuments Online* [TAMO], John Foxe's Protestant Martyrology (Sheffield, HRI Online Publications, 2011): www.johnfoxe.org/index_realm_more_gototype_modern_type_essay_book_essay9.html.

'"Emissaries of Babylon" or "Brothers in Christ"? Charles Wesley and Anti-Catholicism', *Wesley and Methodist Studies*, 2 (2010), 3–23.

'The Changing Legacy and Reception of John Foxe's "Book of Martyrs" in the "Long Eighteenth Century": Varieties of Anglican, Protestant and Catholic Response, c. 1760–c. 1850', in Robert D. Cornwall and William Gibson (eds), *Religion, Politics and Dissent, 1660–1832: Essays in Honour of James E. Bradley* (Farnham: Ashgate, 2010), pp. 219–47.

'The Oxford Movement and the Legacy of Anglican Evangelicalism', in Joris van Eijnatten and Paula Yates (eds), *The Dynamics of Religious Reform in Church, State and Society Northern Europe, 1780–1920. II: The Churches* (Leuven: Leuven University Press, 2010), pp. 53–66.

'Das Oxford Movement und das Vermächtis des Anglischen Evangelikalismus. Religiöse Reform in der Church of England des frühen 19 Jahrhunderts', in Claus Arnold, Bernd Trocholepczy and Knut Wenzel (eds), *John Henry Newman: Kirchenlehrer der Moderne* (Freiburg im Breisgau: Herder, 2009), pp. 25–53.

'Oriel and the Making of John Henry Newman – His Mission as College Tutor', *Recusant History*, 29:3 (2009), 411–21. An earlier version of this article was published in the *Oriel College Record* (2008), 44–51.

'The Changing Legacy of John Foxe's Book of Martyrs: Varieties of Protestantism and Anti-Catholicism', in Kathryn Duncan (ed.), *Religion in the Age of Reason: A Transatlantic Study of the Long Eighteenth Century* (New York: AMS Press, 2009), pp. 211–25.

'The Oxford Movement and its Historiographers: Brilioth's "Anglican Revival" and "Three Lectures on Evangelicalism and the Oxford Movement" Revisited', in Michel Desjardins and Harold Remus (eds), *Tradition and Formation: Claiming an Inheritance. Essays in Honour of Peter C. Erb* (Kitchener, Ontario: Pandora Press, 2008), pp. 173–93. An earlier version of this article was published in *Kyrkohistorisk Årsskrift*, 106 (2006), 132–42.

'The Oxford Movement as Religious Revival and Resurgence', in Kate Cooper and Jeremy Gregory (eds), *Revival and Resurgence in Christian History*, Studies in Church History, 44 (Woodbridge: Boydell Press, 2008), pp. 214–24.

'Charles Wesley, Catholicism and Anti-Catholicism', in Kenneth G. C. Newport and Ted A. Campbell (eds), *Charles Wesley: Life, Literature and Legacy* (Peterborough: Epworth Press, 2007), pp. 141–65.

'Newman and Oxford', in Philippe Lefebvre and Colin Mason (eds), *John Henry Newman in His Time* (Oxford: Family Publications, 2007), pp. 21–46.

'Recreating the History of the Church of England: Bishop Burgess, the Oxford Movement and Nineteenth-Century Reconstructions of Protestant and Anglican Identity', in Nigel Yates (ed.), *Bishop Burgess and his World: Culture, Religion and Society in Britain, Europe and North America in the Eighteenth and Nineteenth Centuries* (Cardiff: University of Wales Press, 2007), pp. 233–89.

'The Oxford Movement', in Jonathan Hill (ed.), *The New Lion Handbook: The History of Christianity* (Oxford: Lion Hudson, 2007), p. 366.

'The Wilkinson Lecture, 2006: "Floreat Vigornia!": Worcester College and the Oxford Movement', *Worcester College Record* (2007), 63–88.

'Anglicanism "Represented" or "Misrepresented"? The Oxford Movement, Evangelicalism, and History: The Controversial Use of the Caroline Divines in the Victorian Church of England', in Sheridan Gilley (ed.), *Victorian Churches and Churchmen: Essays Presented to Vincent Alan McClelland*, Catholic Record Society: Monograph Series (Woodbridge: Boydell & Brewer, 2005), pp. 308–69.

'The Waning of Protestant Unity and Waxing of Anti-Catholicism? Archdeacon Daubeny and the Reconstruction of "Anglican" Identity in the Later Georgian Church, c. 1780–c. 1830', in William Gibson and Robert G. Ingram (eds), *Religious Identities in Britain, 1660–1832* (Aldershot: Ashgate, 2005), pp. 179–230.

The Oxford Dictionary of National Biography, H. C. G. Matthew and Brian Harrison (eds), 60 vols (Oxford: Oxford University Press, 2004 and www.oxforddnb.com/): articles on Richard Bagot, John Bowdler, Richard Lynch Cotton, George Croft, Charles Daubeny, Ashurst Turner Gilbert, Alexander Knox, Thomas Lathbury, Henry Handley Norris, William Patrick Palmer, Edward Pearson, Henry John Rose, Hugh James Rose, William Stevens, Joshua Watson, Samuel Wix.

'"Survivals or New Arrivals"? The Oxford Movement and the Nineteenth-Century Construction of Anglicanism', in Stephen Platten (ed.), *Anglicanism and the Western Christian Tradition: Continuity, Change and the Search for Communion* (Norwich: Canterbury Press, 2003), pp. 144–91.

'A Disputed Legacy: Anglican Historiographies of the Reformation from the Era of the Caroline Divines to that of the Oxford Movement', *Bulletin of the John Rylands Library*, 83:1 (2001), 121–67.

'Introduction' to a new edition of Christopher Dawson's 1933 *Spirit of the Oxford Movement and Newman's Place in History* (London: Saint Austin Press, 2001), pp. xv–xxxiv.

'Anglicanism' and 'Horsley, Samuel (1733–1806)', in Iain McCalman, *An Oxford Companion to the Romantic Age: British Culture, 1776–1832* (Oxford: Oxford University Press, 1999), pp. 406–7 and 548–9.

'Church or Protestant Sect? The Church of Ireland, High Churchmanship, and the Oxford Movement, 1822–1869', *Historical Journal*, 41:2 (1998), 457–93.

'"The Difficulties of Protestantism": Bishop Milner, John Fletcher and Catholic Apologetic against the Church of England in the Era from the First Relief Act to Emancipation, 1778–1830', *Recusant History*, 24:2 (1998), 193–236.

'"Lost Causes and ... Impossible Loyalties": The Oxford Movement and the University', in M. G. Brock and M. C. Curthoys (eds), *The History of the University of Oxford, Volume VI: Nineteenth-Century Oxford, Part I* (Oxford: Clarendon Press, 1997), pp. 195–267.

Contributor to: F. L. Cross and E. A. Livingstone (eds), *The Oxford Dictionary of the Christian Church*, 3rd edn (Oxford: Oxford University Press, 1997).

'A Review Article: David Newsome, *The Convert Cardinals: John Henry Newman and Henry Edward Manning*', *Anglican and Episcopal History*, 66:1 (1997), 100–6.

'A Review Article: Rowan Strong, *Alexander Forbes of Brechin: The First Tractarian Bishop*', *Anglican and Episcopal History*, 66:3 (1997), 391–9.

'Church and King: Tractarian Politics Reappraised', in Paul Vaiss (ed.), *Newman: From Oxford to the People: Reconsidering Newman and the Oxford Movement* (Leominster: Gracewing, 1996), pp. 93–123.

'"Our Brethren of the North": The Scottish Episcopal Church and the Oxford Movement', *Journal of Ecclesiastical History*, 47:4 (1996), 655–82.

'Sources of English Conversions to Roman Catholicism in the Era of the Oxford Movement' and 'Newman and Early Tractarian Politics', in V. Alan McClelland (ed.), *By Whose Authority? Newman, Manning and the Magisterium* (Bath: Downside Abbey, 1996), pp. 1–40 and 79–111.

'Aspects of Cathedral Life, 1828–1898', in Patrick Collinson, Nigel Ramsay and Margaret Sparks (eds), *A History of Canterbury Cathedral* (Oxford: Oxford University Press, 1995), pp. 256–96.

'The Anglican Newman: A Reappraisal'. Review article: Recent Studies of John Henry Newman, *Anglican and Episcopal History*, 63:1 (1994), 73–86.

The Oxford Movement in Context: Anglican High Churchmanship, 1760–1857 (Cambridge: Cambridge University Press, 1994).

'Church Parties in the Pre-Tractarian Church of England, 1750–1833: The "Orthodox" – Some Problems of Definition and Identity', in John Walsh, Stephen Taylor and Colin Haydon (eds), *From Toleration to Tractarianism: The Church of England, c. 1689–c. 1833* (Cambridge: Cambridge University Press, 1993), pp. 334–59.

'An Academic Counter-Revolution: Newman and Tractarian Oxford's Idea of a University', in Laurence Brockliss (ed.), *History of Universities* 10 (Oxford: Oxford University Press, 1991), pp. 137–97.

'Oxford, Tract 90 and the Bishops', in David Nicholls and Fergus Kerr (eds), *John Henry Newman: Reason, Rhetoric and Romanticism* (Bristol: Bristol Press, 1991), pp. 28–87.

'The Oxford Movement: Historical Background, 1780–1833', in Geoffrey Rowell (ed.), *Tradition Renewed: The Oxford Movement Conference Papers* (London: Darton, Longman & Todd, 1986), pp. 24–50.

'Pusey and the Question of Church and State', in Perry Butler (ed.), *Pusey Rediscovered* (London: SPCK, 1983), pp. 255–97.

Notes

We would like to thank Stewart J. Brown for his helpful comments and suggestions that we have incorporated into this introduction.

1 P. B. Nockles, 'Continuity and Change in Anglican High-Churchmanship in Britain, 1792–1850' (University of Oxford DPhil thesis, 1982).

2 See, in particular, the admiring review article by Boyd Hilton: '*Apologia pro Vitis Veteriorum Hominum*', *Journal of Ecclesiastical History*, 50:1 (1999), 117–30. One indication of the book's ongoing influence is that Google Scholar lists 357 citations of it in books and articles (as of March 2021).

3 'Oriel and Religion, 1800–1833', and 'A House Divided: Oriel in the Era of the Oxford Movement, 1833–1860', in Jeremy Catto (ed.), *Oriel College: A History* (Oxford: Oxford University Press, 2013), pp. 291–370; 'Worcester College and the Oxford Movement',

in Jonathan Bate and Jessica Goodman (eds), *Worcester: Portrait of an Oxford College* (London: Third Millennium Publications, 2014), pp. 58–67.
4 For example, Peter B. Nockles and Vivienne Westbrook (eds), *Reinventing the Reformation in the Nineteenth Century: A Cultural History, Bulletin of the John Rylands Library* 90:1 (2014); Peter B. Nockles and Stewart J. Brown (eds), *The Oxford Movement: Europe and the Wider World, 1830–1930* (Cambridge: Cambridge University Press, 2012).
5 Stewart J. Brown, Peter B. Nockles and James Pereiro (eds), *The Oxford Handbook of the Oxford Movement* (Oxford: Oxford University Press, 2017).
6 This bibliography does not include dozens of book reviews written by Peter. Details on some of these reviews can be found on his pages on the University of Manchester and Manchester Wesley Research Centre websites.

Engines of Tyranny: The Court Sermons of James II

WILLIAM GIBSON, OXFORD BROOKES UNIVERSITY

Abstract
This article considers the sermons preached by royal chaplains at the court of James II and the organisation of the chapel royal by James as a Catholic organisation. In doing so, it addresses the question of where James's assurance and certainty came from that he was ruling as God wished him to do. The evidence presented here is that James organised his Catholic chapel royal to be a conscious source of guidance and support. His chaplains reciprocated by addressing him as a Catholic king whose duty was to bring to heel a recalcitrant and stubborn people. His chaplains used historical precedent and theological argument to press on James his determination to bring his Protestant subjects to obedience. This is a study of the Catholic milieu of James's court and of the theological impetus behind his rule.

Keywords: James II; Catholicism; chapel royal; sermons; preaching

James II's reign was one of the high watermarks of the influence of religion on politics and constitutional development. The Revolution of 1688 saw the English nation choose their Church over their King. It was a choice that had aftershocks in British politics for decades. James II is not one of Britain's best-loved kings; indeed he must be very low on that list. Equally, he must have felt that his subjects were among the most sullen and stubborn that a king had to face. For historians also, despite some implausible attempts to rehabilitate James as a paragon of religious toleration, he remains a problematic figure. If we consider his political and constitutional methods, it is difficult to contest the Whig view of his reign advocated by Macaulay in 1848.[1] James used the *Godden* v. *Hale* spurious legal case to extract a judgment endorsing his right to suspend laws; he exploited the *quo warranto* proceedings to rig elections to Parliament; he used wholesale dismissals of lords lieutenant, magistrates and militia commanders to punish those who disagreed with him, and evicted all the fellows of Magdalen College, Oxford as punishment for following the statutes of their College.[2]

In short, his methods were those of a tyrant who would brook no opposition. But if James's methods were unprincipled, no one could challenge the sincerity of his aim. James's conversion to Catholicism in 1668 was genuine and he was undoubtedly a pious believer – notwithstanding his persistent predilection for mistresses and the fathering of illegitimate children. It was from his faith that James derived a determination to return England from Anglicanism to the Roman Catholic Church. This was his providential mission. Yet he was singularly unsuccessful in doing so; rather than being greeted with the adulation he expected, his subjects were uncooperative. The nobility grudgingly accepted their expulsion from the county militias, lieutenancies and magistracy rather than convert; the universities risked expulsion and deprivation of fellows rather than concede; and the poor seemed much more attracted by anti-Catholic sermons than by the propaganda of his Jesuit clergy.

In addition James's wife, Mary of Modena, repeatedly experienced miscarriages and stillbirths – between 1674 and 1688 she had ten such pregnancies. As time went on, James became more splenetic and less tolerant. After his army deserted him on Salisbury Plain in November 1688, he suffered a complete mental breakdown with physical symptoms including crippling headaches and severe nosebleeds.

What sustained James during the repeated disappointments of his reign? Undoubtedly, inner conviction played a central part. James certainly believed that he had been chosen by God for a special purpose: why else had he survived the exile of the 1650s, the attempts to exclude him from the throne in the 1670s, the assassination attempt of 1683, and later the Monmouth rebellion of 1685? Surely the hand of Providence was protecting him for a special purpose. A report on the Rye House assassination attempt that he commissioned in his first months as king said as much. The account included the claim that James had been saved 'by God's Providence continually watching over his Majesties and these Nations safety . . . many of the Traytors soon after fell into the Hands of Justice'. James himself was 'deeply sensible he has been now once more preserv'd by the immediate hand of God; and therefore looks on himself afresh obliged to manifest his gratitude to Heaven, by promoting the Glory of his Preserver'. James regarded himself as the recipient of 'divine favour'.[3] More significantly, perhaps, he wanted those who opposed him to 'be convinc'd by that very Providence which used to be their own principal and best-loved argument'.[4] One aspect of James's motivation which has not been fully explored is the influence of the sermons that he heard in the chapels royal, converted in his reign to Catholic chapels. Twenty-eight of the sermons preached before James survived the Revolution and were reprinted, probably as Jacobite propaganda, in 1741.[5]

The sermon culture of the seventeenth century was very strong and, despite repeated injunctions from successive rulers, preachers frequently spoke about the political issues of the day. Indeed, the pulpit was one of the sources for guidance for rulers and ruled. By the time of the Restoration, sermons had become a key part of the burgeoning print culture of the late seventeenth century, supported in part by the right of bishops and the universities to license publications.[6]

The Coronation and the Chapels Royal

Before turning to the Catholic sermons, however, it is important to note that James took the coronation oath to protect the Church of England, but he regarded many Anglican sermons as entirely unacceptable. He often railed at the anti-Catholic preaching of Anglican clergy – and suspended Bishop Henry Compton of London for failing to discipline anti-Catholic preachers. In March 1686, James ordered Anglican bishops to suppress anti-Catholic sermons. A few months later, he established a Licensing Office to sell certificates of dispensation from penal legislation to Protestant Dissenters and Catholics.[7] This seemed to observers to be the start of James ignoring his coronation oath and suspending the Test Act illegally. Tony Claydon claimed that James had a serious problem with sermons. On the one hand he attended few Anglican services during his reign; on the other, he had a large Anglican ecclesiastical household with a full complement of chaplains and preachers, but they delivered their sermons in the chapels royal in which the sovereign's pew was empty.[8]

At James's coronation, his former chaplain, Bishop Francis Turner of Ely, preached an extraordinary sermon which cannot have been welcome to the King. The sermon grappled with a problem that affected many Anglicans: whether James would abuse his power and whether this damaged the nature of the Anglican doctrine of passive obedience to the King.[9] Turner's text for his sermon was the coronation of Solomon in the Book of Chronicles. Turner compared James's and Solomon's coronations because, like Solomon's, James's title was 'firm and good', and 'his people were an obedient people'. But Turner's sermon struck some discordant notes. He asserted that no usurper could expect to 'reign prosperously' and that any questioning of James's claim was dangerous 'else there will be competitors'. Turner went on with discordant similes: he suggested that 'management of the sceptre' had to be as strong as the King's claim, and pointed to the precedents of 'the second Edward and Richard' as kings who had indisputable claims to their thrones but lost them through misgovernment. Drawing attention to these precedents seemed infelicitous. On the issue of the loyalty of subjects, Turner came close to contract theory when he claimed: 'since the wills of men are free, tis confest their leaves must be asked, whether they be happy or no; whether they will obey . . . For want of a people obedient and willing to be ruled by a gentle hand, the best of kings was most vilely cast away.' Turner also argued that people ceased to be good and religious when they rebelled.

He then turned to the issue of James's claim and said that, having been at Charles II's deathbed, he could attest that the King had wanted to be succeeded by his brother. He spoke of the deliverance 'from that abominable Excluding Bill', and warned those who would challenge James: 'take heed of destroying your country to build your own house'. At the end of the badly conceived sermon, Turner's audience must have felt that James's title to the throne was questionable, his peace dependent on his subjects' compliance, and his own success dependent on his wise rule. This cannot have been James's intention in choosing his former chaplain to preach his coronation sermon.[10]

Turner's coronation sermon may be one reason why James so quickly turned to Catholic priests as preachers in the chapels royal. From early in 1685, the chapel royal in St James's Palace was converted to a Catholic place of worship. James continued to hear Anglican sermons there, usually from Tory Anglican clergy who could be relied on to be uncontroversial, including Thomas Ken.[11] But, having dismissed the bishop of London, Henry Compton, as dean of the chapels royal in September 1685, he instituted Catholic masses in the chapel and appointed Catholic priests to preach. The old Whitehall Chapel remained in Anglican use by Princess Anne, but James usually attended Catholic services at St James's Palace, where his Queen, Mary of Modena had her chapel. The chapel royal at St James's Palace, though used by both James and Mary, was principally the Queen's chapel.[12] However, its role was greatly expanded and it was used for sermons, masses, and later for the consecration of Catholic bishops for England. James also worshipped sometimes at Somerset House, where his sister-in-law the dowager Queen, Catherine of Braganza, had a chapel. The provision of Queen Catherine's Catholic chapel at Somerset House, had been agreed in her marriage treaty. As part of this, she established a Benedictine community with priests drawn from various European religious houses. There was also a Franciscan friary next to the chapel which, though technically not part of her household, was overlooked by most and treated as if it was included in the marriage treaty. She also had three Portuguese Catholic chaplains in her service.[13] Queen Catherine's chapel was 'targeted by the Jesuits as a ready way to influence the King and Queen at first hand ... the Chapel thus became a tool in their struggle to re-convert the nation from the top down'.[14] On occasion, James also attended mass at Windsor, at the Spanish ambassador's chapel, or those of Catholic peers, such as Lord Petre at Ingatestone Hall, northeast of London.[15]

James also built a new Catholic chapel at Whitehall Palace in 1685 close to the existing Tudor chapel royal. John Evelyn commented when he saw James's new elaborate Catholic chapel at Whitehall with six or seven Jesuit priests attending and a tabernacle on the altar that he came away 'not believing I should ever have lived to see such things in the K[ing] of England's palace'.[16] James's new chapel royal established a second ecclesiastical hierarchy, including Father Edward Petre as clerk of the closet.[17] James, as Duke of York, had already established a corps of about thirty Jesuit missioners in London; from 1685 this number grew dramatically.[18] The new chapel royal at Whitehall was unmistakably a political statement of James's restoration of a Catholic monarchy.[19] James was forced to disguise the costs of the building and fitting out of the chapel as secret service money to avoid political opposition to it.[20] James also established a Catholic chapel in the Palace of Holyrood House in Edinburgh and spent £8,000 on plate for the celebration of the mass.[21]

Philip Ellis

The first sermon James heard in the chapel royal at St James's was a fortnight after the death of Charles II. The preacher was Philip Ellis, brother of Sir William Ellis who was appointed Secretary of State by James. Ellis was a Catholic convert who had entered the Benedictine order at Douai and had a reputation as a brilliant preacher. He had come to England as preacher-general a few weeks before James's accession. He was soon appointed chaplain by James and came to play an important part in his Catholicising policy. Ellis preached frequently before the King and seven of his sermons were printed at the King's command. In particular he preached an important sermon in November 1686 reassuring English landowners that James had no intention of taking back former monastic lands; Ellis had also persuaded James to appoint the Catholic John Massey as dean of Christ Church, Oxford.[22]

Ellis's sermon on 24 February 1685 was on the three types of sin: sins of ignorance, inadvertence and obduracy. But his specific theme was the preaching of Jonah to convert the Assyrians. It was a parable adapted for the circumstances of the time: Jonah had converted the King of the Assyrians and the King bound his people to comply with Jonah's preaching. But the people were obdurate and in the end Nineveh was destroyed. Ellis was explicit in his meaning: 'But where is it that I speak? Is it not to a Christian Assembly, to a Christian Town, an ancient Theatre of Religion? People will not believe daily experience, will not credit their common sense, will not hearken to their own reason and conviction; but despite of sense, reason, conscience and experience, will still persist in a vain and groundless presumption'.[23] His conclusion was that James should 'not be ashamed to correct and blot out this errata'.[24] This was a clarion call to the King to press on with his Catholicising policies, and the use of Jonah seemed to endorse the right of preachers to address political issues to a monarch. The dangers of a stubborn people who refused to follow their king was the centrepiece of his sermon and it must have been clear that Ellis intended to point out that the alternative to obeying James was national destruction.

A year later, at Easter 1686, Ellis returned to the topic of what should be done about wayward apostates from the Catholic Church. He said the biblical example was to break down idols, in the Old Testament they had 'banish'd the artificers, demolish'd the altars, but also cut down the groves, to efface even the memory of idolatry'.[25] Effacing the memory of the existence of the Church of England was an alarming prospect for the majority of the country. Nevertheless, James ordered that the sermon should be published by his printer, Henry Hills, so that his Anglican subjects could read Ellis's comments.[26] The sermon coincided with an intensive period of prayer and reflection by James, during which he spent many hours with the priests of his chapel and there were reports of conferences with the priests after the prayers.[27] Moreover, James was troubled by the recalcitrant Anglicanism of his people. When touring the country in 1686 and 1687, he sometimes bent to local feeling and allowed the Anglican liturgy to be used when he worshipped because he was told that public opinion would not tolerate the use of the Catholic liturgy.[28]

The tendency of preachers, of all religious denominations, to preach by analogy and parable was a very common practice in the seventeenth and eighteenth centuries, and so it was with the Catholic sermons preached before James.[29] On 25 October 1685, two months after the Duke of Monmouth met his grisly end in a badly botched beheading, the Jesuit John Pearsall preached before James in the chapel royal at St James's Palace.[30] Pearsall preached on the episode from St John's Gospel of a young nobleman who was sick. Pearsall might well have brought Monmouth to the mind of his audience when he referred to 'a rich, noble, young dying prince who lies groaning at death's door ... I wish that the followers of sensuality, who make pleasures their God, live as they were never to die, imagine time to stand and laugh at discourses of another world ... would turn their thoughts hither a little while.' If they were in any doubt, Pearsall added that wealth and position often led to 'restlessness and dissatisfaction'. It led to a sickness of the soul that he warned his audience to avoid.[31]

Ellis's sermon on 1 November 1685, also preached at St James's Palace, was perhaps intended to stiffen James's resolve. It coincided with James's exasperation at the refusal of Parliament to repeal the Test Act, which led to the proroguing of Parliament. Ellis's theme was the invocation of saints, a useful opportunity to advance a distinctively Catholic practice that was often attacked by Anglican preachers. Ellis pointed out that some of James's forebears were among the company of saints: 'many of your Royal Ancestors and mighty predecessors inherit a never fading crown of glory and possess a Kingdom which they do not transmit'. In such a company of saints, Ellis said, 'the red and white roses are twisted in the same garland, the Edwards and the Henrys embrace and the fierce Briton rejoices that the Royal Blood of Scotland runs in English veins'. Ellis emphasised that James's reward for his religion would come in heaven.[32] The sermon seemed designed to enable James to cope with setbacks and to focus on the reward he would receive in heaven rather than the obstructions he faced on earth.

The sermons preached a month later, during Advent 1685, addressed James's political agenda even more explicitly. On 13 December, Ellis preached on the idea of liberty. He said of people that they, 'stand in need of a strong rein to keep you from rushing into an endless series of irregularities and transgressions. And therefore you must be often warned that the rod is upon your back ... God is in the midst of us ... but that we know him not is the specific crime of man, an apostasy that discriminates you from all other creatures.' The demand for liberty, claimed Ellis, led to 'blood revenges, scandalous reflections, black calumnies, shameless commerces and unbridled liberties'.[33] On Christmas day, Thomas Godden preached at the chapel royal at Somerset House on the idea of the law.[34] According to Godden, the law of God required men 'to conform our wills to His, quickly whilst we are in the way of this life, lest at any time ... He delivers us to the judge and the judge to the officer and we be cast into prison.' But God had left a body on earth to guide people in the form of the Church, and the Church's teaching was 'Learn of me to be obedient to your superiors.'[35] The warning was underscored by Ellis on New Year's Day 1685/86 at St James's Palace when he emphasised that humankind was sinful and his particular sin was to disobey God. Godden and Ellis were normalising James's experience: he would naturally face demands for liberty from fallen and sinful men and women and had to rely on the authority of the Church.

Five days later, at Somerset House before Queen Catherine, John Bentham, another Douai alumnus who was a doctor of the Sorbonne, preached on the arrival of the wise men in St Matthew's Gospel.[36] The theme of Bentham's sermon was the rebellious nature of the Jews and their apostasy of the golden calf. Many of his observations were as apt for the case of Anglicans as for Jews: 'To indulge such as once faithfully served him [God], though so unhappy as sometimes to run astray; to bless that race whose ancestors have been loyal, to preserve a country which never wanted some true servants of God, although many failed in their duty, seems worthy a divine bounty.' Bentham went on to suggest that if two servants were equally negligent and undutiful: one who had been turned out of your house but the second who had been part of your family, you would regard the second 'as infinitely more criminal'.[37] It seems likely that many in the chapel royal would have regarded this as equally applicable to Anglicans as to Jews.

Obedience from the Pulpit

By Whitsun 1686, Catholic royal chaplains were getting into their stride and politics became even more explicit in their sermons. William Hall, a Carthusian who had studied at Lisbon and was said to be the best preacher in England, addressed politics in a sermon at Somerset House, in which he made an aside that beasts revolt against their owners because they lack reason.[38] Soon after he was made a chaplain in ordinary to James. But it was Ellis who took these bat-squeaks and amplified them in an explicit attack on those who might oppose James. Obstinacy was, said Ellis, an 'execrable crime', though he indicated that God would forgive those who were rebellious: 'He hath a tender compassion for the most rebellious sinner; and in spite of all provocations, acts of hostility and defacing the beauty of a heart ... the print of his finger still remaining on the creature.' But, he continued: 'If a people should depose their prince, they would commit the foulest, the most unjust and most unchristian action in the world ... but if the giddy multitude proceed to a new election and put up the mortal enemy of their lawful sovereign then 'tis a contempt of [the Holy Ghost].'[39]

The drum of obedience was sounded at almost any opportunity in chapel royal sermons. Thomas Codrington, a particularly well-connected priest who had been secretary to Cardinal Howard in Rome and was personally commissioned by Innocent XI to return England to Catholicism, preached before James in November 1686 on the importance of confession. Codrington recounted the story of the Emperor Charles V who confessed his sins, to which his confessor replied: 'You have confessed the sins of Charles, now confess the sins of Caesar.' Codrington emphasised that while rulers were only accountable to God, 'the subject [was responsible] for his behaviour to those in authority'.[40] Codrington's sermon clearly placed the onus of obedience on both James and his subjects. A week later Philip Ellis touched on the theme of the monarch's duty in a sermon on Herod's imprisonment of John the Baptist. Ellis denounced Herod's corrupt ministers, but his wrath was aimed at Herod's assertion that the time was not right to proclaim Christ because it might cause some disturbance in the state.[41] This was a veiled attack on James's ministers who had counselled the same and argued that James should temper his Catholicising policies with time for people to accommodate them.[42] Ellis was in no doubt that this was the same advice that had corrupted Herod.

The most full-throated sermon of James's reign was preached by the Jesuit Edward Scarisbrike, at the Whitehall chapel on 30 January 1687, on the anniversary of the martyrdom of Charles I. Scarisbrike had been educated at the English College at St Omer and had been named by Titus Oates as a conspirator during the Popish Plot. In 1687 he left his mission in Lancashire to join a new Jesuit establishment in the Savoy, founded by James. His 30 January sermon was published under the title 'Catholick Loyalty: Upon the Subject of Government and Obedience'. Scarisbrike made a clear statement of the divine right of kings: kings ruled by God's commission and were only bound to obey Him. The death of Charles I was a 'treasonable and barbarous regicide; a regicide committed in face of the sun, in cold blood, and under a pretext of law; nay and to consummate the wickedness, by the hands of rebellious subjects ... a diabolical violence upon the person and dignity of a lawful, a just, a merciful and most excellent prince'. He argued that it would not have happened if the people had understood the biblical injunction to obey rulers, and that divine authority and subjects' obedience to their rulers were not conditional: 'It is not in the power of the person to un-king the office; and much less in the power of the people to call God's immediate minister to an account . . . there is no room for intruders betwixt the King of Kings and his Vice-gerents.'

Indeed, Scarisbrike seemed as keen to instruct James in his duties as to demand obedience from his subjects; he said to the King that God's teaching was: 'you hold your commission at My will and pleasure; there is no other power that hath any thing to do with you. I have placed you in the throne of my greatness; invested you with the robes of dignity. I have armed you with the sword of justice, I have deposited all the ensigns of majesty in your hands, not for yourselves to alienate or dispose of, but in truth as you shall answer for them at my tribunal. Who then shall dare to oppose you?' If this was not clear enough, Scarisbricke ended by making a direct comparison between the start of the rebellion against Charles I with the complaints and demands for liberties under James.[43] It was an astonishingly political sermon which can have left James and his subjects in no doubt about the nature of the divine right that the Catholic Church expected of James. It was followed a week later by Thomas Codrington who claimed that those who had opposed Charles I had suffered from 'spiritual blindness'.[44]

The frailty of human understanding was a theme taken up by other preachers. James Ayray, chaplain to the Spanish ambassador, preached at Somerset House, on 10 April 1687, on the importance of obedience. Ayray claimed that since men and women have 'veiled' judgement, they should be led by the Church through mysteries 'which do surpass the reach of human understanding'.[45] The most advanced form of this position was adopted by Bonaventure Gifford. Gifford came from an old English Catholic family and in January 1687 was consecrated bishop at St James's Palace and appointed vicar apostolic for the Midland District of England. He had also criticised James for having the Countess of Dorchester as his mistress, which the King took in good part. On the fourth Sunday after Easter 1687 he preached before the King at Whitehall. His theme was the infallibility of the Church and the warnings in the Bible to those who refused to hear it. But his argument was also designed to propel James to action; he said, 'I am persuaded, and not without good grounds, that there are many in this nation who . . . would most willingly embrace the Catholick faith, and who wish nothing more, than that things were brought to that pass, that they might do it without danger of reproach from their friends and acquaintances.'[46] He went on: 'I appeal to all you, that have been converted to our Church, whether you have not found its doctrine and practice very different from what it was represented to you? You therefore that are yet kept out of the Communion of this Church by the like misrepresentations, you owe this justice and charity both to us and yourselves.'[47] With the nation's leading convert sitting in his congregation, Gifford went on to compare Anglicans who would not convert to 'Turks and Jews'.[48] The alignment of political obedience to James with spiritual obedience to the Catholic Church was one which was clearly a powerful theme in the sermons James heard.

Promoting Catholicism

In the second half of James's reign, court sermons advanced a strong defence of the Catholic Church. On 24 August 1687, Sylvester Jenks preached a sermon before James on his visit to Worcester. Jenks was a Douai professor who recalled that Worcester had played an important part during the Civil War. Jenks used that example to claim: 'we shall always be ready to expose our lives and fortunes in your Majesty's service. It is not in the power of subjects to give their prince a more convincing assurance that they will always be loyal, that they always have been so. I only wish with all my heart that we had ever been as loyal to the Church as to the State; and that we had as zealously opposed the Reformation.'[49] But his central thrust was to denounce attacks that had recently been advanced by Anglican clergy on the doctrine of transubstantiation. Jenks saw this as an example of human pride and dismissed Anglicans as the latest in a line of schismatics.

Jenks clearly impressed James as he was asked to preach before the King on the theme of transubstantiation, on 14 June 1688 and 26 August 1688, at Whitehall and Windsor. In the first sermon, preached four days after the birth of James's son, Jenks argued that enemies of transubstantiation were the enemies of the Church.[50] The second sermon was a much stronger attack on the Church of England, decrying its 'pretended reformation'. He argued that transubstantiation was a 'Mystery . . . above their small capacity; their weak imaginations could not reach it. See here an ancient model of the modern Reformation!' He called on Anglicans to: 'acknowledge the injustice of the Reformation; return home joyfully to their old Mother church and full of admiration of God's mercy to them shew forth the praises of him, who call'd them out of darkness into his wonderful light'.[51] These sermons came as James's reign was approaching its crisis, with the trial of the seven bishops in June and the imminent threat of invasion from William of Orange.

In an extraordinary melodramatic performance on 13 April 1688, Angel Bix, a Franciscan and chaplain to the Spanish ambassador, who was installed at James's new friary near Lincoln's Inn Fields, preached a blood-drenched sermon on rebellion and treason against God. The sermon included numerous mentions of bloodletting and frequent ejaculations such as 'Ha!' The printed version included all these as well as many exclamation marks. Bix argued that Judas was the chief rebel, who abused the kiss, the sign of peace, for his treachery. He railed at those who betrayed Christ and compared them to Adam's rebelliousness. His only comforting words were for his Catholic listeners, to whom he said: 'at least you Catholicks, you the faithful children of my Church, you that so often eat the flesh and drink the blood of the lamb, do not you increase my pains.'[52] Of course, such sermons were of little comfort to James when William invaded. Father Edward Petre had already packed his goods and left in November and abandoned James.[53] Other preachers, including Gifford and Ellis were briefly imprisoned, as Catholic bishops, but were released and fled with the others to France.

When James left Britain at the end of 1688, there was of course the question as to what would happen to his Catholic chapels. Those which had been Anglican chapels were simply returned to their former use and Catholic items removed. William of Orange's decision to hold a number of meetings at the end of 1688 and early 1689 in the Queen's chapel at St James's was clearly a signal that the Catholic use of the building was ended. William also granted James's new Catholic chapel at Whitehall to the French Protestant congregation in London for their use.[54] The fires at Whitehall Palace in 1691 and 1698 meant that James's Catholic chapel was destroyed.[55]

Other than the horror and distaste of many of James's Protestant ministers and other observers, there is little evidence of the direct impact of the court sermons on James or his policies. Lord Ailesbury, a gentleman of the bedchamber, complained of James that 'too much of his time was taken up at holy exercises'.[56] It cannot be said that James followed one or other policy directly because of the impact of the sermons. Nevertheless, the sermons preached at the chapels royal created an ambient expectation of James's Catholicising policies. They provided a theological and soteriological justification for James. If he experienced moments of faint-heartedness or loss of confidence, the sermons reminded him that he was doing what the Church and God held to be right. Those who opposed him were overturning the natural order by their resistance to an anointed king to whom they owed obedience. None of these ideas were new to James, but the consistency with which this message was broadcast from the pulpit with the sanction of divine authority may have had an effect on him.

Certainly to contemporaries and historians, the influence of his priests on James has been regarded as strong. In particular, historians have detected James's strong commitment to the Jesuit Order. Moreover the Jesuits themselves saw the significance of their position at court. By 1687, they were exasperated by the apolitical position of James's confessor, Father Mansuet, and forced him out, replacing him with the Jesuit John Warner. Father Petre admitted to Father La Chaise, confessor to Louis XIV, that the Jesuits exerted a considerable influence over James.[57] The Jesuits were only one of a number of Catholic influences on James; Benedictines and Dominicans also seemed to urge James along the same path.[58] The Catholic clergy preaching before James also knew that their sermons were potent. Father Lewis Sabran's letters back to his provincial in 1688 acknowledged that his repeated preaching about the time of the birth of the Prince of Wales were consciously controversial sermons.[59] Moreover, by October 1688, politicians like Lord Sunderland realised how much political clout James's Catholic priests exerted. At that time it was he, as minister, who had to seek out and beg for the support of Lord Melfort and Phillip Ellis, now a bishop.[60] Even Nathaniel Crewe, bishop of Durham, who collaborated with James for most of his reign and sat on the Ecclesiastical Commission, found himself unable to tolerate the Catholic priests' influence. When Father Petre was appointed to the Privy Council in November 1687 Crewe refused to attend meetings as a result.[61] The impact of the priests on James was not lost on the lowly members of the royal household. Mr Dixie, James's coachman, said as he drove the King to exile: 'God damn Father Petre! But for him, we had not been here!'[62]

The sermons preached before James were a potent expression of the Church's expectations of the King. It is not possible to establish a direct line between each sermon and a course of action. Nevertheless, James's serious attention to preaching and the timing of some sermons to coincide with political events is suggestive. If Mr Dixie saw priests as responsible for James's problems, perhaps that was a view shared more widely in Britain. What can be asserted is that the court sermons of James II created a theological matrix closely attuned to the Catholicising policies that triggered his downfall.

Notes

1. Thomas Babington Macaulay, *The History of England from the Accession of James the Second* (London: J. W. Lovell, 1848).
2. William Gibson, *James II and the Trial of the Seven Bishops* (Basingstoke: Palgrave Macmillan, 2009), chapters 2 and 3.
3. At the same time, James was tormented by the failure of his Queen, Mary of Modena, to carry a baby to term. She repeatedly miscarried, and this seems to have been associated by James with his failure to re-establish Catholicism in England. David John Peter Baldwin, 'The Politico-Religious Usage of the Queen's Chapel, 1623–1688' (Durham University, MLitt thesis, 1999), p. 140.
4. Thomas Sprat, *A True Account and Declaration of The Horrid Conspiracy against the late King, His Present Majesty and the Government* (London: Thomas Newcomb, 1685), pp. 19, 158–9.
5. Christoph Ketterer's *To Meddle with Matters of State: Political Sermons in England, c. 1660–c. 1700* (Göttingen: V&R Unipress, 2020) discusses court sermons preached before James II in the context of public sermons before Charles II and James II. Ketterer argues that the principal purpose of the sermons was to resist anti-Catholic preaching. He does not examine them from the viewpoint of their impact on James II himself.
6. For the sermon culture, see Hugh Adlington, Peter McCullough and Emma Rhatigan (eds), *The Oxford Handbook of the Early Modern Sermon* (Oxford: Oxford University Press, 2011); Keith A. Francis and William Gibson (eds), *The Oxford Handbook of the British Sermon, 1689–1900* (Oxford: Oxford University Press, 2012); Joris van Eijnatten, *Preaching, Sermon and Cultural Change in the Long Eighteenth Century*, A New History of the Sermon 4 (Leiden: Brill, 2009).
7. Bernard and Margaret Pawley, *Rome and Canterbury Through Four Centuries* (London: Mowbray, 1974), pp. 46–7. Even the Pawleys, who were sympathetic to Catholicism, called James's policy 'a fork-tongued policy of universal toleration, intending in this way to bring in justice for his fellow-religionists by a side-wind'.
8. Tony Claydon, 'The Sermon Culture of the Glorious Revolution: Williamite Preaching and Jacobite Anti-Preaching, 1685–1702', in Adlington, McCullough and Rhatigan (eds), *The Oxford Handbook of the Early Modern Sermon*, pp. 487–8.
9. James Ellesby, *The doctrine of passive obedience asserted in a sermon preach'd on January 30, 1684* (London: William Crooke, 1685).

10 Francis Turner, *A Sermon Preached Before their Majesties K. James II and Q. Mary at their Coronation in Westminster Abby, April 23. 1685* (London: Richard Clavell, 1685), *passim*. James's problems with Turner's sermon must have paled in comparison with those with his chaplain Thomas Jones ('sometime Domestick and Naval Chaplain to his R. Highness the Duke of York'), who wrote *Elymas the Sorcerer: Or, a Memorial Towards the Discovery Of the Bottom of this Popish-Plot, And How Far His R. Highness's Directors have been Faithful to His Honour and Interest, Or the Peace of the Nation. Publish'd upon Occasion of a Passage in the Late Dutchess of York's Declaration for Changing Her Religion* (London: H. Jones, 1682).

11 Gibson, *James II and the Trial of the Seven Bishops*, pp. 42–3.

12 Oxford, Bodleian Library, MS Rawlinson 978 details the costs of provisions for the Queen's chapel at St James's.

13 Baldwin, 'Queen's Chapel', pp. 144, 148, 159. The pulpit in Queen Catherine's chapel was said to be one of the tallest in London with seven steps up to the platform.

14 *Ibid.*, p. 170.

15 Such new chapels were highly controversial and the creation of a Catholic chapel in the City of London led to a riot in 1686. Ernest Testa, *James II: Bigot or Saint?* (Lewes: Book Guild, 1987), p. 57.

16 Patrick Dillon, *The Last Revolution: 1688 and the Creation of the Modern World* (London: Jonathan Cape, 2006), pp. 73, 74.

17 London, The National Archives, LS/13/255, Lord Steward's warrants of appointments for the chapel royal.

18 Henry Foley, *Records of the English Province of the Society of Jesus*, 7 vols (London: Burns and Oates, 1879), vol. 5, p. 215. James had ignored the 1674 Order in Council which banished all Catholic clergy then in England and which led most secular priests to withdraw to the Continent.

19 Arthur T. Bolton and H. Duncan Hendry, *The Seventh Volume of the Wren Society, 1930: The Royal Palaces of Winchester, Whitehall, Kensington, and St James's* (Oxford: Oxford University Press, 1930), pp. 73, 120.

20 Baldwin, 'Queen's Chapel', p. 157.

21 Duncan Thomson *et al.*, *Dynasty: The Royal House of Stewart*, ed. Rosalind K. Marshall (Edinburgh: National Galleries of Scotland, 1990), p. 84.

22 Geoffrey Scott, 'Ellis, Philip (1652–1726)', *Oxford Dictionary of National Biography*. Early in 1688 Ellis was appointed the first vicar apostolic of the Western District, and was consecrated on 6 May 1687 by Ferdinand d'Adda, archbishop of Amasia *in partibus*, at the chapel royal in St James's, where the King had founded a monastery of fourteen Benedictine monks. Baldwin suggested that Ellis's sermon on monastic lands must have been the product of close negotiation with James to attempt to ameliorate anti-Catholic sentiment among the landowning classes, although there is also evidence that it troubled James who once again ascribed his wife's miscarriage to his failure to establish Catholicism in England. Baldwin, 'Queen's Chapel', p. 142.

23 *A Select Collection of Catholick Sermons, Preach'd before their Majesties, King James II, Mary Queen-Consort and Catherine Queen-Dowager*, 2 vols (London: n.p., 1741), vol. 1, pp. 306–8.

24 *Ibid.*, vol. 1, p. 296.
25 *Ibid.*, vol. 2, p. 53.
26 Worldcat does not have a record for the publication of the sermon, but it may be one of those recorded in the Bielefeld Academic Search Engine (BASE).
27 Testa, *James II*, p. 54.
28 Stephen Brogan, *The Royal Touch in Early Modern England: Politics, Medicine and Sin*, Royal Historical Society Studies in History: New Series (London: Royal Historical Society/Boydell Press, 2015), p. 116.
29 One of the religious works that had most offended James while Duke of York was Samuel Johnson's work on Julian the Apostate, which was a thinly veiled attack on James as an apostate from Anglicanism, and which endorsed the legitimacy of resistance to him. Samuel Johnson, *Julian the Apostate: Being A Short Account of his Life, the Sense of the Primitive Christians about His Succession, and their Behaviour Towards Him, Together with A Comparison of Popery and Paganism* (London: Langley Curtis, 1682).
30 Pearsall was one of the Jesuits attached to Queen Catherine's chapel. Baldwin, 'Queen's Chapel', p. 183.
31 *Catholick Sermons*, vol. 2, pp. 463–9.
32 *Ibid.*, vol. 1, pp. 6–7.
33 *Ibid.*, vol. 1, pp. 74–84.
34 Godden was almoner of Queen Catherine of Braganza and had achieved some notoriety during the Popish Plot when he was one of the falsely accused. In 1686 Godden was one of the Catholic priests who defended the Real Presence at a conference before the King against William Jane and Simon Patrick. *Catholic Encyclopedia* online edition www.catholic.org/encyclopedia/view.php?id=5224 (accessed 29 April 2018).
35 *Catholick Sermons*, vol. 1, pp. 136, 154.
36 It is unclear whether sermons preached at Somerset House were solely before the Queen Dowager. The chapel was reserved for her use but it seems likely that on some occasions the Queen, Mary of Modena, and James himself were present. Two months later Bentham was to preach before James in a highly defensive sermon which emphasised 'The Catholick Church was always careful to put just bounds and limits to that honour which her children paid to the Virgin Mother' and seemed designed to answer Anglican concerns about Mariology. *Catholick Sermons*, vol. 2, p. 22. A similar sermon by the Jesuit Henry Humberstone – delivered at Worcester – defended the Catholic practice of making the sign of the cross. *Ibid.*, vol. 2, p. 71.
37 *Ibid.*, vol. 1, pp. 200, 212.
38 James Hogg, 'Hall, William (1655–1718)', *Oxford Dictionary of National Biography*. *Catholick Sermons*, vol. 2, p. 107. The Jesuit Edward Scarisbrike in a sermon on the third Sunday after Pentecost made the same point: that those who suffered from 'spiritual leprosy' 'tend to mutinies or rebellion, they are presently check'd and forced to remain in due subordination to reason, and to follow the train of princely virtues'. *Ibid.*, vol. 2, pp. 346–7.
39 *Ibid.*, vol. 2, pp. 239, 249.
40 *Ibid.*, vol. 1, pp. 49–50.
41 *Ibid.*, vol. 1, p. 70.

42 Paradoxically, Ellis was sceptical when, in June 1687, Lord Sunderland converted to Catholicism; he did not believe Sunderland's was a genuine embrace of Catholicism and was simply a political expedient to retain the King's favour. John Philipps Kenyon, *Robert Spencer, Earl of Sunderland, 1641–1702* (London: Longman Green & Co., 1958), p. 198.
43 *Catholick Sermons*, vol. 1, pp. 228, 231, 237, 240, 251.
44 *Ibid.*, vol. 1, p. 263.
45 *Ibid.*, vol. 2, p. 107.
46 *Ibid.*, vol. 2, p. 172.
47 *Ibid.*, vol. 2, p. 174.
48 *Ibid.*, vol. 2, p. 176.
49 *Ibid.*, vol. 2, p. 346.
50 At the same time, Father Petre had dissuaded James from granting a general pardon for refusal to read the Declaration of Indulgence. Testa, *James II*, p. 85. It was soon after this that Nottingham and Clarendon refused to attend Privy Council meetings at which Petre was present. *Ibid.*, p. 103.
51 *Catholick Sermons*, vol. 2, pp. 282, 335, 342.
52 *Ibid.*, vol. 1, pp. 427–8.
53 Stuart Handley, 'Sir Edward Petre, 3rd Baronet', *Oxford Dictionary of National Biography*.
54 Edgar Sheppard, *Memorials of St James's Palace*, 2 vols (London: Longmans, 1894), vol. 2, p. 237.
55 The sculptures from the chapel were taken to Westminster Abbey and in 1820 relocated to Burnham-on-Sea, where the dean was also rector: Robert Dunning (ed.), *Somerset Churches and Chapels: Building, Repair and Restoration* (Tiverton: Halsgrove, 2007), p. 67.
56 Chandos Sydney Cedric Brudenell-Bruce Cardigan, *The Life and Loyalties of Thomas Bruce, a Biography of Thomas Earl of Ailesbury and Elgin ...* (London: Routledge & Kegan Paul, 1951), p. 110.
57 Oxford, Bodleian Library, MS Rawlinson letters 62, fos 5–8.
58 John Miller, *Popery and Politics in England, 1660–1688* (Cambridge: Cambridge University Press, 1973), pp. 235–6.
59 Foley, *Records of the English Province of the Society of Jesus*, vol. 5, p. 292.
60 Kenyon, *Robert Spencer, Earl of Sunderland*, p. 222.
61 Charles Edwin Whitting, *Nathaniel, Lord Crewe, Bishop of Durham (1674–1721) and His Diocese* (London: SPCK, 1940), p. 167.
62 Cardigan, *The Life and Loyalties of Thomas Bruce*, p. 139.

Engraved Clerical Portraiture in England, c. 1660–1850: An Introductory Survey

RICHARD SHARP

Abstract
Architecture and visual arts in general have been subjects of a growing body of recent scholarship connected with the ecclesiastical history of the 'Long Eighteenth Century', but little attention has been given to portraiture. Although honourable mention should be made of pioneering work by John Ingamells on painted episcopal portraits, and by Peter Forsaith, very recently, on Methodist portrait prints, other aspects of this extensive subject still await investigation. The article outlines the development of engraved portrayal of clergy, mainly of the Church of England, during the two centuries before production of multiple images was taken over by photography, and indicates how the quantity, variety, and dissemination of such material can provide some index of the priorities of a pre-photographic age. It does not aim to be a comprehensive or a complete survey of the corpus of engraved portraiture; nevertheless, this article provides an initial guide to the abundance of previously unexplored illustrative material, and may suggest a framework for further exploration. It is hoped that future scholars will build on this initial work to enable a complete catalogue of such images to be developed and further explored.

Keywords: engraving; Evangelical; mezzotint; nonjurors; portraiture; printselling

This article surveys previously unexplored examples of engraved clerical portraiture in England, c. 1660–1850. The purpose is to show the development of engraved portrayal of clergy to indicate its quantity, variety and dissemination in a pre-photographic age. It is not a comprehensive or a complete survey of the corpus of engraved portraiture, but provides evidence of the abundance of such images as a framework for future scholars to build on and explore.

The English print trade, which had grown considerably during the reigns of James I and Charles I, was severely disrupted during the Civil War and Interregnum. By 1660, at the Restoration of the monarchy and the Church of England, business was dominated by a small number of London printsellers, of whom the most important was Peter Stent (fl. c. 1640–65), whose catalogue of engraved imagery, issued in 1654, is the oldest surviving example of its kind. Stent's successor, John Overton I, traded at the White Horse without Newgate from 1669 to 1707.[1] Much of their stock, including a high proportion of portraits, comprised material engraved before the outbreak of the Civil War and originally sold by earlier publishers.[2] Thus, for example, the post-Restoration publication lines of Stent and Overton continued to appear on portraits of Jacobean bishops first engraved by Simon de Passe (c. 1595–1647),[3] Francis Delaram (fl. 1615–24),[4] John Payne (fl. 1620–39)[5] or originally published by William Peake, the successor to Sudbury and Humble.[6] Portraits such as these, seldom measuring more than 7" × 5" (178 × 127 mm), had been produced for separate sale, but were also bound into books as frontispieces. Other early clerical portraits, smaller still in size, had featured in collections such as Robert Boissard's *Bibliographia Chalcographica* (1650).[7] Examples of this kind included work by the etchers Wenceslaus Hollar (1607-77),[8] Richard Gaywood (*fl.* 1644-68)[9] and William Marshall (*fl.* 1617-48), the most prolific engraver of the Caroline era, with 254 attributable prints, of which half were portraits.[10]

However, after 1660, such portraits of the English School, engraved or etched on small and increasingly worn copperplates, were rapidly superseded as printmaking in England underwent a transformation, due largely to the arrival of Continental engravers. Some accompanied the restored court, while others arrived later, seeking refuge from Louis XIV's invasion of the Netherlands in 1672 and his persecution of French Huguenots. Even before the Restoration itself, the finest engraver working in England during the 1650s was a Frenchman, Pierre Lombart (1613-82). During 1651-53 and in 1655 he produced notable engraved portraits of Oliver Cromwell, having originally come to notice in 1650 as the engraver of a title page to Jeremy Taylor's *Rules and Exercises of Holy Dying*, where the author appeared as the focal figure in a theatrically contrived tableau.[11] This was followed by a larger, but more conventional, frontispiece to Taylor's *Ductor Dubitantium* in 1660. Lombart's most notable clerical portrait represented Brian Walton (**Figure 1**), as the frontispiece to his *Biblia Polyglotta* published by Thomas Roycroft in 1657, surpassing all earlier examples of the genre in both quality and size.

By 1663, Lombart had returned to France, but large clerical portraits of high quality continued to be engraved in England, mainly by artists from overseas. David Loggan (1634-92), of English descent, but born in Danzig, had trained with Wilhelm Hondius and Crispijn de Passe the Younger before returning to London in *c.* 1658, becoming naturalised in 1675. Best known for his meticulous architectural views of the colleges of Oxford (1675) and Cambridge (1690), Loggan also engraved many portraits, the finest being a series of large half-length studies of leading members of the English episcopate, taken from his own drawings and published directly from his home in Leicester Fields.[12] In 1673, encouraged by Loggan, Abraham Blooteling (1640-90), a talented Dutch engraver who had been trained by Cornelis van Dalen, was brought to England, where his engraved portraits included the bishops John Wilkins, Edward Stillingfleet and John Tillotson. The first was from an original painting by Mary Beale, while the latter two were after Sir Peter Lely, the plates being reworked and retitled when the sitters were promoted, respectively, to the bishopric of Worcester and to the archbishopric of Canterbury. In *c.* 1674, Loggan and Blooteling were joined by Peter Vandrebanc (1649-97), who had trained in Paris under the distinguished engraver François de Poilly.[13] A study of Thomas Lamplugh (**Figure 2**), originally published in 1689, is a fine example of Vandrebanc's work.[14]

Following the overshadowing of Lamplugh's reputation after the Revolution and his death in 1691, the publisher Christopher Browne caused the plate to be reworked, presumably in an attempt to recover the costs of its original commissioning. A second state was published in 1695, with the sitter's identity altered to represent the new archbishop of Canterbury, Thomas Tenison.[15]

Figure 1 Dr Brian Walton. Engraving by Pierre Lombart, 1657. 328 × 232 mm.

Figure 2 Archbishop Thomas Lamplugh. Engraving by Peter Vandrebanc after Sir Godfrey Kneller, published 1689. 400 × 288 mm.

One of the leading English engravers of the late seventeenth century was Robert White (1645–1703). David Loggan's foremost pupil, he was later said to have had 'so vast a genius in drawing and engraving a face ... that perhaps he has not left his equal in Europe behind him'.[16] Like Loggan, White frequently based engravings on his own drawings made *ad vivum*. Examples of clerical portraits of this kind included folio size studies of Gilbert Burnet (1687), John Sharp (1691) and Simon Patrick (1700).[17] But in 1691, when White engraved a portrait of Archbishop John Tillotson of Canterbury, he worked from an original painting by Mary Beale.[18] An advertisement for this print provides valuable information about White's distribution methods and also about the price charged for a separately published portrait engraving of this size and quality: 'The true Effigies of his Grace, John, Lord Archbishop of Canterbury. Engraven by Rob. White, on a large sheet of Paper, from the Original lately painted by Mrs Mary Beale. Price 12*d*. Sold by B. Aylmer in Cornhill; W. Rogers in Fleet Street; and most Booksellers and Picturesellers in London and Westminster.'[19]

Further work for engravers was created by the growing publishing trade, documented in detail after Michaelmas 1668 in the Term Catalogues, increasing demand for book illustrations and portrait frontispieces. A leading engraver of this kind was William Faithorne (*c*. 1620–91), who had published his first work with Robert Peake shortly before they both gave up business to join the King's army, in which they served together until their capture in October 1645 at the siege of Basing House. After banishment in France, Faithorne returned to London in 1652 and resumed his career as an engraver specialising in portraits, with examples of his clerical output including frontispieces for Ralph Brownrig (*Sermons*, 1661), Jeremy Taylor (*Holy Living*, 1663), John Hacket (*Sermons*, 1675) and Henry More (*Opera Theologica*, 1675).[20] David Loggan engraved a series of fine frontispiece portraits, including Isaac Barrow (*Sermons*, 1678 and *Works*, 1683), Henry More (*Works*, 1679), John Pearson (*Exposition of the Creed*, editions of 1683 and 1692) and Richard Allestree (*Sermons*, 1684). Robert White was a prolific engraver of frontispiece portraits, including Brian Duppa (*Holy Rules*, 1674), Peter Heylyn (*Historical Tracts*, 1681), Simon Patrick (*Paraphrase on Job*, 1685), John Tillotson (*Sermons*, 1688 and 1694), Edward Stillingfleet (*Sermons*, 1696 and *Works*, 1710), Benjamin Whichcote (*Discourses*, 1701), Jeremy Collier (*Dictionary*, 1701), Robert South (*Sermons*, 1694) and George Hickes (*Linguarum Veterum*, 1703). Other frontispieces were produced by lesser engravers, such as Frederick Van Hove[21] and John Sturt (1658–1730), now best remembered for his virtuoso edition of the Book of Common Prayer (1717), engraved entirely on silver plates.[22]

The decade after the Restoration also saw the introduction into England from the Continent of a new printmaking technique. Unlike the line processes of engraving and etching, mezzotint achieved effects through variations in tone.[23] Among the earliest clerical sitters to be portrayed in the new medium were Humphrey Henchman and Gilbert Sheldon, both by unidentified engravers after Sir Peter Lely.[24] When knowledge of the new technique spread, Isaac Beckett (d.1688) produced mezzotints of Henry Compton, after Riley,[25] and of Gilbert Burnet,[26] while prints issued by the publisher Richard Tompson included portraits of John Dolben, after Huysmans, George Morley (**Figure 3**), after Lely, and Titus Oates.[27]

Figure 3 Bishop George Morley. Mezzotint published c. 1675–79. 332 × 283 mm.

David Loggan also experimented with mezzotint, most notably in a large group depicting Richard Allestree, John Dolben and John Fell,[28] while collaboration between Francis Place (1647–1728), a York-based gentleman amateur, and Pierce Tempest (1653–1717)[29] produced several fine portraits of prominent northern clergy, including Nathaniel Crewe, bishop of Durham,[30] Richard Sterne, archbishop of York,[31] and Thomas Comber, dean of Durham.[32]

Public interest in the trial of the seven bishops in 1688 generated demand for commemorative portraits on an unprecedented scale. The bishops 'were placed with the Primitive Confessors, if not above them; they were compared to the Seven Golden Candlesticks, and to the Seven Stars in Christ's Right Hand, and their Pictures publickly Sold in all Printsellers Shops, and bought up in vast Numbers, as the Portraits of the Guardians of the Laws, Liberties and Religion of their Country'.[33] An instantly recognisable composition was a grouping with Archbishop William Sancroft at its centre surrounded by six bust-length oval portraits of his suffragans: Ken, Lake, Lloyd, Trelawney, Turner and White. Numerous versions of this image were published in England and in Holland, both as line engravings[34] and mezzotints.[35] Sets of small portraits of the individual bishops were also produced,[36] with images of Sancroft in particular demand.[37]

Similar levels of interest were stimulated by the prosecution of Dr Henry Sacheverell in 1710. As the date of his trial approached, rival printsellers issued competing versions of the doctor's portrait.[38] The leading examples were engraved in mezzotint by John Smith[39] and Gibson, with two further mezzotints by Andrew Johnston.[40] An advertisement in the *Post Boy* announcing the publication of one of the latter prints was accompanied by a warning from the publisher, Philip Overton, that 'whatever Grav'd prints come out are false and spurious'. Overton reissued this advertisement a fortnight later with an additional warning: 'There is a Counterfeit Copy of this Print lately published; the true one as done from the painting has Andrew Johnston at the bottom of it, besides the Painter's Name.'[41]

Versions of Sacheverell's portrait continued to proliferate after his trial. Some of these prints, several of which incorporated polemical verses or similar text, are listed and described in the British Museum catalogue of engraved satires. See, for example, the anonymous engraving of Sacheverell holding a portrait of Charles I, published by Sutton Nicholls *c.* 1710, with verses:

> What though to Preach Obedience ben't in season
>
> It's but a Misdemeanour, not High Treason
>
> But since it is ungrateful to Obey,
>
> View Him whose life Rebellion took away.[42]

Some made an explicit comparison between the prosecution of Sacheverell and that of the seven bishops in 1688, adopting the familiar composition in which the principal character was depicted surrounded by smaller oval portraits of his supporters (**Figure 4**), the figures in this case being Sacheverell and the six bishops (Compton, Crewe, Dawes, Hooper, Sprat and Sharp) who had voted against his impeachment.[43]

Figure 4 Dr Henry Sacheverell and his supporters. Anonymous engraving. 357 × 267 mm.

Other prints revived memories of past conflicts. A mezzotint by John Simon, after Hargrave, showed Bishop Compton holding a miniature portrait of the Royal Martyr, King Charles I, and an elaborate engraving by George Vertue, after Lely, depicted James Sharp, the archbishop of St Andrews murdered by Presbyterian Covenanters in 1679, with a martyr's crown.[44] Party feeling ran high. On 5 July 1710 the Oxford Jacobite Thomas Hearne recorded the derision which greeted Whig attempts to promote a rival image:

> As Dr Sacheverell's Picture has been ingrav'd several Times, & great Numbers have been and are constantly sold, so the Faction, who are mightily concern'd at ye Reception Dr Sacheverell meets with, out of pure opposition & the more to gain upon the Mob have got that vile Rascal Hoadly's Picture ingrav'd and printed, not at all like him, but in a full, plump posture, whereas he is a thin, meagre, soure Fellow, more like a scare-Crow than a Man.[45]

By contrast, the Bangorian controversy of 1717–19 was contested primarily with words rather than pictures. No portrait was engraved of William Law, author of the *Three Letters to the Bishop of Bangor*, although Andrew Snape was portrayed in a mezzotint attributed to John Faber Sr,[46] published by Philip Overton on 1 February 1718 and advertised as representing 'a Strenuous Defender of the Doctrines and Discipline of the Church of England against the Opinions of the Bangorists'.[47] A subsequent advertisement for this print declared it could also be purchased from provincial sellers in Oxford, Exeter and Eton, where Snape was Headmaster.[48] Three weeks later, a rival mezzotint portrait of Benjamin Hoadly, by John Simon,[49] was published by Edward Cooper.[50] This plate had formerly shown Hoadly as rector of St Peter-le-Poer, but was now reworked to represent him in episcopal attire. Although one printseller, John Garrett at the Angel in Cornhill, held stocks of both images, neither is common, and it has been rightly observed that 'the visual dimension of the Bangorian controversy is notable largely for its paucity'.[51]

By contrast, when Francis Atterbury was arrested in 1722 on suspicion of Jacobite conspiracy, it was recorded that 'The Commitment of the Bishop of Rochester made a great Noise, through the whole Kingdom' and that 'a Print of that Prelate, looking through a Grate, with a Copy of Verses engrav'd under his Effigies, and Comiserating his Lordship's Afflictions, was industriously exposed to Sale; for which Mr Bowen, Engraver and Print-seller, and Mr Edward Ward, who wrote those Verses, were taken up'.[52] They were released after five days' detention. In 1732, following Atterbury's death, Bowen appealed for the return of his confiscated stock, arguing that 'now, the late Bishop of Rochester being dead, the reviving of these Prints, it may be thought, won't produce the like Ill Effect, and therefore they may be sold with Safety'.[53] In addition to this portrait, which had been engraved anonymously, a further large engraving of Atterbury was issued at the time of his trial.[54] Published by Philip Overton and advertised in the *Post Boy* of 30 May–1 June 1723, this was openly acknowledged as the work of Michael Vandergucht, after a portrait by Kneller 'now in the Hand of Mr Morice, his Lordship's Son-in-Law'. Following Atterbury's death this print was reissued with the addition of a five-stanza 'Ode', comparing him to:

> the high-crested Oak, which long had stood
>
> The Tempest's Shock and ye fierce Lightning's Blaze,
>
> Whole Ages flourishing o'er all the Wood . . .
>
> So with unshaken Zeal did he oppose
>
> The factious Insolence, the impious Hate,
>
> The Malice, Rage and Turbulence of those,
>
> Who sought subversion to the Church & State . . .[55]

The establishment of a distinct communion of Nonjurors after initial deprivations in 1690 and the later refusal by other clergy to abjure the exiled Stuart claimants to the British Crown is also well documented in the field of engraved portraiture. Besides the five bishops who continued to adhere to James II, despite having been numbered among the seven who had formerly resisted him in 1688, two further bishops who refused to comply with the post-Revolution order are represented in the engraved record. The bishop of Chester, Thomas Cartwright (d.1689), was depicted in a rare mezzotint by Isaac Beckett after Soest,[56] and in 1704 William Sheridan, bishop of Kilmore and Ardagh, was shown in a small engraving by Sherwin, used as a frontispiece to his *Sermons*.[57] Denis Granville, the deprived dean of Durham who ministered to the exiled court at Saint-Germain-en-Laye until his death in 1703, was portrayed in a French engraving of the highest quality by G. F. Edelinck after Beaupoille, with a Latin inscription which denounced William of Orange as an usurper.[58] John Kettlewell (d.1695) was the subject of numerous engravings, the best being after Tilson, with several versions in line and one in mezzotint by John Smith.[59] An engraving of Henry Dodwell, by Michael Vandergucht, served as the frontispiece to Brokesby's *Life* (1711). Frontispieces to works by Jeremy Collier (1701) and George Hickes (1703) were engraved by Robert White, and Collier was also represented in a mezzotint by William Faithorne.[60]

The Nonjuring controversialist Charles Leslie (d.1722), who from 1711 until 1721 ministered to the court in exile, was portrayed in two large mezzotints by George White and John Simon.[61] During Leslie's time in France, a fine engraving by François Chereau after Alexis-Simon Belle was extensively advertised in England.[62] Richard Welton (d.1724), a provocative non-abjuror, was represented in two engravings, both done anonymously. The larger was separately published; the smaller served as a frontispiece to his *Eighteen Practical Discourses* (1724).[63] Another anonymous engraving depicted the controversial altarpiece installed by Welton in 1713 at St Mary's, Whitechapel, in which White Kennett was portrayed in the character of Judas.[64] That altarpiece had been based on a work by James Fellowes, an artist widely employed by High Tory and Jacobite patrons. His portraits of Humphrey Gower, Master of St John's College, Cambridge, the greatest centre of Nonjurors in either university, and of Laurence Howell, a Nonjuring clergyman who died in Newgate, after denouncing George I as a usurper in *The Case of Schism in the Church of England*

Fairly Stated (1718), were both engraved in large format, the first by George Vertue, the second anonymously.[65]

Little is known about Ralph Taylor (**Figure 5**), who served as a chaplain to the Jacobite court at Saint-Germain and Avignon before returning to England to receive consecration as a bishop in the Nonjuring succession shortly before his death in 1722. However, the size and quality of a commemorative portrait, engraved and published in 1723, indicates that he was a figure of greater significance than his present obscure reputation suggests.[66] Equally interesting is the only portrait print of the distinguished liturgist Thomas Brett (1667–1743), who succeeded Jeremy Collier as primus of the English Nonjurors in 1726. This fine mezzotint, produced after Brett's death by James Macardell after a painting by the little-known artist Charles de Laffontaine,[67] is almost unique in the record of the later Nonjuring movement. The only approximately comparable portrait is a mezzotint of the antiquary Thomas Baker (d.1740), engraved by John Simon after Charles Bridges, whose study had to be done from memory, Baker's modesty being such as to make him decline all invitations to sit.[68]

Besides these separately published prints, many smaller engravings depicted other Nonjurors, most notably the popular devotional authors Thomas Ken[69] and Nathaniel Spinckes.[70] A remarkable grouped frontispiece to *The True Church of England Man's Companion in the Closet* (5th edn, 1728),[71] engraved by Gerard Vandergucht, represented four Nonjurors (Ken, Hickes, Kettlewell and Spinckes) in association with two great seventeenth-century High Churchmen, Lancelot Andrewes and William Laud. A rare engraving by James Cole of Matthias Earbery (d.1740) served as frontispiece to his *History of the Clemency of our English Monarchs* (1717). Two rare mezzotints by John Faber Sr of Henry Shute (*c.* 1720) and Robert Orme (d.1733) employed characteristic formulae employed by Nonjurors, describing the sitters respectively as 'Eccles. Anglia. Presbyter' and 'Priest of the Church of England'.[72]

Production of separately published portraits of conforming clergy continued, in mezzotint and line, throughout the first half of the eighteenth century. The majority of these sitters were bishops, with the most usual format being 'posture' size, approximately 14" × 10" (356 × 254 mm). Leading engravers in mezzotint in the earlier part of this period included John Smith (*c.* 1652–1742)[73] and George White (*c.* 1671–1732);[74] together with John Faber Sr, who came to England from Holland *c.* 1695 and died in 1721,[75] and John Simon (1675–*c.* 1755), a Huguenot refugee.[76] Later, John Faber Jr (*c.* 1695–1756) produced thirty-two clerical portraits between 1722 and 1751. These included Thomas Burnet, Nathaniel Crewe and John Tillotson, all after Kneller; Thomas Herring (an unusually large plate, measuring 20" × 14" (508 × 356 mm), published in 1751 and dedicated to Lord Hardwicke), Matthew Hutton (as archbishop of York, published in 1748 at 2*s.*), Zachary Pearce and Edward Willes, all after Hudson; George Fleming, Edmund Gibson and John Waugh, all after John Vanderbank, and George Stanhope (**Figure 6**) and William Wake, after Ellys.[77]

Between 1749 and 1759 James Macardell (d.1765), originally from Ireland, engraved sixteen clerical mezzotints including Thomas Gooch, Stephen Hales, Edward

Figure 5 Dr Ralph Taylor. Engraving by George Vertue after J. Verelst, 1723. 356 × 252 mm.

Figure 6 Dr George Stanhope. Mezzotint by John Faber Jr, 1729. 317 × 254 mm.

Maurice and Richard Osbaldeston, all after Hudson; Thomas Ashton and John Garnett, after Gainsborough, and Archbishops Thomas Herring and Thomas Secker, respectively after Webster and Wills; while his compatriot John Brooks produced the best portrait of George Berkeley, a mezzotint after a painting by Latham, depicting the philosopher-bishop with a Bible and copies of his work *Siris and the Minute Philosopher*.[78] The most prominent line engravers of this period were George Vertue (1684–1756)[79] and Michael Vandergucht (1660–1725), both of whom were also responsible for a substantial output of smaller engraved frontispieces.[80] Other notable portraits of the period included studies of Benjamin Hoadly (1743) and Thomas Herring (1750), both engraved by Bernard Baron after William Hogarth, and Thomas Sherlock (1756), engraved by Simon François Ravenet after Vanloo.[81]

A good idea of the various styles of portraiture offered for sale can be found in surviving catalogues issued by printsellers. In 1728, for example, in a catalogue produced by John Bowles, a section of 'Mens Heads in large Metzotinto' included portraits of Bishops Atterbury, Burnet, Gibson, Hoadly and Willis, besides Samuel Clarke and Jonathan Swift,[82] while Atterbury was also available in a larger, but presumably cruder, 'Royal Sheet' format. In 1754, Henry Overton I, who had succeeded John Overton at the White Horse without Newgate in 1707, listed an engraving of Bishop Hoadly by Vertue, priced 1s.,[83] together with 'Large Metzotinto Heads' of John Tillotson,[84] John Wesley[85] and Thomas Gooch.[86] A catalogue issued in 1764 by the bulk distributors Cluer Dicey and Richard Marshall from their 'Printing Warehouse' in Bow Churchyard offered an insight into a more popular end of the market, characterised by big engravings and woodcuts, whose crudity, cheapness and consequent ephemeral nature has meant that survivals of this genre are now rare.[87] This catalogue included a 'Copper Royal' representation of 'Bishop Burnet and John Wesley', offered per quire at the wholesale price of 2s. plain, or 4s. coloured; 'Fool's Cap Sheet Prints' of Bishop Patrick, Archbishop Sharp and 'Archbishop Laud, and six more on one Sheet', 'All very neatly Coloured in Water Colours at 3s. per Quire'; and 'Pott Sheet Prints of Henry Finch, Dean of York (**Figure 7**), Bishop Burnet and John Wesley', at 1s. plain or 2s. coloured per quire.

When Robert Sayer married the widow of Philip Overton in 1748, he took over one of London's largest and longest-established printselling businesses at the Golden Buck in Fleet Street, where he continued to trade until his death in 1794. Sayer's catalogue of 1775, issued in conjunction with John Bennett,[88] included a wide selection of clerical portraiture, ranging from fine mezzotints measuring approximately 16" × 12" (406 × 305 mm), selling at 5s.,[89] through the 'Works of James MacArdell', at 2s.,[90] to 'Metzotintos, Posture Size', at 1s.,[91] and 'Small Metzotintos 6" × $4\frac{1}{2}$" (152 × 114 mm) at 6d. The catalogue also included Royal Sheet size 'Cheap prints, excellently well engraved . . . each beautifully ornamented' of George Whitefield and John Wesley, 'Both upon one plate'; Bishop Sherlock; George Whitefield, alone, and William Romaine.[92]

Similar stock was listed by John Boydell, whose 1773 catalogue was notable for the inclusion of three clerical mezzotints of unprecedented size and quality.[93] Measuring 20" × 14" (508 × 356 mm) and selling for 7s. 6d.,[94] these reflected changing

Figure 7 Dr Henry Finch. Anonymous engraving, published by Thomas Cobb, c. 1730. 332 × 244 mm.

tastes after *c*. 1760, as the use of line processes in portraiture declined,[95] and single published engraved portraits and frontispieces to theological and devotional works became less common.[96] The market for bigger clerical portraits was thereafter dominated by mezzotint, with subjects, usually of episcopal rank or with claims to literary distinction, being engraved after paintings by artists of the first rank, often published by printsellers no longer based in the City of London but in the newly fashionable West End. In 1760, capitalising on the success of *Tristram Shandy*, Edward Fisher (1730–*c*. 1785) published a portrait of Laurence Sterne after Sir Joshua Reynolds for 5*s*.[97] James Watson (d.1790) produced mezzotints of Robert Hay Drummond (1764) and Zachary Mudge, both after Reynolds, and Charles Lyttelton, after Cotes. In 1775 Thomas Watson (d.1781) published a mezzotint of Thomas Newton (**Figure 8**), after Reynolds, from premises in New Bond Street.[98]

An earlier mezzotint of Newton, after Benjamin West, had been engraved in 1767 by Richard Earlom.[99] John Raphael Smith (1752–1812) produced mezzotints of Archbishops Robinson (1775), Markham (1778) and Bourke (1784), all measuring 20" × 14" (508 × 356 mm) and after Reynolds, along with slightly smaller mezzotints of Jonathan Shipley and Joseph Warton, also after Reynolds (1777).[100] William Dickinson (1746–1823) produced portraits of Thomas Percy (1775) after Reynolds, and Edmund Law (1777) after George Romney.[101] Also working from paintings by Romney, John Jones (*c*. 1745–97) issued mezzotints, at 20" × 14" (508 × 356 mm), of Richard Farmer (1785), Shute Barrington (1786), Samuel Parr (1788), William Paley (1792) (**Figure 9**) and Richard Watson (1794).[102]

The impact of the Methodist and Evangelical movements was copiously reflected in engraved portraiture. Reference to the British Museum catalogue is recommended for those who wish to form a complete impression of the range of portraits representing John Wesley and George Whitefield, but special mention should be made of the mezzotints of each sitter by Greenwood after the well-known paintings by Nathaniel Hone,[103] originally published in 1769 and 1770, and widely copied thereafter. Sayer and Bennett's 1775 catalogue listed multiple versions of portraits both of Wesley and of Whitefield, at prices ranging from 5*s*. to 6*d*., together with mezzotints of James Hervey, at 1*s*., and William Romaine, at 1*s*. and at 6*d*., and also in a large 'Royal Sheet'.[104]

Between 1772 and 1777 a remarkable sequence of Evangelical and Protestant Dissenting portraits were engraved by Richard Houston and published by Carington Bowles.[105] Measuring 14" × 10" (356 × 254 mm) and selling for 2*s*. each, many of these portraits are shown in Bowles's shop window as represented in Robert Dighton's mezzotint droll 'A Real Scene in St Paul's Church Yard, on a Windy Day', published in June 1783.[106] Carington Bowles also published the only substantial portrait of Augustus Montague Toplady,[107] a strikingly large mezzotint of the Countess of Huntingdon[108] and several mezzotints by Jonathan Spilsbury, an engraver of Evangelical sympathies. These latter included Richard de Courcy (1770) and Andrew Kinsman (1772), both after Russell, and Torial Joss (1771).[109] Spilsbury also engraved a portrait of the Moravian leader John Gambold after Brandt,[110] published

Figure 8 Bishop Thomas Newton. Mezzotint, 1775. 405 × 329 mm.

Figure 9 Archdeacon William Paley. Mezzotint by John Jones, 1792. 468 × 375 mm.

by West in 1771, besides the only substantial image of John William Fletcher, vicar of Madeley, published in 1786, the year after Fletcher's death.[111]

Until superseded by the development of photographic processes in the mid-nineteenth century, mezzotint continued to dominate the field of large format reproductive portraiture. Such prints, still by leading engravers after portrait artists of the first rank, usually measured around 18" × 14" (457 × 356 mm), with sitters including the foremost clergy of the period. Examples of work by Charles Turner (d.1857) included Beilby Porteus (1807, after Hoppner), Shute Barrington (1817, after Lawrence), William Howley (1817 and 1829, after Lawrence), Henry Bathurst (1820, after M. A. Shee) and Charles Manners Sutton (1830, after Hoppner).[112] Samuel William Reynolds (d.1835) engraved Brownlow North (1819, after Howard), Thomas Burgess (1820, after Owen) and Reginald Heber (1827, after Phillips).[113] William Say (d.1834) engraved Shute Barrington (1812, after W. Owen) and John Eveleigh (1809, after Hoppner, a private plate) and William James Ward (d.1840) engraved C. J. Blomfield (1827).[114] In 1831 a mezzotint of William Van Mildert, the last prince bishop of Durham (**Figure 10**), after the magnificent portrait by Sir Thomas Lawrence, was published by Colnaghi:[115] it was engraved by Thomas Lupton (d.1873), who in 1834 also engraved Edward Maltby, after Beechey.

In the 1840s, Samuel Cousins (d.1887) engraved C. R. Sumner (after Shee), J. B. Sumner (1840, after Carpenter), and G. A. Selwyn (1842) and John Keble (1845), both after Richmond. Perhaps appropriately, some of the last mezzotint clerical portraits represented sitters best known for their aversion to change: Christopher Bethell,[116] Henry Phillpotts[117] and Martin Joseph Routh.[118]

This article has surveyed a range of previously unexplored illustrative material relating to engraved clerical portraiture in England, c. 1660–1850. The development of engraved portrayal of clergy, mainly of the Church of England, has been outlined to indicate how the quantity, variety and dissemination of such material can provide some index of the priorities of a pre-photographic age. Alongside the work of John Ingamells on painted episcopal portraits and Peter Forsaith on Methodist portrait prints, this study can provide a framework for the further exploration of these images.[119]

A Note on Copper Plates

Although most impressions from a copper plate were usually printed and sold soon after engraving, in some instances plates continued to be printed long after the sitters represented were dead. Such impressions are identifiable by bearing the publication line of later printsellers, and are generally of inferior quality, owing to the worn condition of plates after multiple printings and consequent reworking. Late eighteenth- or even early nineteenth-century impressions exist of some mezzotints first issued almost a century earlier by John Smith[120] and John Faber Sr.[121]

In other instances, reworking changed the identity of the sitter entirely. Peter Vandrebanc's engraving of Thomas Lamplugh (1689) was subsequently altered to Thomas Tenison.[122] An engraving of Archbishop James Sharp, by Vertue (1710), was

Figure 10 Bishop William Van Mildert. Mezzotint, 1831. 413 × 327 mm.

later reworked by Vandergucht as Archbishop William Dawes.[123] A mezzotint of Dawes, by John Smith,[124] was later reissued as Atterbury; another by John Faber Sr of Andrew Snape was subsequently altered and sold by Jordan and Bakewell as 'The famous Mr Henly of the Oratory'.[125] A mezzotint of William Wake, by George White, later reappeared as Thomas Herring,[126] while two portraits apparently representing

Charles Wesley were later states taken from plates originally engraved for different sitters.[127]

Rare or Unrepresented Sitters

Caution must be exercised when interpreting the significance of engraved portraiture. It is important to appreciate that most of the prints which have survived into our own times are from the more expensive end of the original market. Yet printsellers' catalogues also list much cheap material, of which hardly any examples now survive. It is difficult now to form a proper notion of the clerical portraiture that once circulated in such ephemeral and cruder forms. Similarly, although the number and quality of surviving portraits may indicate the influence or popular reputation of sitters, this was not invariably so. Some of the most influential clergy of the period, including Henry Hammond, William Cave, William Wall, Joseph Bingham, Joseph Butler, William Law, Charles Wheatly, John Newton and Henry Venn have no contemporaneously published engraved portraits, while Daniel Waterland is represented solely by a single and uncommon mezzotint,[128] issued by R. Manby, a partner in the firm which published Waterland's books, including the *Review of the Doctrine of the Eucharist* (1737).

Notes

All photography for this article was undertaken by George Skipper, Alnwick, from the author's personal collection.

1 Antony Griffiths, *The Print in Stuart Britain, 1603–1689* (London: British Museum Press, 1998).
2 Alexander Globe, *Peter Stent, London Printseller, circa 1642–1665* (Vancouver: University of British Columbia Press, 1985), cited hereafter as Globe; all numbers are catalogue numbers.
3 George Abbot (Globe 1, first published by Compton Holland); Lancelot Andrewes (Globe 11); John King (Globe 202, first published by Sudbury and Humble); James Montague (Globe 235, first published by Henry and Compton Holland).
4 Robert Abbot (Globe 2, previously published by Sudbury and Humble, then by William Peake).
5 Joseph Hall (Globe 165, first published by Philemon Stephens and Christopher Meredith).
6 Walter Curll (Globe 106, engraved by T. Cecill); John Howson (Globe 181, engraved by Martin Droeshout, *fl.* 1601–39).
7 Including Bishops G. Abbot, R. Abbot, Babington, King, Lake, Montagu, White, and Williams; Jean-Jacques Boissard, *Bibliotheca Chalcographica illustrium virtute atque eruditione in tota Europa, clarissimorum Virorum Theologorum, Juriconsultorum, Medicorum, Historicorum, Geographorum, Politicorum, Philosophorum, Poetarum, Musicorum, Aliorumque* (Frankfurt: Iohannis Ammonij Bibliopola, 1650).

8 Including Andrewes, in Freeman O'Donoghue and Henry M. Hake, *Catalogue of Engraved British Portraits in the Department of Prints and Drawings, British Museum* (London: British Museum, 1908–25) 6 [hereafter cited as O'D; all numbers are catalogue numbers], Lake (O'D, 2), Laud (O'D, 6, 9, 22), Overall (O'D, 1) and Williams (O'D, 3).
9 Hewit (O'D, 1) and Laud (O'D, 10).
10 Arthur M. Hind, *Engraving in England in the Sixteenth and Seventeenth Centuries: A Descriptive Catalogue with Introductions, Vol. III: The Reign of Charles I* (Cambridge: Cambridge University Press, 1964), pp. 102–92. Examples of Marshall's ecclesiastical work included George Abbot (O'D, 3), William Laud (O'D, 7 and 30) and James Ussher (O'D, 9).
11 See Griffiths, *The Print in Stuart Britain*, pp. 178–81, nos 116 and 117.
12 Henry Compton 1679 (O'D, 1), Nathaniel Crewe (O'D, 1), Peter Gunning (O'D, 1), John Lake 1688 (O'D, 1), Peter Mews (O'D, 1), William Sancroft 1680 (O'D, 1), Thomas Sprat (O'D, 4) and Seth Ward 1678 (O'D, 2). For the most recent biographical treatment of Loggan see G. Tyack, 'David Loggan (1634–1692)', *Oxford Dictionary of National Biography* (Oxford: Oxford University Press, 2004).
13 E. Benezit, *Benezit Dictionary of Artists* (Paris: Éditions Gründ, 1911).
14 Examples are held by the National Portrait Gallery, London [hereafter NPG], D30882 and D30883.
15 NPG D20240.
16 'Vertue Notebooks IV', *Walpole Society*, 24 (1935/36), p. 108.
17 Respectively NPG D18616, D21351 and D30910.
18 See, for example, D31122, D31123, D31124, and D39616, among others.
19 Edward Arber, *The Term Catalogues, 1668–1709*, 3 vols (London: Edward Arber, 1903–06), vol. 2, p. 383.
20 A. Griffiths, 'William Faithorne, (1670–1703)', *Oxford Dictionary of National Biography*.
21 E.g. John Pearson (*Exposition of the Creed*, 1676).
22 Examples of frontispieces by Sturt include Ezekiel Hopkins (*Sermons*, 1691), John March (*Sermons*, 1693) and Offspring Blackall (*Sermons*, 1706).
23 C. Wax, *The Mezzotint, History and Technique* (New York: H. Abrams, 1996).
24 John Chaloner Smith, *British Mezzotinto Portraits* (London: H. Sotheran, 1878–83), [hereafter cited as CS]: anon. 55 and anon. 109.
25 CS, 26.
26 CS, anon. 11.
27 Carol Blackett-Ord and Simon Turner, 'Early Mezzotints: Prints Published by Richard Tompson and Alexander Browne', *The Seventieth Volume of the Walpole Society* (2008), 1–206.
28 CS, 1.
29 Tempest has been described as 'the most interesting publisher of the 1680s and 1690s': Griffiths, *The Print in Stuart Britain*, p. 244.
30 CS, 4.
31 CS, 11.
32 CS, 'Lumley', 1.

33 Francis Lee, *Memoirs of the Life of Mr John Kettlewell* (London: S. Collins, 1718), pp. 176–7. See the engraving by Simon Gribelin, a Huguenot, published by his fellow-refugee Paul van Somer in June 1688, immediately after the bishops' acquittal, representing the bishops with the apocalyptic imagery of seven stars and seven candlesticks described in Revelation 1:12–20 (Griffiths, *The Print in Stuart Britain*, p. 298).

34 See examples by Loggan (NPG D37133), White (NPG D1333 and D18862, this often serving as a frontispiece to the book of the *Bishops' Tryal*), J. Drapentier (British Museum Prints [hereafter BM] 1877-0811-708) and A. Haelwegh (BM 1872-0608-551).

35 See examples by John Oliver (BM 1902-1011-3565), Jacob Gole (BM 1853-0112-1662), Pieter Schenck (NPG D9286) and Richard Palmer (NPG D9285); also anonymous plates attributed possibly to John Smith (CS, anon. 6) and the 'school of Beckett' (CS, anon. 5).

36 Notably a set of line engravings published by John Overton, including Sancroft (Richard Sharp, *The Engraved Record of the Jacobite Movement* (Aldershot: Scolar Press, 1996), p. 625 [hereafter Sharp; numbers refer to catalogue entries]), White (Sharp, 665), Trelawney, Turner (Sharp, 655), Lake (Sharp, 476) and Ken (Sharp, 461); also a set of small mezzotints done by William Vincent with Lake (CS, 8; Sharp, 477), Sancroft (CS, 10; Sharp, 619), Turner (CS, 12; Sharp, 654) and White (CS, 13; Sharp, 664).

37 See in particular a large mezzotint ascribed to the 'school of Beckett', by whom it was sold (CS, anon. 103; Sharp, 620) and other smaller mezzotints (e.g. CS, anon. 104; Sharp, 621; CS, anon. 105; Sharp, 622; CS, anon. 106, Sharp, 624).

38 Many engraved portraits of Sacheverell were derived from these sources. See, for example, Vertue 1714 (O'D, 12), Nutting (NPG 31476) and Schenck (NPG D4126), anon. mezzotint (NPG D20096).

39 CS, 219.

40 CS, 3 and 4.

41 *Post Boy*, 25–28 February 1710.

42 BM, satires, 1510. See also a mezzotint by John Faber Sr (CS, 63), published in 1710 and entitled 'the 3 Pillars of ye Church', representing the Doctor with other supporters, Francis Higgins and Philip Stubbs.

43 Anonymous engraving, with St Paul's above (BM 1868-0808-13521; Dutch copy BM 1863-0808-53 [O'D, 1 and 2]).

44 Respectively NPG D1501 and D20993.

45 Thomas Hearne, *Remarks and Collections of Thomas Hearne*, 11 vols, ed. C. E. Doble (Oxford: Oxford Historical Society, 1885), vol. 3, p. 20. The portrait of Hoadly to which Hearne alluded may have been the engraving by George Vertue (O'D, 7).

46 CS, anon. vol. 2, p. 97.

47 *Post Boy*, 30 January–1 February 1718.

48 *Evening Post*, 13–15 February 1718.

49 CS, 82.

50 *Post Man*, 20–22 February 1718. An impression of this print is held in the British Museum (1864-0813-96).

51 Andrew Starkie, *The Church of England and the Bangorian Controversy, 1716–21* (Woodbridge: Boydell & Brewer, 2007), p. 59.

52 Abel Boyer, *Political State of Great Britain*, 60 vols (London: J. Baker, 1711–29), vol. 24, p. 281 (September 1722). An impression of this print survives in the Ashmolean Museum, Oxford, and is illustrated in Sharp, *Engraved Record of the Jacobite Movement*, p. 62. It shows Atterbury holding an image of Archbishop Laud, to whom he is compared in eight lines of verse which ascribe his arrest to 'party Spleen and vile Fanatick Rage'. See also *Evening Post*, 15–18 September 1722 and Tim Clayton, *The English Print, 1688–1802* (New Haven, CT: Yale University Press, 1997), p. 78 and plate 89.
53 Cited by Herbert M. Atherton, *Political Prints in the Age of Hogarth* (Oxford: Oxford University Press, 1974), pp. 72–3.
54 Sharp, 284.
55 *The Epistolary Correspondence, Visitation Charges, Speeches, and Miscellanies of Francis Atterbury* (London: J. Nicols, 1783), vol 2, p. 436, by Alexander Pope.
56 CS, 11; Sharp, 372.
57 Sharp, 641.
58 Sharp, 409.
59 Sharp, 465–8; CS, 148; Sharp, 464.
60 Sharp, 390; Sharp, 378; Sharp, 423; CS, 6; Sharp, 377.
61 CS, 25; Sharp, 485.
62 CS, anon. 61; Sharp, 486; Sharp, 484. See *Evening Post*, 23–25 August 1715: 'Next Saturday may be had A curious Print of Mr Charles Lesley, most artfully engraven by F. Chereau at Paris, from the Original of A. S. Bolle [sic] workt upon a superfine French Royal Paper and sold by O. Sawbridge in Little Brittain, and most Booksellers and Printsellers in London and Westminster.' Further advertisements by J. Wilford, successor to Sawbridge, in 1721, for 'A Neat Effigies of the Reverend Mr Lesly, lately brought from Paris. Both Engrav'd, and in Metzotinto. Price of each 2s. 6d.' in *Weekly Journal*, 7 January 1721 and *Daily Journal*, 9 June 1721. Soon afterwards, more advertisements placed by Wilford announced that the 'Effigy of the Reverend and Learned Author of the Snake in the Grass, lately brought from Paris' could be had for 1s. 6d., and indicated that the print was 'of a size proper to be prefix'd to his Theological Works lately printed', a point still being made in 1725, when *Mist's Weekly Journal* announced that this 'very neat and beautiful Effigies of the late Rev. and learned Mr Charles Leslie . . . will serve as a very proper Frontispiece to his *Theological Works* in 2 vols Folio, and may be prefix'd to those which are already bound, as well as to those which may be bound hereafter'. See *Post Boy*, 29 June–1 July 1721; *Daily Journal*, 30 October 1721; *Mist's Weekly Journal*, 2 October and 23 October 1725.
63 Sharp, 660 and 659.
64 Sharp, 714.
65 Sharp, 408 and 426. For Fellowes see L. H. Cust (rev. J. Ingamells), 'James Fellowes (*fl.* 1735–51), *Oxford Dictionary of National Biography*.
66 Sharp, 652. An example of Taylor's portrait is held by the BM1849,1031.87.
67 CS, 29; Sharp, 330.
68 CS, 21; Sharp, 295. See Hearne, *Collections*, vol. 11, p. 178, 28 March 1733, recording 'Mr Murray & Mr Vertue's going to Cambridge, to steal Mr Baker's face', and how

Baker afterwards said to Hearne 'that if I hear of a picture or print, that bears his name ... he desires, I will believe, he had not vanity enough to countenance such a design'.
69 Fifteen examples, all small engravings, are listed in Sharp (nos 449–63).
70 See, for example, the engraving of Spinckes, by Vertue after J. Wollaston, prefixed to 'The Sick Man Visited' (4th edn, 1731).
71 Sharp, 712.
72 Sharp, 395; CS, 69; Sharp, 643.
73 Smith's plates included Henry Aldrich, 1710 (CS, 3) and Edward Fowler, 1717 (CS, 91), both after Kneller; Thomas Knipe, 1712 (CS, 152), a double portrait of Bishop Sprat with his son, 1712 (CS, 243), both after Dahl, and Thomas Burnet (CS, 29), after Riley.
74 White's output included portraits of Francis Atterbury (CS, 1), George Hooper 1723 (CS, 22), Charles Leslie (CS, 25) and William Wake (CS, 52).
75 Faber's plates included Francis Atterbury (CS, 3 and 4), John Hough, 1715 (CS, 44), White Kennett, 1719 (CS, 50), William Talbot (CS, 72 and 73) and Charles Trimnell, 1719 (CS, 74).
76 Simon's plates included Francis Atterbury 1718 (CS, 19) and John Tillotson (CS, 151), both after Kneller, Samuel Clarke (CS, 40), Henry Compton, 1710 (CS, 42), William Fleetwood, 1702 (CS, 59), Benjamin Hoadly (CS, 82), Joseph Wilcocks, 1721, reissued 1731 (CS, 163), Richard Willis (CS, 166) and Thomas Wilson (CS, 168).
77 R. Sharp, 'John Faber (c. 1660–1721)', Oxford Dictionary of National Biography.
78 For Macardell and Brooks see T. Clayton and A. McConnell, 'James Macardell (1727/8–1765)', Oxford Dictionary of National Biography, and A. Puetz, 'John Brookes (c. 1710–1756)', Oxford Dictionary of National Biography.
79 Vertue's principal engravings included portraits, at 14" × 10" (356 × 254 mm), of Bishops Martin Benson (after Richardson, 1739), Philip Bisse (after Hill), Francis Blackburne (after Seeman, 1727), William Dawes (after Murray), Francis Gastrell (after Dahl, 1728), Edmund Gibson (after Ellys, 1727), Benjamin Hoadly (as rector of St Peter-le-Poer, later altered to bishop of Bangor), William Lloyd (first after Forster, then after Weideman, 1714); John Potter (after Dahl, 1727), Richard Smalbroke (after Murray, 1733) and William Talbot (after Kneller: 1720 as bishop of Salisbury, reissued 1722 as bishop of Durham). Vertue also engraved a strikingly large portrait ($17\frac{1}{2}$" × 12"; 445 × 305 mm) of Thomas Wilson, bishop of Man (after Fellowes, 1726), and also a portrait of John Wesley (after J. M. Williams, 1746 [O'D, 19]), the only large line engraving to represent Wesley when young.
80 Examples by Vertue include Anthony Horneck, *Several Sermons upon the Fifth of St. Matthew* (London: B. Aylmer, 1706); Humphrey Prideaux, *Connexion* (Oxford: Oxford University Press, 1716 and 1720); John Kettlewell, *Memoirs of the Life of John Kettlewell* (London: S. Collins, 1718), *Measures of Christian Subjection, the Works of John Kettlewell* (London: S. Collins, 1719); Offspring Blackall, *Works* (London: T. Ward, 1723); Richard Fiddes, *Life of Wolsey* (London: J. Barber, 1724); George Smalridge, *Sermons* (Oxford: at the Theatre, 1724); William Dawes, *Works* (London: n.p., 1733); Atterbury, *Sermons* (London: T. Woodward, 1735); Samuel Clarke, *Works* (London: J. Knapton, 1738); Thomas Tanner, *Notitia Monastica* (London: W. Bowyer, 1744), and many others. Examples by Michael Vandergucht include Daniel Whitby, *Commentary on the New*

Testament (London: J. Churchill, 1700); George Stanhope, *Paraphrase on the Epistles and Gospels* (London: W. B., 1706); William Beveridge, *Sermons* (London: R. Smith, 1709); William Nichols, *Discourse on the Book of Common Prayer* (London: R. Bonwicke, 1710); George Bull, *Life* (London: R. Smith, 1713) and *Works* (London: R. Smith, 1721); Henry Dodwell, *Life* (London: F. Brokesby, 1715); John Moore, *Sermons* (London: W. Taylor, 1715); Offspring Blackall, *Sermons* (London: T. Ward, 1717); William Fleetwood, *Sermons* (London: W. Mears, 1717) and many others. For work by Gerard Vandergucht (c. 1698–1777) see Kettlewell, *Life* (London: S. Collins, 1718) and Tillotson, *Sermons* (London: J. Ware, 1742).

81 For examples of the engravings of Benjamin Hoadly and Thomas Herring by Bernard Baron, see NPG D35870 and NPG35718, and for the engraving of Thomas Sherlock by Simon François Ravenet, see NPG D40703.

82 *A Catalogue of Maps, Prints, Books, and Books of Maps, which are printed for, and sold by J. Bowles* (London: J. Bowles, 1728). The portraits of Burnet (CS, Smith, 29), Hoadly (CS, Simon, 82) and Willis (CS, Simon, 166) had been acquired from the stock of Edward Cooper and were also sold by Thomas Bowles in St Paul's Church Yard. Republication of old plates was common practice: John King (1702–59) at the Globe, Poultry, for example, republished many engravings first done before 1700 (e.g. Robert White's plates of John Sharp [1691] and Thomas Tenison); while Thomas Bakewell (fl. 1729–49) and Timothy Jordan, in Fleet Street to 1745 and later in Birchin Lane, Cornhill, reissued many mezzotints originally produced by John Faber Sr (Kennett, Snape, Talbot, Trimnell, Wallis and Talbot; CS, 50, 70, 72, 74, 76). Thomas Jeffreys and William Herbert, trading from 1747–58 at the Golden Globe on London Bridge, continued to sell impressions of a print of the seven bishops first engraved by Gribelin in 1688.

83 *A Catalogue of Maps, Prints, Copy-Books &c From off Copper-Plates ... Sold by Henry Overton* (London, 1754), p. 56, no. 8.

84 *Ibid.*, p. 62, no. 28, originally published by John Simon (CS, 28).

85 *Ibid.*, no. 41, by John Faber Jr after Williams (CS, 378).

86 *Ibid.*, no. 42, by Macardell (CS, 90).

87 C. Dicey & R. Marshall, *A Catalogue ...* (London: The Printing Office, 1764), now available online at http://diceyandmarshall.bodleian.ox.ac.uk (accessed 8 November 2020). See also Sheila O'Connell, *The Popular Print in England* (London: Museum Press, 1999).

88 *Sayer & Bennett's Catalogue of prints for the year 1775*, republished in facsimile by the Holland Press (London, 1970).

89 *Ibid.*, p. 9: Cornwallis and Terrick, both by Fisher after Dance; Drummond, by Watson after Reynolds; Thomas (Winchester) and Robinson, both by Houston, respectively after Benjamin Wilson and Reynolds; George Whitefield and John Wesley, both by Greenwood after Hone.

90 *Ibid.*, p. 10: Stephen Hales (CS, 94), John Reynolds (CS, 151), Thomas Ashton (CS, 6) and Emanuel Collins (CS, 44).

91 *Ibid.*, pp. 18–19: Secker and Sterne, Whitefield and Wesley (after Hone), William Romaine, James Hervey and Thomas Jones (all by Purcell: CS, 65, 39, 46).

92 *Ibid.*, p. 142, nos 40–3.
93 A catalogue of prints, published by John Boydell, engraver in Cheapside, London (London: J. Boydell, 1773).
94 *Ibid.*, p. 29, no. 14, Thomas Newton (Earlom after West); no. 15, Samuel Chandler (Pether after Chamberlain) and no. 21, Archbishop Robinson (Smith after Reynolds), p. 63.
95 A rare exception is the stipple engraving by John Jones after Romney of Archbishop Moore (1792), NPG 38938. Moore also featured in the series of semi-caricatured whole length etched portraits by Robert Dighton (d.1814) as 'The Principal Arch' (NPG 982e) with others, including Samuel Horsley ('A Trip from Rochester to St Asaph' [1802], NPG D10947, subsequently reissued as 'The late Right Revd …' [1809], NPG D10948). The enduring posthumous reputation of Horsley was further reflected in a large mezzotint, by Meyer after Green, published in 1813 (NPG D35998).
96 However, demand for small portrait engravings, in line or stipple, was sustained by the rise of new publications, such as the *London Magazine*, *European Magazine*, *Universal Magazine* and *Gospel Magazine*.
97 Later mezzotints by Fisher included Frederick Cornwallis, published by Robert Sayer in 1769 at 5*s.*, and Richard Terrick, published by Fisher himself in 1770, both after Nathaniel Dance.
98 For examples, see NPG D35396 (Robert Hay Drummond), BM 1902,1011.6456 (Charles Lyttelton), NPG D38750 (Thomas Newton).
99 NPG D38749.
100 See, for example, NPG D39842 (Archbishop Robinson), NPG D38228 (Markham), BM 1832,1211.112 (Bourke), NPG D4220 (Shipley), NPG D10591 (Warton).
101 See, for example, NPG D39455 (Percy), BM Q,3.3 (Law).
102 See, for example, NPG D36654 (Farmer), NPG D21472 (Barrington), BM 1902,1011.2908 (Parr), NPG D9534 (Paley), BM 1902,1011.2929 (Watson).
103 CS, 5 and 6.
104 See n. 85.
105 Samuel Brewer, Dissenter (CS, 11), Andrew Gifford, Baptist (CS, 47), Joseph Gwennap, Baptist (CS, 58), John Langford, Independent (CS, 68), John Macgowan, Particular Baptist (CS, 73), Henry Peckwell, chaplain to Marchioness Dowager of Lothian (CS, 85), William Percey, chaplain to the Countess of Huntingdon and president of Georgia College (CS, 89), William Romaine, Evangelical (CS, 106), John Trotter, Scotch Presbyterian in London (CS, 117), all after Russell; Thomas Jones, Evangelical (CS, 66), Martin Madan, Evangelical (CS, 74), George Whitefield (CS, 123) all after Jenkin, and John Wesley after Williams (CS, 122).
106 BM 1935-0522-130. A similar row of Evangelical portraits is seen in 'Miss Macaroni and her Gallant at a Print-Shop', published by John Bowles on 2 April 1773, showing his shop at no. 13, Cornhill.
107 Mezzotint by J. R. Smith, 1777 (CS, 164).
108 After Russell, 500 × 350 mm, published 1773 (CS, anon. 90); also a smaller version.
109 CS, 15; CS, 25; CS, 24.
110 CS, 16.

111 NPG D36982.
112 Gillian Forrester, 'Charles Turner (1774–1857)', *Oxford Dictionary of National Biography*.
113 Felicity Owen, 'Samuel William Reynolds (1773–1835)', *Oxford Dictionary of National Biography*.
114 B. Hunnisett, 'William Say (1768–1834)', *Oxford Dictionary of National Biography*.
115 NPG D38817.
116 Thomas Lupton after J. W. Gordon (1849), NPG D31732.
117 William Walker after T. A. Woolnoth (1851), NPG D40209.
118 Henry Cousins after H. W. Pickersgill (1851), NPG D39902.
119 John Ingamells, *The English Episcopal Portrait, 1559–1835: A Catalogue* (London: Paul Mellon Centre for Studies in British Art, 1981); Peter S. Forsaith, *Image, Identity and John Wesley: A Study in Portraiture* (Abingdon: Routledge, 2018).
120 Mezzotints by John Smith of Henry Aldrich (CS, 3), Henry Compton (originally by Beckett: CS, 26), Richard Cumberland (CS, 73), Edward Fowler (CS, 91) and Thomas Sprat and son (CS, 243) were all reissued in a set of 'Illustrious Heads' published by John Boydell in 1811, together with the seven bishops (CS, anon. 6).
121 E.g. White Kennett (CS, 50; republished by Robert Laurie, *c.* 1790), Francis Atterbury (CS, 3) and George Stanhope (CS, 336; republished by Bowles and Carver, 1793–1832).
122 O'D, 1; George Somes Layard and H. M. Latham, *Catalogue Raisonné of Engraved British Portraits from Altered Plates* (London: P. Allan, 1927). NPG item 67.
123 Layard, *Catalogue Raisonné*, p. 100.
124 BM 1902-1011.6953; later as Atterbury, BM 1868-0808.1463.
125 BM 1902-1011.1154; altered state BM 1902-1011.1155.
126 Layard, *Catalogue Raisonné*, p. 111.
127 Engraving by Cole after Fry: (i) as Matthias Earbery (BM 1851-0503.218); (ii) as Charles Wesley (BM 1930-0330.78). Mezzotint by John Faber Jr (CS, 378): states (i–iii) as John Wesley; states (iv) as Charles Wesley. Other examples can be found in Layard, *Catalogue Raisonné*, p. 101; CS, Pelham, 22; CS, Brooks, 15.
128 J. Faber Jr after Phillips (CS, 376).

Thomas Townson and High Church Continuities and Connections in Eighteenth-Century England

NIGEL ASTON, UNIVERSITY OF LEICESTER

Abstract
This article focuses on the career and writings of a neglected eighteenth-century High Church cleric, Thomas Townson (1715–92). It aims to restate his contemporary prominence as a writer and pastor and present fresh research into the intergenerational transmission and reception of High Church ideas and practices within a distinctive religio-political milieu in Staffordshire and Cheshire. In this recovery of contexts, it notes Townson's relatively slight inspirational importance within both the Hackney Phalanx and the earlier Oxford Movement, and argues that, while there were undoubted continuities and connections between the Georgian Church of England and the Tractarians, Townson's marginality for most of the latter serves to confirm Peter Nockles's emphasis on the Oxford Movement as, in many senses, a 'new start'.

Keywords: High Church; pastoralia; Oxford University; Jacobitism; cultural politics

Notions of continuities and discontinuities within the High Church tradition over the century c. 1760–1860 have been fundamental to Peter Nockles's magisterial recasting of the origins and character of the Oxford Movement.[1] Even so, our overall sense of and perspective on High Church trends within the established church in eighteenth-century England remain incomplete.[2] This article might be viewed as an exercise in filling in a further piece of the picture through a focus on Archdeacon Thomas Townson (1715–92) and the loose connection of Midlands-based High Churchmen with whom he was linked. Most of their descendants were associated with the Oxford Movement and up to a point in sympathy with it. But only up to a point. It was their sense that Newman and Pusey were progressively discarding the values of Townson and his generation that prevented figures like Archdeacon Edward Churton and Bishop the Hon. Richard Bagot from finally endorsing it. The focus here then is on the intergenerational transmission and reception of theological and ecclesiological ideas and practices within a distinctive religio-political milieu, one within which Townson made his impact as a pastor and author.[3]

In studying Townson, the article constitutes a minor change of direction that might be usefully imitated in a study of other comparable individuals. For Townson was not part of the University (and later Magdalen) College, Oxford, George Watson/William Jones/George Horne nexus of Hutchinsonians that has been extensively explored by the current author and many others;[4] he preceded them by half a generation at Oxford. Indeed, it may be precisely because Townson was not drawn to Hutchinsonianism theologically that he has been overlooked. His career and his interests underline the point that High Churchmanship and Hutchinsonianism were not coterminous, that this conjunction was the exception not the rule. Townson belonged to another tribe altogether within the loose spectrum of pre-Tractarian High Church groupings.[5]

Townson, a son of the vicarage, was exposed to High Church and Nonjuring cultural and educational influences from boyhood. Born in the year of the Jacobite rebellion, he was educated locally and at Oxford by men with those explicit sympathies and allegiances; his friends at college and in early adulthood confirmed these preferences, and they remained consistently central to his Christian identity. But that is not the whole story. In later life, in a changed political climate, they were tempered by his own scriptural scholarship, his overriding focus on ministry, and the pastoral needs of the rural parish that Townson served for four decades. Young people who came to know him personally in his later years including Ralph Churton (his future biographer) and Reginald Heber, or through his writings (John Jebb),[6] found his values and pattern of ministry influential in moulding their own clerical formation and outlook. The problem for the historian is that these and other churchmen were too ready to elide the contextual differences between the established church in the mid-eighteenth century as Townson experienced it and how it stood several decades later. Thus, while recognising Townson's undoubted pastoral gifts, one should be cautious about seeing in him a prefiguration of some kind of later, Keblesque ideal: his parish of Malpas in the 1770s was quite different to Keble's at Hursley in the 1840s. Fortunately, an understanding of Townson's career in its contemporary settings is assisted by the survival of archival sources that qualify and offset its posthumous reconstruction by his immediate biographers.

Thomas Townson was an Essex boy, born at Great Leighs, the eldest son of the Revd John Townson, rector of the parish, and Lucretia (1683–1760), his wife. Young Thomas's scholastic abilities were apparent when he matriculated as a commoner at Christ Church, Oxford, in March 1733 and lay behind his election to a demyship at Magdalen College the year before he took his BA in 1736. A (probationary) fellowship at the same college followed in 1737 and he held it for fifteen years, the university recognising him through his nomination as senior proctor in 1749.[7] Meanwhile, Townson had been ordained (deacon, September 1741; priest, September 1742), taken his BD degree in 1750 and was beginning to gather benefices; he followed his father at Hatfield Peverel in 1746 and remained there for just three years because it was impracticable to do duty conscientiously at that distance from Oxford. Townson moved in August 1749 to the rectory of Blithfield, Staffordshire; in 1752 he added the lucrative rectory of the lower mediety of Malpas, Cheshire. But again, holding the two livings in plurality proved problematic and he seized the opportunity to resign Blithfield (though not his Blithfield connections) in 1758, when he was fortunate enough to benefit from a bequest of £8,000 and the contents of his extensive library from William Barcroft, rector of Fairstead and vicar of Kelvedon, both Essex parishes. Thereafter Townson contented himself with the parish of Malpas until, in 1781, he accepted the huge archdeaconry of Richmond in the Chester diocese at the behest of Bishop Beilby Porteus.[8] He fulfilled his duties painstakingly until his death at the age of 77 in the spring of 1792.[9]

Townson was never a man with many enemies. Personal modesty, cheerfulness, enjoyment of recreation and an unfailing sense of humour (commonly at his own expense) brought him friends at every stage in his life.[10] And he was politique enough to keep out of most theological controversies. He never paraded his high Tory political leanings and these were not allowed to overshadow his primary pastoral concerns for his pupils, his parishioners and his friends.[11] He also got on well with women and was not short of female admirers. Yet, when he left Oxford for parish life in the 1750s he opted for celibacy. He still took delight in the families of his friends and, in a large measure, became an honorary member of several. His sixteen-year residence in Oxford had introduced him to Tory High Church families up and down the western Midlands. These were characterised by intermarriage, regular socialising, a lingering cultural regard for Jacobitism lately mutated from a political one, and an ancestral attachment pre-dating the Civil War to the Church of England that before 1760 was coupled with marginalisation within the mid-Hanoverian clerical establishment.

In south Buckinghamshire, at Shardeloes in the Chilterns, Townson was a welcome guest, having acted as a 'bear-leader' (i.e. guide, chaperone and tutor) on two Grand Tours successively to the two wealthy William Drakes (1723–96 and 1747–95) in their youth. Both were products of Westminster School and Brasenose College, and both in due course independently inclined Tory MPs for Amersham (where the family was Lord of the Manor).[12] The elder William Drake was the friend and contemporary of (1719–1806), MP for Oxford University 1751–80, and very much the lynchpin of the Tory or 'Old Interest' in the Midlands at mid-century. His country seat, Arbury Hall near Nuneaton in Warwickshire, was a place of constant resort for travelling Tories, and Townson regularly enjoyed his hospitality and conversation. As Newdigate told him in 1787, 'we will never forgive you if you pass us by in your annual rambles, as in our central situation you can take no road that will not bring you near us'.[13]

Forty-five miles northwest of Arbury lay Blithfield in Staffordshire, the home of his closest lifelong friends, allies and supporters, the Bagot family. The latter had ancestral roots in the county that pre-dated the Norman Conquest and, unsurprisingly, they had been loyal to Charles I during the Civil War in which Colonel Richard Bagot was mortally wounded at Naseby.[14] Townson encountered the Bagots initially through teaching William Bagot at Magdalen and his care and dutifulness sufficiently endeared him to William's father, Sir Walter Wagstaffe Bagot, 5th baronet (1702–68), that he awarded Townson the family living of Blithfield. Walter was a consistent upholder of the family tradition of Toryism that was never far from overt Jacobitism as MP for Newcastle-under-Lyme (1724–27) and Staffordshire (1727–54), and he ended his career as Sir Roger Newdigate's fellow MP for Oxford University (1762–68).

Townson encountered the Roman Catholic Church on the Continent at first hand from having made three 'Grand Tours' in France and Italy, the first with Drake the elder and (partially with) James Dawkins (1722–57) between 1742 and 1745; the second with William Bagot from 1750 to 1752, and the third with Drake the younger between 1768 and 1769.[15] Townson imparted to Bagot a particular love of Italy that never left him and, by their many visits to churches and convents and attendance at some services there and in France, taught him that consternation was not an appropriate response to the Catholicism of the 'polite'.[16] Townson recognised Christian integrity in individual Catholics as much as in Protestants when he encountered them at first hand and was delighted, while on his travels in 1743, to have seen Henri François Xavier de Belsunce de Castelmoron, bishop of Marseille (1671–1755) (who had ministered heroically in person during the plague of 1720–21 in the city) 'where He lives in Health-full old age as I judged, and happy in the veneration of his Flock which he has lived to see not only repair its loss of forty thousand Souls, but increase half as many more'.[17] Indeed, at no point in Bagot's later public speeches or private papers does he anywhere make casual anti-Catholic comments, though it was a given for him – as it was for Townson – that the 'corruptions' of the papacy had deprived that communion of the pristine lustre that uniquely belonged to the Church of England. Townson took pains to emphasise that purity when he made it a condition of travelling with Drake the younger that he should, on each Sunday, read the service of the day as liturgically prescribed by the Book of Common Prayer.[18] But Townson also made sure that their party had left Naples in sufficient time to observe the election and coronation of Lorenzo Ganganelli as Pope Clement XIV in May 1769.[19]

Townson was very much a typical Oxonian clerical product of the 1730s, Tory by family background, and exposed to persistent Jacobite influences at Magdalen College via his pupils, his colleagues and his clerical connections. Magdalen was, of course, Henry Sacheverell's college, and it was struggling half-heartedly to come to terms with the Hanoverian order.[20] One of its finest scholars, the Virgilian expert and Sacheverell's one-time pupil, Edward Holdsworth (1684–1746), had resigned in 1715 rather than take the oaths to George I and thereafter made his living as travelling tutor in Italy.[21] It was Holdsworth who accompanied Townson – as senior bear-leader – on his first Grand Tour in 1742–44 where they were painted by James Russel in a conversation piece with their charges.[22] Whigs were convinced of Holdsworth's malign influence: he was, claimed Horace Walpole's friend (Sir) Horace Mann, 'notoriously attached to the Pretender ... and known to debauch the sentiments of the young English that he is acquainted with'.[23] But, as far as Townson was concerned, he could admire Holdsworth as a man of principle without subscribing unconditionally to his politics. He was aware, even as a young man, that it would be expedient for any sort of clerical progress to look for preferment in the direction of conformist bishops like John Hough of Worcester (1651–1743, Magdalen's defender as president against the encroachments of James II), Edmund Gibson and Thomas Sherlock.[24]

Amid his many Magdalen friends, Townson was especially close to Dr Thomas Winchester (1712–80), from Faringdon, Berkshire, whose temperament, good humour and mild Tory inclinations matched his own. The bond between them was cemented in 1761 when Winchester gave up the vice-mastership of Magdalen and married Townson's sister, Lucretia, having the previous year taken the college living of Appleton, then in Berkshire, further south in the Thames valley.[25] Winchester was not an original theologian like his brother-in-law, but, as a parish priest and a benign presence, he was quietly inspirational.[26] And he was also willing to be Townson's polemical collaborator in defence of the ecclesiastical establishment in the late 1760s and early 1770s. The Oxford 'fathers' of the 1830s and 1840s would not have found much to inspire them in Thomas Winchester – he was too obviously a high and dry Tory for that. What they did begin to see, because of the exceptional longevity of Martin Routh's presidency of Magdalen and his connection back to the George Horne generation, was the relatively advanced flavour of the worshipping life of the college, a character that influenced Townson's personal churchmanship.

Services at Magdalen took place within a large ornate chapel and were, by contemporary standards, quite ceremonial with echoes of Laudian practices in the 1630s.[27] The Prayer Book liturgical year was observed to the letter and the music and choral tradition (there was a permanent choir) was the equal of anything to be found at Christ Church or New College. And at the east end, in 1745, just when Townson returned from his first Grand Tour and resumed teaching at the College, President Edward Butler installed a large painting of Christ bearing the cross as an altarpiece. Within the obvious limits, Townson would later use Magdalen as a template for worship in his own parish churches at Blithfield and Malpas, particularly its sedulously rubrical liturgical uses. It was his invincible conviction thereafter that 'a certain decency and solemnity of form were of great use in giving life and effect to religious offices intrinsically excellent'.[28]

High Churchmanship and Jacobite proclivities tended to be seen as part and parcel together by those who did not profess them and there were certainly those in early Hanoverian Magdalen who fitted that description. Townson was not among them and may be considered representative of a generation where that link was broken. Throughout his life, he upheld Tory values, those of the 'Old Interest' as they were becoming, and respected those in public life such as Sir Walter Bagot and Sir Roger Newdigate, who conspicuously did so.[29] His regard for the monarchical character of the established church and its spiritual integrity was influenced by, but was never in thrall to, die-hard Jacobite loyalism; he was too emollient by nature to cultivate antipathy towards Low Churchmen or papists, and he steered clear of attracting attention through any kind of political showmanship of the Sacheverell kind. Thus Townson stayed on the margins while still resident in Oxford and acted as senior proctor in 1749, the same year the Radcliffe Camera was opened with magnificent academic pageantry and a notoriously indiscreet speech from William King that was easily susceptible to Jacobite interpretation.[30] For all his Toryism, Townson sought out other Oxford scholars irrespective of party affiliation, and he was particularly drawn to the great Hebraist, Robert Lowth (1710–87); indeed, Townson was considered by many second only to Lowth for academic prowess in their generation.[31]

By the time of the divisive Oxfordshire election of 1754, Townson had left the university, returned from his second Grand Tour with William Bagot, and settled into residence in his rectory in Cheshire with regular journeys into Staffordshire to his other living at Blithfield. He was learning how to be a parish priest and the *opus Dei* and his mesh of friendships across the Midlands seems to have suited him well. Having had the good fortune to be left the Barcroft library in 1758, residence in a country parsonage also offered opportunities for his own writing and he does not appear to have regarded his parishes as being merely a springboard for early promotion into the upper reaches of the Church. He also avoided being drawn into polemic. Until, that is, an extended controversy erupted after publication of Archdeacon Francis Blackburne's *The Confessional*, published anonymously in May 1766, with its plea for a relaxation in subscription to a simple profession of belief in the scriptures as the Word of God.[32] Why did Townson become involved? He was not an obvious candidate of the sort being encouraged by Archbishop Thomas Secker to take up the cudgels on behalf of the ecclesiastical status quo and gain metropolitical goodwill in consequence: Townson was rather advanced in years (he was 51 in 1766), at a remove from university circles, and probably too much of an outright Tory for Secker's liking.

Townson did not underestimate Blackburne's persuasive power or the challenge he posed to Anglican identity and dogmatics by his provocative assault on subscription requirements to the Thirty-nine Articles.[33] He, like scores of clergy colleagues, could not risk letting Blackburne claim the field by default in what turned out to be 'the most serious intellectual challenge to the established Church during the mid eighteenth century'.[34] In effect, Blackburne was calling for a new Reformation. Townson was joining a goodly company for, it was estimated at the time, orthodox responses by 1768 filled ten volumes, much of it taking the form of quite vituperative *ad hominem* argumentation.[35] Townson chose a different angle, gently pointing out in *Doubts Concerning the Authenticity of the Last Publication of the Confessional* (1767) discrepancies between what Blackburne claimed to find in sources such as Charles II's Declaration of Breda, and works by Bishop John Conybeare and Daniel Waterland that Blackburne was adducing to support his case, and what Townson found when he consulted the originals himself. In so doing, Townson was attacking the trustworthiness of Blackburne's whole enterprise.[36] Blackburne opted to defend himself in another pamphlet and Townson felt obliged to reiterate his objections in *A Defence of the Doubts ... in Answer to Occasional Remarks etc* (1768).[37] He therein displayed his thorough textual familiarity with seventeenth-century English history against the 'Remarker' (as Blackburne had styled himself), whom he disingenuously treated as an entirely separate author to that of *The Confessional*.

For his third riposte to Blackburne, Townson opted for a fictive dialogic form which, he obviously considered, afforded a means of obtaining prominence in a crowded polemical field. This was *A Dialogue between Isaac Walton and Homologistes; in which the Character of Bishop Sanderson is Defended Against the Author of the Confessional* (1768). Townson was determined not to allow any aspersions by Blackburne to dent the reputation of that unlikely favourite Caroline divine of Georgian High Churchmen, Robert Sanderson, bishop of Lincoln (1587–1663),[38] and cast himself in the persona of another admired figure, Isaac Walton, the better to achieve his objective and vindicate Sanderson in every instance where he was attacked.

Townson was always a reluctant public controversialist and, even when he did make a contribution, preferred it to be anonymous. This is not to say that the multiple challenges to the stability of the established church in his lifetime did not concern him; rather that personal pastoral witness was his primary response. As his friend Dr William Falconer, the physician to Chester Infirmary between 1767 and 1770, noted 'It is certain, [that] he never obtruded his notions upon any one.'[39] It hints at an inadvertent ineffectuality, of self-imposed limitations in Townson's make-up that goes some way to explain his marginalisation. Yet even he could not stand back when Joseph Priestley began to write against the doctrine of the Trinity in the early 1780s and Samuel Horsley, archdeacon of St Albans, emerged as Priestley's would-be Anglican nemesis.[40] Horsley's visitation charge to the clergy of his archdeaconry was published in 1783 and widely circulated. Townson entirely endorsed Horsley's case that there was no significant change in the doctrines of the Church from apostolic times to the post-Nicene era and, in a letter dated 2 March 1784, thanked the archdeacon on behalf of others while expressing the hope that 'for the sake of the Christian church in general, [he] will again exert the abilities and learning with which he is blest, in contending for the faith, which was once delivered to the Saints'.[41] He included his own remarks on Priestley's letters and these strictures appeared (though without attribution) as an appendix when Horsley further published *Letters from the Archdeacon of St Albans in Reply to Dr Priestley* in late 1784.[42]

Townson's own New Testament scholarship was not, in the first instance, polemical. Having returned from his third and last Continental tour in 1770, he settled down to work on what was eventually published as *Discourses on the Four Gospels, Chiefly with Regard to the Peculiar Design of Each, and the Order and Places in which They Were Written* (1778), in effect, the expansion of a sermon he had preached before Oxford University in 1771. There were eight 'Discourses' in all, constructed around the central claim that the evangelists wrote their Gospels in the order contained in the Bible, each written with a special purpose and a design as assigned to them by the early Fathers and the tradition of the Church.[43] It was a fairly conventional thesis, patristically based, but also one that drew on four more recent commentators, interestingly, only one of them an Anglican, John Mill, whose Greek edition of the New Testament (1707) was a collation of readings of the principal manuscripts both in England and on the Continent. The others were Jean Le Clerc's *The Harmony of the Evangelists* (1701), the Independent Jeremiah Jones's *A New and Full Method of Settling the Canonical Authority of the New Testament* (1726), and the neo-Arian Nathaniel Lardner's *The Credibility of the Gospel History* (1727–55).

The volume was well received within the Anglican establishment and Townson in 1779 was awarded an Oxford DD *nem. con.* on the basis of it. His old friend and former pupil, Sir William Bagot, predicted that fresh glories lay in store: 'I look upon what has happened only as a Prelude to higher titles intended you by the King, & that you will soon be the Right Reverend, & his Grace the Most Reverend, as it is now impossible you can remain any longer concealed at Malpas, & all your nolo episcopari will avail you nothing.'[44] For all the bantering note, Bagot was not mistaken: Lord North – who had met him at Oxford and at Blithfield – came calling with an offer in 1783 wearing two hats, one as Home Secretary in the coalition with Charles Fox, and the other as Chancellor of the University of Oxford. For most of the century, the workings of the patronage system had failed to throw up a divinity professor who combined talent and communicative skill and North (who knew Townson personally) judged that he had found the right man. He was to be disappointed. Townson, at 68, turned down the offer of the Regius Chair of Divinity on the grounds of age (despite being only a year older than his predecessor, Thomas Randolph, when he accepted the post).[45] But it may be, that having taken on the archdeaconry of Richmond only two years previously, he considered that his gifts as a priest were best deployed in parochial and diocesan contexts. He had also started work, after publishing the *Discourses*, on an account of Christ's resurrection life on earth that attempted to reconcile the Gospel accounts.[46]

Personal modesty and scrupulous scholarship played their part in holding Townson back from publishing regularly, but the principal reason was the priority he gave to his ministry as a parish priest during four decades in Malpas.[47] As a mediety, Townson shared the benefice with a colleague who held the Upper Mediety so that the geographically extensive parish with its twenty-four hamlets or townships functioned, for ecclesiastical purposes, as something approximating to a team ministry.[48] Each rector had a curate, with two chapels as well as the parish church to serve, so there was no shortage of duty for them to cover.[49] Though officially one co-rector officiated alternate Sundays, Townson was insistently diligent in leading worship Sunday by Sunday and on the major festivals at either the parish church or one of the chapels, and divided the preaching duty with his curate. Holy Communion was celebrated on the first Sunday of the month and on the great feasts of the Church when he insisted on a minimum of two clergy being present at the altar. Townson's Eucharistic convictions and devotionalism were typical of a wide range of the orthodox clergy in his generation.[50] He taught his people, in the words of one of his sermons, that the Eucharist is not only 'a remembrance and commemoration of the death and sacrifice of Christ, but a feast upon this sacrifice'.[51]

Townson also prepared young people thoroughly for confirmation and expected them to know at least the Lord's Prayer, Ten Commandments, and Apostle's Creed before he would give them a ticket to be confirmed. As he explained to William Bagot:

> But if they could say the belief &c, I proceed upon this ground to explain to them as well as I was able and thought them capable of comprehending me the nature of the Christian faith, asking them some plain questions out of the creed . . . Explaining the terms where I thought they did not fully understand them, reading to them at the same time some parts of the office of baptism, and confirmation, that they might be a little apprized of what they had promised in one, and were going to take upon themselves in the other.[52]

In his own household, morning and evening prayer were read daily with an hour of reading and meditation on scripture every Sunday. Not that Sunday was either gloomy or dull. On the contrary, Townson invited members of his congregation to his rectory on what was for him, according to his biographer, 'a day of peculiar hospitality and equal cheerfulness'.[53]

At all times, he sought to be pastorally accessible to his parishioners by visiting regularly, distributing Bibles and pious tracts, establishing people's material needs and trying to guide and relieve them and, through the avoidance of any sort of ostentation or preening, encouraging parishioners to feel that in him they had an ally in both their temporal and spiritual lives. Townson was a constant though concealed almsgiver in Malpas, quick to offer money to those who struggled to clothe and feed themselves.[54] He interested himself in the affairs of Malpas Grammar School and had an eye for academically talented pupils whose family financial resources would be likely to hold them back from achieving success. The most striking instance of his intervention was in the case of his future biographer, Ralph Churton.[55]

After 1781, Townson's commitment to his parish and to his studies was offset by his appointment to the archdeaconry of Richmond. It covered vast tracts of northern England and was a long way from Malpas but, given Townson's seniority, the esteem of his fellow clergy, and pastoral reputation within the diocese, he was an explicable choice for the energetic Beilby Porteus (bishop, 1776–87). After becoming archdeacon, Townson, on behalf of his bishop, lost no time in making himself aware of conditions in this jurisdiction at first hand (including the state of churches and parsonages). He issued a special commission on 25 April 1782 and visited all five of the northern deaneries within the archdeaconry that summer, riding a total of 572 miles. He was also prominent in the charitable society Porteus had constituted in Kendal in 1778 to provide 'necessitous relief' for clergy in the many unremunerative livings in the Richmond archdeaconry.[56]

Despite his pastoral commitments in his archdeaconry and in his parish, Townson's scholarly fervour remained high in the 1780s and early 1790s. In these later years, his encounters with some of the many Roman Catholics in the northern part of the Chester diocese led him to a fresh examination of the claims of Rome to primacy.[57] It was, of course, a perennial question for Anglicans of Townson's disposition, given further currency during the pontificate of Pius VI by the controversial religious reforms of Holy Roman Emperor Joseph II, the spread of Febronianism across Germany and, after 1789, the remodelling of the Gallican Church and the passing of the *Civil Constitution of the Clergy*.[58] It was by no means impossible for commentators to conclude that the institutional papacy would wither away and that national Church settlements (along loosely Anglican lines) would become normative across Catholic Europe.

As so many had done before him, Townson read contemporary events in the light of the Book of Revelation concerning the city of Babylon and prepared a text on the subject that was published posthumously as *Babylon in the Revelation of St. John as Signifying the City of Rome*.[59] He explicitly identified the Church of Rome, not just the city (with which he was familiar from his own Italian travels) with Babylon. In this work, Townson evidenced a familiarity with the Tridentine decreees, the writings of controversialists including Robert Bellarmine and, above all, took his cue on the illegitimacy of papal jurisdiction from the leading protagonist of the Catholic Enlightenment, Ludovico Antonio Muratori. He may have been steeped in the sources but this was essentially an anti-Roman tract. That said, like many High Church contemporaries he could see aspects of primitive Church order and apostolicity in the Roman Catholic Church, so that Townson may properly be considered an anti-papalist rather than an anti-Catholic. It might be noted that he referred favourably in his essay to the Catholic 'dissenters' petitioning Parliament for civil relief in May 1789.[60] However, *Babylon* was not the sort of text likely to endear the author in due course to Newmanites.

Townson remained intellectually and pastorally vigorous into his seventies but, as one who had always depended on his friendship networks, found that the death of his old Magdalen contemporary, John Loveday, in May 1789, shook him badly. In 1790 he suffered a malady that prevented him travelling any distance, and what turned out to be his last illness began in December 1791 when he was afflicted by dropsy and asthma.[61] Though Townson continued to be sociable and saw much of his brother-rector Richard Heber and his family, his health still declined steadily over the next three months; he received Holy Communion on Easter Day 1792 (8 April), and died peacefully a few days later.[62] He left precious little personal wealth. As one bereft neighbour and friend noted:

> This neighbourhood has had an irreparable loss by the death of Dr Townson his Eulogium is general both from rich and poor that a better man never either lived or dyed and he has the happiness of taking all his riches with him as excepting one 30 guineas in the house to Bury him, and £1000 in the funds left in annuitys to those to whom he had before been a benefactor ... and ... they fear his Library which is very valuable must be sold.[63]

Townson died without either ever having taken an Oxford chair or completed a sufficient corpus of writings that would confirm his importance and influence. An academic career was there for the taking but Townson was never particularly ambitious and chose instead to devote himself to parish ministry. His preoccupation with the spiritual and material well-being of his parishioners (as he conceived it to be) appears genuine enough. He brought them, from Oxford, an unimpeachable love of the Church as a spiritual body, rooted in scripture, tradition and the sacraments, a persuasion not at odds with his concern to maintain the constitutional standing of the Church of England. But he lacked polemical bite in defence of these convictions. His ideals married a regard for the Protestant leaders of the English Reformation Church with Caroline divines (principally Bishop Sanderson) and the Nonjurors, some of whom (such as Edward Holdsworth) he had known personally. This confection was not an unsullied mixture for the average Tractarian. Nevertheless, it represented a very mainstream flow of Georgian High Churchmanship, respectful of the foundational Protestant nature of Anglicanism.

Whatever the convictions of their fathers, Townson's generation was, by and large, not Jacobite although, as a watchword or subversive jibe, the label could be deployed as an outlet for present discontents towards the Whig status quo. And that progressive transition from a political to a much looser, cultural Jacobitism (itself, after 1760, to be transmuted into unbending Hanoverian loyalism) was to be found not just in him but in the whole Bagot/Newdigate nexus from as early as the late 1740s. It had become an irrelevancy, a distraction from the interests of the Church, possibly inimical to her recovery or deliverance from latitudinarian bishops. Instead, like so many of his High Church contemporaries, Townson focused his energies unheroically on the parish ministry of the Church for, as he wrote to his friend and fellow pastor, Richard Congreve: 'The Gospel, as Bishop Sherlock says somewhere, is the religion of sinners; and a blessed religion it is for them, if they endeavour to make a right use of it by a sincere though imperfect obedience; as such I have received it, and hope ever to abide by it.'[64]

Ralph Churton, Townson's principal disciple, never ceased in print to advertise his mentor's gifts;[65] and the younger John Jebb, bishop of Limerick, who worked on Townson's unpublished manuscripts, concluded that 'His works ... will probably be regarded among our first theological productions, by judicious divines and scholars, in an age to come.'[66] But Jebb's prophecy proved to be excessively sanguine: Townson's impact on both the Hackney Phalanx and the mainstream of the Oxford Movement was quite limited, especially on the latter.[67] Townson's beliefs and values were right on the fault lines between the High Churchmen of the mid-eighteenth century and their advanced counterparts of the 1840s. Certainly, there was Tractarian respect for the devotional, overtly sacramental character of Georgian clergy who had held on to a partially Catholic understanding of their inheritance, but it came too closely associated with the monarchical state and was just too ineradicably Protestant in their sight. As for Townson personally, his low profile for posterity had much to do with his leaving Magdalen before Horne and William Jones had registered their presence and the Hutchinsonians had made their maximum impact on Oxford in the 1750s, with his rejection of the Regius Chair in 1783, and the advancing influence of German biblical scholarship in the early nineteenth century.[68]

If there was one very moderate Tractarian who held on to what he believed Townson and his like represented and constantly argued that this deposit should not lightly be repudiated by their successors it was Ralph's second son, Edward Churton, rector of Crayke in Yorkshire from 1836 until his death in 1874. He could find his Tractarian colleagues exasperating and would in time maintain that 'All went wrong at Oxford from the time that the leaders [Newman and Pusey] began to form a party.'[69] But Churton was a rare voice because, as Peter Nockles has always insisted, the Tractarians had 'their own theological agenda'.[70] That recognition should inspire the further, properly contextualised recovery of the different tribes of Georgian High Churchmen such as Thomas Townson and his circle. In so doing it will at last move the scholarly focus on and away from the High Church Hutchinsonians, one that has afforded many insights, but has also left its other, more mainstream manifestations under-explored.

Notes

I wish to thank Grayson Ditchfield and an anonymous reader for their helpful comments on earlier versions of this article.

1 See, above all, Peter B. Nockles, *The Oxford Movement in Context: Anglican High Churchmanship, 1760–1857* (Cambridge: Cambridge University Press, 1994).
2 William Jacob, 'Being High Church in the Early Eighteenth Century', Lecture to the Anglo-Catholic History Society, vol. 15 (2005), n.p., is a helpful introduction to the subject.
3 As Nockles points out, 'if ideological cohesion was often lacking, a sense of cultural and social cohesion in pre-Tractarian High Churchmanship was fostered by patronage and family networks'. *Oxford Movement*, p. 15.
4 Derya Gurses Tarbuck, *Enlightenment Reformation: Hutchinsonianism and Religion in Eighteenth-Century Britain* (Abingdon and New York: Routledge, 2017); Nigel Aston, 'From Personality to Party: The Creation and Transmission of Hutchinsonianism, c. 1725–1750', *Studies in the History and Philosophy of Science*, 35:3 (2004), 625–44; C. D. A. Leighton, 'Hutchinsonianism: A Counter-Enlightenment Reform Movement', *Journal of Religious Studies*, 23:2 (1999), 168–84.
5 F. C. Mather, *High Church Prophet: Bishop Samuel Horsley (1733–1806) and the Caroline Tradition in the Later Georgian Church* (Oxford: Clarendon Press, 1992), pp. 200–19; James J. Sack, *From Jacobite to Conservative: Reaction and Orthodoxy in Britain c. 1760–1832* (Cambridge: Cambridge University Press, 1993), pp. 188–98; Nigel Aston, 'High Church Presence and Persistence in the Reign of George III (1760–1811)', in Stewart J. Brown, Peter B. Nockles and James Pereiro (eds), *The Oxford Handbook of the Oxford Movement* (Oxford: Oxford University Press, 2017), pp. 51–66.
6 Ralph Churton (1754–1831), Fellow of Brasenose College, Oxford, 1778; rector of Middleton Cheney, Northants., 1792; archdeacon of St David's, 1805–31; Reginald Heber (1783–1826), educated in Malpas; fellow of All Souls College, Oxford, 1805; prebendary of St Asaph, 1815; bishop of Calcutta, 1822–26; John Jebb (1775–1833), educated Trinity College Dublin, archdeacon of Emly, 1820; bishop of Limerick, 1822–33. The general consensus was that when Churton first brought out his edition of *The Works of the Reverend Thomas Townson, DD* in 1810 (there was a long biographical introduction), he had done a fine job in editing, and that the volumes should 'find a place in every theological library'. *Gentleman's Magazine* (hereafter *GM*), vol. 80 (1810), 47–52. Cf. *The Quarterly Review*, 6 (1811), 98–103.
7 Joseph Foster (ed.), *Alumni Oxonienses 1715–1886*, 4 vols (Oxford: Oxford University Press, 1891), vol. 4, p. 1432.
8 Collated 30 October 1781. See Map of the Chester diocese 1750, Lancashire Record Office, ARR/10/1.
9 *GM*, 62 (1792), 473, 573–4. Adam Jacob Levin, 'Townson, Thomas (1715–1792)', *Oxford Dictionary of National Biography*.
10 For his race-going in Oxford, see Staffordshire Record Office, Stafford (hereafter SRO) Congreve Papers, D1057/M/I/14/9, Townson to Richard Congreve, [July] 1738.
11 *GM*, 62 (1792), 573.

12 John Ingamells, A *Dictionary of British and Irish Travellers in Italy 1701–1800* (New Haven, CT: Yale University Press, 1997), pp. 312–13. See letters of Townson to William Drake the Elder in Aylesbury, Buckinghamshire Archives (hereafter BA), Drake MSS, D/DR/8/16/1–16. It was the elder Drake who awarded the rectory of Malpas in 1752.

13 Newdigate to Townson, Arbury, 7 February 1787, in *The Correspondence of Sir Roger Newdigate of Arbury Warwickshire*, ed. A. W. A. White, Dugdale Society Publication, vol. 37 (Hertford: Stephen Austin and Sons, 1995), p. 244.

14 George Wrottesley, *A History of the Family of Bagot* (London: Harrison and Sons, 1908), pp. 105–9.

15 Details in Ingamells, *Dictionary*, pp. 283, 312–13, 949; John Nichols, *Literary Anecdotes of the Eighteenth Century*, 9 vols (London: John Nichols, 1815), vol. 9, p. 481.

16 Mrs Charles Bagot [Sophy Louisa Percy Bagot], *Links with the Past* (London: Edward Arnold, 1901), p. 193. In later life Sir William Bagot bought Italian religious paintings for display at Blithfield, including purchases made for him by Townson in Rome 1768–69. For Drake the younger's admiration for the Catholic religious art he encountered in French churches, see Jeremy Black, *France and the Grand Tour* (Basingstoke: Palgrave, 2003), p. 171. For evolving attitudes to Catholicism among the travelling elite, see Clare Haynes, '"A Trial for the Patience of Reason"? Grand Tourists and Anti-Catholicism after 1745', *Journal of British Studies*, 33:2 (2010), 195–208; Rosemary Sweet, *Cities and the Grand Tour: The British in Italy, c. 1690–1820* (Cambridge: Cambridge University Press, 2012), pp. 147–83.

17 SRO, Congreve Papers, D1057/M/I/14/14, Townson to Richard Congreve, Rome, 10 January 1743.

18 R. H. Cholmondeley, *Heber Letters, 1782–1832* (London: Batchworth Press, 1950), p. 187; BA, Drake MSS, D/DR/8/31, Townson to Drake, 12 October 1768.

19 SRO, Congreve Papers, D1057/M/I/14/24, Townson to Richard Congreve, Venice, 5 July 1769; Ingamells, *Dictionary*, p. 313. Townson had also seen Benedict XIV 'in great splendour' at the conclusion of the Jubilee year of 1750 in Rome. SRO, Bagot Papers, D5121/1/10/13, William Bagot to Sir Walter Wagstaffe Bagot, 19 January 1751.

20 Robin Darwall-Smith, 'The Monks of Magdalen, 1688–1854', in L. W. B. Brockliss (ed.), *Magdalen College Oxford: A History* (Oxford: Magdalen College, 2008), pp. 334–45.

21 Ibid., pp. 508–9.

22 'William Drake, Dr Thomas Townson, and Edward Holdsworth', private collection (1744). Ralph Edwards, 'A Conversation Piece by James Russel', *Burlington Magazine*, 93 (1951), 126–7.

23 *The Yale Edition of Horace Walpole's Correspondence*, 48 vols (New Haven, CT: Yale University Press, 1937–83), vol. 19, p. 112.

24 SRO, Congreve Papers, D1057/M/I/14/7, dated *c*. 1734/35.

25 Sarah Markham, *John Loveday of Caversham 1711–1789: The Life and Tours of An Eighteenth-Century Onlooker* (Wilton: Michael Russell, 1984), p. 429. Townson's friend, Richard Congreve, was chaplain to Bishop Hough, a living link to the 1680s.

26 Winchester was Gibbon's bugbear in his posthumous *Autobiography* because of his tutor's perceived slackness. Winchester's connection to William Blackstone has led to his inclusion in a putative eighteenth-century Oxford Enlightenment: Ian Doolittle,

'William Blackstone, Edward Gibbon and Thomas Winchester: The Case for An Oxford Enlightenment', in Anthony Page and Wilfrid Prest (eds), *Blackstone and his Critics* (London: Bloomsbury, 2018), pp. 59–76.

27 Cf. Darwall-Smith, 'The Monks of Magdalen', pp. 337–8. The Magdalen ritual practices (such as they were) would develop further under Horne and Routh. For ceremonialism generally, see Nockles, *Oxford Movement*, p. 211.

28 *The Works of the Reverend Thomas Townson: To which is Prefixed An Account of the Author by Ralph Churton*, 2 vols (London: Rivingtons, 1831), vol. 1, p. xxiii.

29 Townson's disgust with the pro-American opposition was undisguised. 'In forty five, associations were constitutional and right; Why? because the Whigs had the reins of sovereignty. In seventy eight, subscriptions in favour of government were discouraged. Why? because they have not this government exclusively in their hands.' SRO, Bagot Papers, D5121/1/13/6, Townson to Sir William Bagot, 23 February 1778. For the old Tories and politics in the 1760s and 1770s, see Paul Langford, 'Old Whigs, Old Tories, and the American Revolution', *Journal of Imperial and Commonwealth Studies*, 8:2 (1980), 106–30.

30 David Greenwood, *William King: Tory and Jacobite* (Oxford, Clarendon Press, 1969), chapter 6.

31 Lowth was at New College and Professor of Poetry, 1741–50. Though generally considered a moderate Whig (originally patronised by Bishop Hoadly) attached to the Cavendish interest, allegations of Jacobitism were made against Lowth in his time. Jonathan Lamb, *Rhetoric of Suffering: Reading the Book of Job in the Eighteenth Century* (Oxford: Clarendon Press, 1997), 119; Scott Mandelbrote, 'Lowth, Robert (1710–1787)', *Oxford Dictionary of National Biography*.

32 For Blackburne's publication and the responses to it, see B. W. Young, *Religion and Enlightenment in Eighteenth-Century England: Theological Debate from Locke to Burke* (Oxford: Clarendon Press, 1998), pp. 47–53, 62–8.

33 For their foundational nature, see John Walsh, 'The Thirty-Nine Articles and Anglican Identity in the Eighteenth Century', in Christine d'Haussy (ed.), *Quand religions et confessions se regardent* (Paris, 1998), pp. 61–70.

34 Robert G. Ingram, *Religion, Reform and Modernity in the Eighteenth Century: Thomas Secker and the Church of England* (Woodbridge: Boydell Press, 2007), p. 104. Blackburne and Townson both held benefices in the Chester diocese.

35 Francis Blackburne, *Memoirs of Thomas Hollis*, 2 vols (London: n.p., 1780), vol. 1, pp. 371–2, 406.

36 The *Doubts* took issue with the second (1767) edition of the *Confessional*, and not the first.

37 In Part I of Blackburne's fifty-six page *Occasional Remarks upon Some Late Strictures On the Confessional*, he did his best to dismiss the author of the *Doubts* as one of a tribe of intellectual 'dwarfs' (p. 18), and clearly felt that no further refutation was necessary.

38 Robert Sanderson (1587–1663), Fellow of Lincoln College, Oxford, 1606; Regius Professor of Divinity at Oxford, 1642–48, reinstated 1660; bishop of Lincoln, 1660–63; moderator at the Savoy Conference with the Presbyterians, 1661, and took the lead in

revising the 1662 Book of Common Prayer. J. Sears McGee, 'Sanderson, Robert (1587–1663)', *Oxford Dictionary of National Biography*. Townson, who relied on Walton's *Life of Sanderson* (1681), was almost certainly unaware of Sanderson's Calvinist conformity.

39 Churton, *Works of the Reverend Thomas Townson*, vol. 1, p. xlvii.
40 Mather, *High Church Prophet*, pp. 55–60.
41 Townson considered the Athanasian Creed 'a very fine composition'. Churton, *Works of the Reverend Thomas Townson*, vol. 1, p. xxii.
42 *Ibid.*, p. xlviii; SRO, Bagot Papers, D5121/1/15/3, Townson to Sir William Bagot, 20 February 1784. Townson's aversion to Socinianism was pronounced, thus, he deprecated the 'new religion' of William Tayleur (1712–96), who settled a large annuity on the Unitarian chapel at Shrewsbury. SRO, D1057/M/I/14/37, Congreve Papers, Townson to Richard Congreve, Malpas, 16 November 1779. Thomas Belsham, *Memoirs of the Late Theophilus Lindsay* (London: Johnson, 1820), pp. 103–4, 243, 342.
43 Townson, 'Discourses on the Four Gospels', in *Works of the Reverend Thomas Townson*, vol. 1, pp. 27–8.
44 New Haven, Connecticut, Beinecke Rare Book and Manuscript Library, Yale University, Osborn Shelves c.57, 5 March 1779.
45 In a letter of 30 January 1793 to Ralph Churton, Bagot insisted he had had no hand in the 1783 offer. Churton, *Works of the Reverend Thomas Townson*, vol. 1, p. xlvii, n.
46 The manuscript entitled *Discourse on the Evangelical History from the Interment to the Ascension of our Lord* was finally in a state acceptable to the author just two days before his death in April 1792.
47 It says much of Townson's *beau idéal* that, on his deathbed he had by him George Herbert's *Country Parson*. Churton, *Works of the Reverend Thomas Townson*, vol. 1, p. lxxiii.
48 The rector of the Upper Mediety after 1770 was Reginald Heber (1726–1804), a Fellow of Brasenose College until 1766.
49 These were Whitewell chapel in Iscoyd, about five miles away, and Chad chapel in Tushingham, about three miles distant. George Ormerod, *The History of the County Palatine and City of Chester*, 3 vols (London: Lackington *et al.*, 1819), vol. 2, p. 347.
50 For an argument that Tory Anglicans more widely and, indeed, Whig ones were similarly influenced, see Brent S. Sirota, 'Robert Nelson's *Festivals and Fasts* and the Problem of the Sacred in Early Eighteenth-Century England', *Church History*, 84:3 (2015), 556–84.
51 A sermon on I Cor. 10:16 written in December 1780. *Ibid.*, p. lxviii. For Eucharistic doctrine, see Nockles, *Oxford Movement*, pp. 236–9; Mather, *High Church Prophet*, pp. 204–6, 210. William J. Bulman, *Anglican Enlightenment: Orientalism, Religion and Politics in England and its Empire, 1648–1715* (Cambridge: Cambridge University Press, 2015), pp. 180–1, 183, argues that the doctrine of the Eucharist as a sacrifice was justified by many 'enlightened' Anglicans in terms of both civil and sacred history.
52 New Haven, Connecticut, Beinecke Rare Book and Manuscript Library, Yale University, Osborn Shelves, c.57, 15 July 1762, fol. 9.
53 Churton, *Works of the Reverend Thomas Townson*, vol. 1, p. xxiv.
54 Lancashire Record Office, DDKE/1/1/149/18, Margaret Hanmer to Lady Kenyon, 28 April 1792. Churton estimated that a quarter of Townson's annual income of

approximately £800 p.a. at his death went on charity. *Works of the Reverend Thomas Townson*, p. lxxxvii.

55 *GM*, 80 (1810), 50. Both Churton's parents had died when he entered the school; Townson stepped in to buy him books and direct his studies so that Churton could enter Brasenose College, Oxford, in 1772. Townson also paid half of Churton's academic expenses at Oxford.

56 Townson gave it an annual benefaction of £10. Churton, *Works of the Reverend Thomas Townson*, vol. 1, p. lxxv.

57 *Ibid.*, vol. 1, p. lxxiv.

58 A few days before his death in 1792 he dropped a hint that 'if the papal power was to be destroyed by the sword, the French probably were the people who should accomplish its downfall'. *Ibid.*, p. xxviii. Townson was no friend of the Revolution. He deplored the 'blind fury for liberty' of the revolutionaries on New Year's Day 1791 and endorsed Burke's *Reflections* saying, 'I look on it as a wonderful work.' New Haven, Connecticut, Beinecke Rare Book and Manuscript Library, Yale University, Osborn Shelves c.57, 1 January 1791, fol. 35; SRO, Bagot Papers, D5121/1/16/28, Townson to Lord Bagot, 1 January 1791. He was particularly struck by Burke's compelling defence of monasticism and had earlier rhetorically asked Lord Bagot: 'If you do not approve of his arguments against the abolition of the monastic orders, be so good as to show me how to answer them; for I find my own reason too weak to answer what he says.' New Haven, Connecticut, Beinecke Rare Book and Manuscript Library, Yale University, Osborn Shelves c.57, 9 December 1790, fol. 34.

59 Thomas Townson, *Babylon in the Revelation of St. John as Signifying the City of Rome Considered with Reference to the Claims of the Roman Church* (Oxford: Fletcher, 1797). It was a theme that interested many other High Churchmen, for instance Charles Daubeny, with his applause in apocalyptic terms in 1797 for the fall of Rome to French forces. Peter B. Nockles, 'Daubeny, Charles (bap.1745, d.1827)', *Oxford Dictionary of National Biography*, and cf. his comments in *Oxford Movement*, pp. 167–9.

60 Townson, 'Discourses', in *Works of the Reverend Thomas Townson*, vol. 2, p. 276.

61 Oxford, Bodleian Library, MS Eng. lett. d. 198, fol. 3, Richard Heber to Elizabeth Heber, 9 January 1792; Churton, *Works of the Reverend Thomas Townson*, vol. 1, pp. lxix, lxxx, lxxxii; *GM*, 62 (1792), 474.

62 For an account of his death in Ralph Churton's presence, see SRO, D5121/1/17/1, 16 April 1792.

63 Lancashire Record Office, DDKE/1/1/149/18, Margaret Hanmer to Lady Kenyon, 28 April 1792.

64 SRO D1057/M/I/14/37, Congreve Papers, Malpas, 16 November 1779.

65 Churton believed the Church of England represented the purest organisation of Christianity in the world. See his *A Short Defence of the Church of England* (1795) written against Francis Eyre, the Roman Catholic. *GM*, 101:1 (1831), 562–5.

66 Thomas Townson, *Practical Discourses: A Selection from the Unpublished Manuscripts of the Late Venerable Thomas Townson, Archdeacon of Richmond*, ed. John Jebb (London: J. Duncan, 1834), p. vii.

67 Clive Dewey, *The Passing of Barchester: A Real Life Version of Trollope* (London: Hambledon, 1991), chapter 8. Ralph Churton's son Edward was, admittedly, curate of John James Watson, the rector of Hackney and member of the 'Phalanx', afterwards his father-in-law.
68 A few years after his death, the Revd Charles Dunster (1750–1816), who published various works on the Gospels, was critical of Townson's scholarship in [A Country Clergyman], *Discursory Considerations on the Supposed Evidence of the Early Fathers, that St Matthew's Gospel Was the First Written* (London: J. Nichols & Son, 1806).
69 Letter to W. Gresley, 20 July 1847, quoted in Nockles, *Oxford Movement*, p. 277, n. See also, G. Martin Murphy, 'Churton, Edward (1800–1874)', *Oxford Dictionary of National Biography*. When Thomas Townson Churton, another son, embraced Evangelicalism in the mid-1830s and expressed disapproval of Newman's Tract 90 in 1841, brother Edward charged him with forsaking their father's friends and the principles they had learned at Malpas. See Nockles, *Oxford Movement*, pp. 17–18.
70 *Ibid.*, p. 275.

George Horne, the Hutchinsonian

DERYA GURSES TARBUCK, BAHÇEŞEHIR UNIVERSITY

Abstract

Hutchinsonianism, a set of ideas developed by John Hutchinson, did not necessarily command considerable respect among intellectuals in the eighteenth century. Hutchinson held that science was divine in origin and was rooted in the Old Testament. He denied the Newtonian principle of gravity and argued that God was necessary for the application of physical laws. He also developed a highly symbolic interpretation of religious ideas. George Horne (1730–92) was an exception in taking Hutchinsonianism seriously. Horne's ideas aimed at uniting Christian orthodoxy against a common enemy, particularly those who undermined Trinitarian Christianity. This article examines Horne's ideas as a Hutchinsonianism and explores his debt to Hutchinson. Horne also can be regarded as the most important representative of the Oxford Hutchinsonians of his generation, in the sense that his orthodoxy and adherence to Hutchinson's ideas were aimed at finding a common ground between the two.

Keywords: George Horne; Hutchinsonianism; William Jones; Oxford

Although Horne is regarded as one of the most respected intellectuals of his time, there has been little historiographical assessment of his writings. Nigel Aston, along with other historians who have touched on the subject of the Hutchinsonian response in this period, locates Horne and William Jones within a context of 'pastoral response to an intellectual attack'.[1] The attack was a heterodox response to certain cosmological as well as religious issues, which are discussed in this article.

George Horne (1730–92) was born at Otham, near Maidstone, on 1 November 1730. He was the son of Samuel Horne, rector of the parish. He received his early education from his father, and was sent to Maidstone school for two years. In his sixteenth year he won a Maidstone scholarship to University College, Oxford. During his undergraduate course Horne became acquainted with William Jones (1726–1800), his future chaplain and biographer. He graduated BA in October 1749, and was elected to a Kentish fellowship at Magdalen College in 1750. Here he passed the greater part of his life; he graduated MA in 1752, and was ordained by the bishop of Oxford in 1753; he was made junior proctor in 1758; and in 1768 he was elected president of Magdalen. From 1771 to 1781 he was chaplain in ordinary to the king. In 1776 he became vice-chancellor of the University. In June 1790, he accepted the bishopric of Norwich. He died at Bath on 17 January 1792.

Hutchinsonianism in Horne's Early Years

When in Oxford, Horne developed an interest in Hutchinsonianism and became a follower of this movement alongside Walter Hodges and William Jones of Nayland. Hutchinsonianism was a counter-Enlightenment High Church evangelical movement which was both highly intellectual and a reforming movement within the Church of England. It was critical of scientific advances and highly scriptural in approach to ideas. The Oxford connection has been noted by historians, especially after the 1750s, but few have elucidated the place of the early Hutchinsonians in Oxford. A defining point for the Oxford circle was the companionship of Horne and William Jones, which needs to be explored further. Vivian Green noted: 'Hutchinsonianism, a somewhat freakish movement, had only a small following at Oxford, but it had there at least one influential spokesman in the kindly and estimable George Horne . . . Horne had a close friend in William Jones, who had studied with him at University College and with whom he collaborated in writing *A Full Answer to the Essay on Spirit* in 1753.'[2] It will become clear that this friendship created a much milder version of Hutchinsonianism among the Oxford circles.

Horne started to build a reputation as a Hutchinsonian, for better or worse, in his early years. His friend, William Jones, wrote: 'It is known to the public, that he [Horne] came very early upon the stage as an author, though an anonymous one, and brought himself into some difficulty under the denomination of an Hutchinsonian; for this was the name given to those gentlemen who studied Hebrew and examined the writings of John Hutchinson Esq., the famous Mosaic Philosopher, and became inclined to favour his opinions in Theology and Philosophy.'[3] Horne's Hutchinsonianism was not just about being a staunch critic of Newton's cosmology, it aimed at uniting orthodoxy and Hutchinsonians in a common cause: combating threats against Trinitarian Christianity.

Horne and William Jones were patronised by, and on familiar terms with, important political figures, such as Lord Bute and the Earl of Liverpool, neither of whom can be categorised straightforwardly as Tories. Both Jones and Horne were certainly active in the Tory politics of the revolutionary period, but this embraced many who would originally have been classed as Whigs. It may well be asked to what extent the political views of Hutchinsonians rested on counter-Enlightenment foundations. Although the followers of Hutchinsonianism were politically diverse, the religious agenda of the movement was pretty much the same: to restore revelatory religion back to its place.

The *Elahim* Controversy

The Hutchinsonian interest in, and belief in the centrality of, Hebrew to the Christian faith, emerged in the controversy over the word *Elahim* in the Old Testament. On this debate seemed to hang the authority of scripture as a source of revelation. Horne, with his commentary on the Book of Psalms, was one of the most popular exegetes of his age, which helps to explain why he was so widely read. The fact that Jewish addition of vowel points to the Hebrew text appalled Hutchinsonians is not under dispute, but Hutchinsonian mistrust of the Jewish Talmudic tradition has not yet been investigated. One obvious reason for undertaking such an investigation is the fact that Jewish Massoretic traditions were seen by Christians as a conspiratorial effort to hide the promised Christian truth in the Old Testament. Hutchinsonians were not unique in this attitude, nor was their biblicism uncommon. It was the

Hutchinsonians who initiated a long-lasting controversy on the etymology of certain words in Hebrew, which lasted for decades with considerable publicity.[4] The so-called *'Elahim* Controversy' is a definitive point of contact between Horne and Oxford Hutchinsonians, in the sense that this controversy enabled them to locate themselves in discussions about what is dear to Anglican orthodoxy, especially revelation and Trinitarianism. Although Horne was not a primary player in the *Elahim* Controversy, this experience altered his vision of being a Hutchinsonian to a more moderate end aimed at unifying the wider orthodox cause.

After the *Elahim* Controversy, Horne's attention was directed initially towards David Hume and Joseph Priestley. He published a critique of Hume.[5] He also started, but could not finish, a tract, *A Defence of the Divinity of Christ*, against Priestley. His *Letters on Infidelity* is an early example of the renewed Hutchinsonian response to the resurgence of heterodoxy and its association with revolutionary ideas.[6]

Combatting Heterodoxy

Horne as well as other Hutchinsonians took heterodoxy to be a threat just as much political as religious in nature. Religion, government and laws, as William Stevens, the High Church layman and follower of Horne and Jones, put it, were subject to the same danger that, in Hutchinsonian eyes, branched out from infidelity:

> Some Gentlemen, who are undoubted friends to our civil and ecclesiastical constitution as by law established, having farther considered the state of things, as set forth in a late *Proposal for a Reformation in Principles*; and seeing how many ill-affected and seditious associations are formed and forming amongst us, to the corruption of religion, learning, and good manners; the disturbing of the public peace, the endangering of life and property, and of every thing that can be dear to Englishmen and Christians, do resolve, to the utmost of their power, to take such measures, in a literary way only, as shall be thought most conducive to the preservation of our *religion, government*, and *laws*. And they do most earnestly and affectionately call upon all persons, who are disposed as they are, to assist them herein; as conceiving that there is not, at this time, an object of greater importance than that which they are now recommending to the attention and support of their countrymen.[7]

Horne and Van Mildert elaborated on this much further. Horne's *Letters on Infidelity* (1784) and Van Mildert's *Boyle Lectures on the Rise and Progress of Infidelity* (1806) are expositions of similar thinking. Hutchinsonians, in their treatment of current political and religious affairs, were not much different from other orthodox members of the Hanoverian Church.

The third generation of Hutchinsonians displayed characteristics different from the earlier followers. William Jones, Horne, William Stevens and William Van Mildert have been regarded as members of this later phase of the Hutchinsonian movement.[8] Horne can be viewed as the man who tried most to moderate the Hutchinsonian profile. William Jones's letter to his biographer William Stevens testifies to this notable change. Jones stated that Horne wrote against Benjamin Kennicott's view that the Hebrew scriptures had complete integrity 'without any fear or reserve', but went on to explain that 'from the moderation and farther experience of both parties ... though their acquaintance began in hostility, they at length contracted a friendship.'[9] Jones as Horne's biographer knew about the later Horne and his feelings then about Hutchinsonian militancy. Horne, on one occasion, stated that: 'Mankind are tired and sick (I am sure I am for one) with the fruitless squabbles and altercations about etymologies and particularities. In the meantime, the great plan of Philosophy and Theology, that must instruct and edify, lies dormant.'[10]

The Oxford group, which included Horne, occupied a transitional role, linking the early followers of Hutchinson and the later ones. Horne should be credited for building this link. The Oxford following was active between the 1730s and the 1790s. Oxford Hutchinsonianism initially exhibited all the traits of early Hutchinsonianism in general – the Trinitarian agenda, the anti-Newtonianism and, most of all, concentration on the Hebrew of the Old Testament. However, the interests of the Oxford followers shifted over time, as did Horne's. While the early Oxford followers were willing to understand and embrace the whole Trinitarian system as offered by Hutchinson, the later ones including Horne, differed by taking up some aspects of Hutchinsonianism within a wider, not exclusively Hutchinsonian, set of ideas. Also, while most of the Oxford Hutchinsonians began their careers by engaging in the Hutchinsonian Hebraic enterprise, later on, Hebrew ceased to be a major tool in Oxford Hutchinsonian hands. For Horne and his Hutchinsonian companions, the grand project of defending Trinitarian Protestant Christianity remained the main goal.

The anti-Newtonian aspect of the movement soon transmitted itself to the Oxford circle. In his early career Horne was very much interested in taking up the anti-Newtonian cause. However, in time this evolved into, or perhaps even out of, a more general interest in natural philosophy that continued to exhibit itself. The friendship of Jones and Horne demonstrates their mutual interest in the theological aspects of the movement, but Horne, in his later years, unlike Jones, dropped altogether the philosophical and cosmological aspects of his interests and concentrated on finding a unifying principle to unite Trinitarian Christians.[11]

Hebraic studies was a key element in this effort. David Patterson has noted that the only other British university that had a chair in Hebrew at this time was Trinity College, Dublin.[12] In Cambridge, as Wordsworth observed, 'the formal teaching of the language seems by the mid-eighteenth century to have become desultory, being entrusted substantially to a single lecturer, Israel Lyons'.[13] Oxford, on the other hand, provided a lively environment for Hebraic studies, so much so that 'their energies were dissipated in the controversy about vocalization – "points" – which raged in the eighteenth century'.[14] So it should come as no surprise that Horne and Walter Hodges, two Oxford Hutchinsonians, published their early pamphlets on Hebrew as a part of this controversy.

The Oxford academic environment was fertile ground for Horne to disseminate his moderate Hutchinsonianism. In addition to the already existing interest in Hebraic studies, there was a commitment to read and teach varieties of eighteenth-century thought: ultra-Lockeanism, which can be seen as a Hutchinsonian feature, was a welcome subject of discussion in the curriculum of the university. The Irish Bishop Peter Browne's *The Procedure, Extent and Limits of the Human Understanding* (1728), a study with Lockean underpinnings, as far as intellectual enquiry was concerned, contained a significant emphasis on the authority of revelation over human reason, and was suggested reading for students alongside Locke's work on the theory of knowledge, *An Essay Concerning Human Understanding* (1690).[15] Browne, a contemporary of Hutchinson, was ultra-Lockean in his theory of knowledge and, like Hutchinson, he advocated dependence on revelation for more certain knowledge and especially 'knowledge of divine things'. The fideist readings of Browne were probably introduced to the Oxford students Horne and Jones before their encounter with Hutchinson's writings.[16]

The earliest Oxford scholar interested in, and familiar with, Hutchinsonianism seems to have been Benjamin Holloway, who had known Hutchinson personally. In the early 1730s, Hutchinson used to visit Oxford and stay at Holloway's home at Middleton Stoney. After one of those visits, in 1734, Hutchinson informed Alexander Stopford Catcott Senior, in a letter, of an emerging Hutchinsonian group at Oxford.[17] Also at Oxford was Walter Hodges, who taught Horne. His most notable work was a commentary on the Book of Job in 1750.[18] However, Hodges was important long before this. William Gardner, the husband of Hutchinson's niece and himself a follower, provides in one of his letters to Catcott Senior valuable information for answering the question of how the Hutchinsonian movement was introduced to wider academic circles at Oxford. In the letter from Gardner to Catcott Senior dated 26 January 1737, Hodges's interest in Hutchinson's works is mentioned.[19] It is apparent in the Gardner-Catcott Senior correspondence that Hodges's interest in Hutchinsonianism was initiated a decade before the publication of Hutchinson's *Works* in 1748. By 1744, the Hutchinsonian movement was well established at Oxford. Beginning in that year, an Oxford journal called *Student* published various pieces relating to Hutchinsonian concerns.

With figures such as Horne, Jones and Catcott Junior we see a continuation of the Hutchinsonian interest in arguments against Newtonian natural philosophy. This activity in its very early stages was vehemently, even violently, anti-Newtonian. The young Horne was very much influenced by Hutchinson's opposition to Newtonian physics and the view that it was inadequate and incompatible with the Genesis account in the Old Testament. Horne's early publications echoed faithfully Hutchinson's anti-Newtonianism.[20] Reflecting upon the negative reputation of Hutchinson's thoughts on cosmology, Horne believed he could explain it: 'One great reason why Mr Hutchinson's discoveries have not been received, at least examined to see whether they deserve it or no, I am fully persuaded, upon a thorough consideration of the matter, is this – It has been an opinion for some time entertained, that Sir Isaac's philosophy is absolutely certain and infallible.'[21] It was enough, cried out Horne, that 'The Newtonian system has now been in possession of the chair for some years.'[22] He argued that, in the meantime, Hutchinson had come up with a more sensible philosophy.

Horne's main anti-Newtonian argument was that in a cosmology such as Newton's, the causes of natural phenomena were left without any explanation. One reason for this was that Newton's mathematical system was not, according to Horne, compatible with the physical world. It was all about effects, and that left holes in the system. All the criticisms of Newtonian cosmology ended up with one ultimate accusation: the fact that his thought led to infidelity, neglected revelation and ignored the Trinity. Horne, in his tracts on natural philosophy, 'argued trenchantly against the Newtonian concept of a vacuum, implicit in his theory of gravitation, as conducive to atheism'.[23] Also, on another occasion, one can easily see the resemblance with Hutchinson's uncompromising and offensive style. Horne, referring to the Newtonian concept of the vacuum, made it clear that he was on Hutchinson's side: 'Who is that vain, presumptuous wretch, that shall dare to say or think they are in a *vacuum*, even supposing such a thing ever was, or is possible to be?'[24] William Warburton noticed this daring and strongly worded pamphlet of Horne's and recommended it, in his correspondence in 1751, to Bishop Richard Hurd. In the letter, Warburton expressed his astonishment at Horne's unashamed anti-Newtonianism and presented *The Theology and Philosophy in Cicero's Somnium* as the definitive study of Hutchinsonianism. Warburton's witty approach to Horne's anti-Newtonianism is worth noting:

> Mr. [Alexander] Pope used to tell me, that when he had any thing better than ordinary to say, and yet too bold, he always reserved it for a second or third edition and then nobody took any notice of it.

> But there is one book, and that no large one, which I would recommend to your perusal; it is called 'The Theology and Philosophy of Cicero's Somn. Scip. Examined.' It is indeed the *ne plus ultra* of Hutchinsonianism. In this twelve-penny pamphlet Newton is proved an *Atheist* and a *Blockhead*. And what would you more?[25]

It is obvious that Horne inherited the early Hutchinsonian antipathy for, and concern at, deist and Arian tendencies that tended to strip scripture of its authority regarding the truths of nature. The reasons for surviving anti-Newtonianism in England were not restricted to this, and Horne was by no means alone in arguing against acceptance of Newton.[26] However, Horne's anti-Newtonianism essentially represented part of the Hutchinsonian agenda that was aimed at restoring the Trinity to the centre of Christian dogma. In his later years, Horne, while certainly not abandoning Hutchinsonian aims, was to drop his anti-Newtonian stance for reasons that are discussed later.

After the decades-long row aimed at using the unpointed Hebrew to establish the fundamental points of Christianity, especially the Trinity, individuals such as Horne longed for a more peaceful environment in which to further the Hutchinsonian undertaking concerning the heart of the matter: 'Enough has been given to the arts of controversy – let something be given to the studies of piety and a holy life. If we can once unite in these, our tempers may be better disposed to unite in doctrine.'[27] Horne was the first Hutchinsonian to state the necessity of abandoning the militancy of Hutchinson and his early followers. His own Hutchinsonianism illustrates the transition, which was not a change in the ultimate aim, but in how to pursue the 'Grand Undertaking'. In his early years Horne had not hesitated to reveal the Hutchinsonian traits that had offended Newtonians in matters of natural philosophy (even Newtonians who were perfectly orthodox in theological matters), had offended Hebraists with no Arian, Socinian or deist tendencies, and had upset perfectly orthodox, traditional exegetes in matters of interpreting the Old Testament. Nevertheless, in his later years, Horne expressed a reluctance to maintain this militant approach. Referring to the long Hutchinsonian controversy on the etymology of the word *Elahim*, which he had joined with various pamphlets, he demanded a better medium than Hebraic studies for furthering Hutchinsonian aims. His intention in doing so was related to his willingness to dispose of the conflict-ridden features of the Hutchinsonian undertaking.[28]

When Hutchinsonianism gained ground in places such as Oxford, Horne observed the difficulty of being simultaneously a Hutchinsonian and a respected divine. Horne realised the hostility towards himself and his fellow Hutchinsonians in his early career: 'These [are] poor gentlemen, the Hutchinsonians, because they'll never get any preferment. The bishops ... all entered into a league never to promote them ... [yet] we are not of the numbers of them who preach Christ for gain or take orders because we are likely to get more by that than anything else.'[29] On another occasion, Horne worried about religious dissent and how frowned upon it was to display partisanship, among the orthodox, in matters of religion. In a letter to Catcott Junior, Horne asked whether Catcott had read William Dodd's treatise, *A Conference*.[30] In the letter, Horne made sarcastic comments on Dodd's efforts to clear himself of all labels so as to make promotion more likely, but this was to be a strategy that Horne was to pursue in his later years, not for promotion perhaps, but in the cause of moderation and unity:

> Have you seen the Conference between the five worthies of different persuasions, a mystic, a Hutchinsonian, A Calvinist, a Methodist, and a Churchman? It is said to be Master Dodd's, who has been employed for some time in scrubbing and scouring himself clean of all the isms, for preferment. The parties in this conference are poor fools indeed, and pin one another down like so many ninepins ... The pamphlet shows one very melancholy truth, which is, that we are crumbling every day more and more into sects and divisions, and by and by it will be a difficult matter to get half a dozen people together who shall agree in matters spiritual.[31]

It is obvious that the issues Horne was referring to here were a part of a larger debate, beyond the Hutchinsonian scheme of things. The breaking down of Anglicanism into various factions, the Methodist challenges and the problem of Calvinism were all causing concern in orthodox circles.[32] Here Horne's comments were more than just a personal slant. However, it shows that Horne was perhaps beginning to appreciate that his own undertaking, his own Hutchinsonianism, could be contributing to the totality of the assault on the unity and strength of the Church of England.

This desire to moderate or soften the profile of Hutchinsonians and to avoid divisions in the Church can be seen in Jones's account of Horne's life. *The Life of Dr Horne* was very much an apologetic work, virtually an effort to clear away all the charges of Hutchinsonianism against Horne. On one occasion, Jones almost denied that Horne was interested in Hutchinson's Hebrew method, despite the fact that Horne produced pamphlets defending it and that his interest in Hutchinsonianism had been initiated through Hutchinson's Hebrew method: 'I do not recollect, that his writings anywhere discover a professed attachment to the Hebrew criticisms of Mr. Hutchinson; and I could prove abundantly, from his private letters to myself, that he was no friend to the use of such evidence either in philosophy or divinity.'[33] On the other hand, we see Jones, in a late work, acknowledging Hutchinson's undeniable influence on Horne's career: 'I know it to be true, that he owed to him the *beginning* of his extensive knowledge; for such a beginning as he made placed him on a new spot of high ground; from which he took all his prospects of religion and learning.'[34]

The beginnings of Horne's extensive knowledge were Hebraic studies under the direction of his Hutchinsonian teacher George Watson. As discussed, the early Horne joined in the controversy over *Elahim* to defend the Hutchinsonian Hebraic method. Horne also acknowledged Hutchinson as a general inspiration. In his later years Horne would engage in a public enterprise to drop the label 'Hutchinsonian', for both himself and for Jones, even though in his private correspondence it appears that Hutchinson never ceased to be an influence on him.[35]

The true nature of the movement itself was not subject to a radical change, but one can see the concealment of attachment to Hutchinson. The use of other non-Hutchinsonian material was, at least to some extent, a part of this concealment rather than a real change of heart. There was a point, however, in the last decades of the eighteenth century, where one can observe a real disintegration of the movement, and the Hutchinsonians' eclectic search for the defence of orthodoxy did undergo change.

A remark made by Horne represents his intentions as to how the teachings of Hutchinson should be restructured. His call for a change of course in promoting Hutchinson is evident here. Right after the defeat in the controversy over *Elahim*, Horne commented: 'I had much rather the name of Hutchinson were dropped, and the useful things in him recommended to the world, with their evidence, in another manner than they have been.'[36] Although it was possible for Horne's generation to relate to a general orthodoxy, it was inevitably a hard thing to do through Hutchinson's aggressive stance.

A change of method for Horne was to use Hutchinson without mentioning him. Horne gave one reason for such a necessity in his private correspondence with Catcott Junior. In a letter written in 1761, Horne complained that in the age they lived in there were amazingly few people who 'will take the trouble to read any book which requires thought and attention'. Talking about Hutchinson as a member of a fraternity, Horne proceeded: 'A writer on philosophy and divinity, brother John, in such times, comes across with great disadvantages.'[37] It seems likely that Horne and his fellow Hutchinsonians did not want to face the 'great disadvantages' that would not only hinder their own public profiles, but also the credibility of their undertaking.

Horne's intentions to integrate the learning and influences he had from non-Hutchinsonians, as writers in one melting pot, is evident by his extensive use of material from Charles Leslie. Jones commented on this in his biography of Horne. It was after the publication of *An Essay on Spirit* (1750) by Robert Clayton, the bishop of Clogher in Ireland, that Jones and Horne first encountered the works of Leslie. While preparing an *A Full Answer to the Essay on Spirit* in 1753, they consulted Leslie's works and appreciated them. However, these were early days for Horne and Jones in terms of the moderating of their Hutchinsonianism. Later on, in the late 1760s, the demise of the Hutchinsonian Hebrew method led them to realise that Hutchinson's influence should be concealed if their message was to be put across. One could therefore say that first came the use of additional resources, beyond Hutchinson, while the dropping of Hutchinson's name, in public, came later.[38]

Jones much later, in 1799, felt the need to explain their appreciation of the writings of Leslie and others, alongside those of Hutchinson: 'When the writings of Leslie, or Law, or Hutchinson, were before Mr. Horne, he used them with judgement and moderation, to qualify and temper each other: he took what was excellent from all, without admitting what was exceptionable from any.'[39] Again one senses some economy with the truth here. The early Horne does not seem to have regarded Hutchinson as just another fruitful resource. The use of other writers by Horne and Jones in mid-century did not necessarily demonstrate any departure from Hutchinson as such, but would increasingly become an invitation to other intellectuals to join their speculation and to incorporate sanitised Hutchinsonian thinking with the rest of contemporary orthodox thought. Thus, the movement was undergoing both a gradual and subtle change in its nature.

Horne and Jones benefited from other writers in preparing their *A Full Answer to the Essay on Spirit* in 1753, but the overriding aim of defence of the Trinity remained intact, and was in fact the driving force in the *Answer*. William Jones's collected works, which were edited by William Stevens, provide certain clues as to the ways in which he adopted Horne's suggestion of dropping Hutchinson's name. Jones preferred to talk about Hutchinson's influences and targets. In a tract called *A Short Way to Truth, or The Christian Doctrine of a Trinity in Unity*, Jones gave a long definition of Trinitarian analogy, as used by Hutchinson, without ever mentioning his name. He referred instead to other thinkers who promoted more or less the same argument, such as Bishop Samuel Horsley and Charles Leslie, as influences.[40] In matters of cosmology, Jones again referred to other anti-Newtonian thinkers such as Herman Boerhaave, without giving any explicit references to Hutchinson.

Although Jones was reluctant to present both Horne and himself as devoted followers of Hutchinson, his private opinion of Hutchinson did not differ markedly from anyone in the earlier circle of followers, except that he felt the need to discard Hutchinson's vehemence: 'he [Hutchinson] was a man of a warm and hasty spirit, like Martin Luther; who, to certain modern speculations in Philosophy and Theology, could preserve no more respect than Luther did to the errors of Popery'.[41] Ironically, this is in fact the way that Hutchinson wanted to be perceived. He always thought of himself as a reformer of religion like Luther.

In another way, the anti-Newtonianism of Horne may have diminished as a part of his Hutchinsonian interests, but this change did not necessarily prove that a significant transformation had occurred in his basic ideas. The freedom of movement allowed by the Hutchinsonian system enabled later followers to pursue one particular Hutchinsonian interest without putting stress on the others. Did this make someone less of a Hutchinsonian? One might be inclined to think so, but this could also be interpreted as the endurance of the movement in adapting to the need for change and to personal specialisms. Yes, Horne may have eventually desired that Hutchinson's name should be dropped, but this did not stop him praising his grand design. Horne's Hutchinsonianism can hardly be doubted, and by reflecting on his example of trying to keep his private devotion and public persona separate in his later years, it can be suggested that this may well have been the pattern for a considerable number of Hutchinsonians in the second half of the eighteenth century.

Anti-Newtonianism became an optional personal interest of individual Hutchinsonians like Horne, rather than a required component of the Hutchinsonian system of thought. Later in the century, Horne would state what had come to matter the most for them, as indeed in one sense it had always done: 'the question seems really to have been this; whether Christianity, in the truth and spirit of it, ought to be preserved; or whether a spiritless thing, called by name of Christianity, would answer the purpose better: in other words, whether the religion of Man's Philosophy, or the religion of God's Revelation, should prevail'.[42] Horne died in 1792. However, Horne's edited works, which were published in 1799 by Jones, put him at the heart of the Hutchinsonian discussions, even at the end of the century. This allows him to be assessed within a wider orthodox context than just the Hutchinsonian concerns highlighted by the work of Peter Nockles. Study of Horne within this wider context could bear fruit in future research.

Notes

Parts of this article have been taken with permission from chapter 5 of my book titled *Enlightenment Reformation: Hutchinsonianism and Religion in Eighteenth-Century Britain* (Abingdon: Routledge, 2017). Discussions I had with Peter Nockles during the preparation of my PhD, which were the genesis of chapter 5, prompted me to write this article as an expression of gratitude to Peter. Many thanks, Peter!

1 Nigel Aston, *Christianity and Revolutionary Europe, 1750–1830* (Cambridge: Cambridge University Press, 2002), p. 102; Nigel Aston, 'Horne and Heterodoxy: The Defence of Anglican Beliefs in the Late Enlightenment', *English Historical Review*, 108:429 (1993), 895–919.

2 V. H. H. Green, 'Religion in the Colleges 1715–1800', in L. S. Sutherland and L. G. Mitchell (eds), *The History of the University of Oxford, Volume V, The Eighteenth Century* (Oxford: Oxford University Press, 1986), pp. 456–7.

3 William Jones, *Memoirs of the Life, Studies, and Writings of the Right Reverend George Horne, D.D. Late Lord Bishop of Norwich* (London: G. C. and J. Robinson et al., 1795), p. 22.
4 See Derya Gurses, 'The Hutchinsonian Defence of Old Testament Trinitarian Christianity: The Controversy over Elahim', *History of European Ideas*, 29:4 (2003), 393–412.
5 George Horne, *A Letter to Adam Smith LL.D. On the Life, Death, and Philosophy of His Friend David Hume Esq. By One of the People Called Christians* (Oxford: Clarendon Press, 1777).
6 George Horne, *Letters on Infidelity. By the Author of A letter to Doctor Adam Smith* (Oxford: Clarendon Press, 1784).
7 William Jones, *The Theological, Philosophical, and Miscellaneous Works of the Rev. William Jones*, 12 vols, ed. William Stevens (London: F. and C. Rivington, 1801), vol. 12, pp. 382–3.
8 See Peter B. Nockles, *The Oxford Movement in Context: Anglican High Churchmanship, 1760–1857* (Cambridge: Cambridge University Press, 1994), pp. 203–4; B. W. Young, *Religion and Enlightenment in Eighteenth-Century England: Theological Debate from Locke to Burke* (Oxford: Clarendon Press, 1998), pp. 138–47.
9 Jones, *Works of the Rev. William Jones*, ed. Stevens, vol. 12, p. xii.
10 Horne, quoted in Jones, *George Horne*, pp. 55–6.
11 Derya Gurses Tarbuck, *Enlightenment Reformation: Hutchinsonianism and Religion in Eighteenth-Century Britain* (Abingdon: Routledge, 2017), pp. 85–105.
12 D. Patterson, 'Hebrew Studies', in Sutherland and Mitchell (eds), *The History of the University of Oxford*, vol. 5, p. 549.
13 Christopher Wordsworth, *Scholae Academicae: Some Account of Studies at the English Universities in the Eighteenth Century* (Cambridge: Cambridge University Press, 1877), pp. 162–70, n. 215.
14 Patterson, 'Hebrew Studies', p. 549.
15 J. Yolton, 'Schoolmen, Logic and Philosophy', in Sutherland and Mitchell (eds), *History of the University of Oxford*, vol. 5, pp. 581–2.
16 Peter Browne, *A Letter in Answer to A Book Entitled, Christianity Not Mysterious As Also, to All Those Who Set Up for Reason and Evidence in Opposition to Revelation & Mysteries* (Dublin: Joseph Ray, 1697); Peter Browne, *The Procedure, Extent, and Limits of Human Understanding* (London: William Innys, 1728). For Browne's influence on later Hutchinsonians, see C. D. A. Leighton, '"Knowledge of Divine Things": A Study of Hutchinsonianism', *History of European Ideas*, 26:3–4 (2000), 159–75.
17 Bristol, Reference Library, Catcott Correspondence, B 26063, John Hutchinson to Catcott Senior, September 1734, fo. 9.
18 Walter Hodges, *Elihu or an Inquiry into the Principal Scope and Design of the Book of Job* (London: James Hodges, 1750).
19 Bristol, Reference Library, Catcott Correspondence, B 26063, William Gardner to Catcott Senior, 26 January 1737, fol. 20.
20 George Horne, *The Theology and Philosophy in Cicero's Somnium ... Explained, Or, An Attempt to Demonstrate that the Newtonian System is Perfectly Agreeable to the Notions of the Wisest Ancients* (London: E. Withers, 1751); George Horne, *A Fair, Candid and Impartial State of the Case between Newton and Mr. Hutchinson. In which is Shown, How*

Far A System of Physics is Capable of Mathematical Demonstration; How Far Sir Isaac's ... Has that Demonstration, etc. (Oxford: S. Parker, 1753).

21 Horne, *Fair, Candid and Impartial State of the Case*, p. 6.
22 *Ibid.*, p. 4.
23 Patterson, 'Hebrew Studies', p. 457.
24 Horne, *Theology and Philosophy*, pp. 7–8.
25 [William Warburton], *Letters from a Late Eminent Prelate to One of His Friends* [Richard Hurd], 2nd edn (London: T. Cadell and W. Davies, 1809), p. 86.
26 For a discussion of the critique of Newton by Daniel Waterland, Richard Grey, William Warburton and George Berkeley, see Scott Mandelbrote, 'Newton and Eighteenth-Century Christianity', in I. Bernard Cohen and George E. Smith (eds), *The Cambridge Companion to Newton* (Cambridge: Cambridge University Press, 2002), pp. 409–31.
27 *Aphorisms and Opinions of Dr. George Horne, With Notes and A Biographical Sketch* (London: John W. Parker, 1857), pp. 34–5.
28 Gurses, 'Hutchinsonian Defence', pp. 408–9.
29 Cambridge, University Library, MS 8134/B/1, 'Commonplace Book', quoted in Margaret C. Jacob, 'Christianity and the Newtonian Worldview', in David C. Lindberg and Ronald L. Numbers (eds), *God and Nature: Historical Essays on the Encounter Between Christianity and Science* (Berkeley: University of California Press, 1986), p. 252. Parts of the manuscript are also quoted in Aston, 'Horne and Heterodoxy', p. 899.
30 William Dodd, *A Conference Between A Mystic, An Hutchinsonian, A Calvinist, A Methodist, A Member of the Church of England, and Others. Wherein the Tenets of Each Are Freely Examined, and Discussed* (London: L. Davis and C. Reymers, 1761).
31 Bristol, Reference Library, Catcott Correspondence, B 26063, George Horne to Catcott Junior, 23 June 1761, fo. 54.
32 On Wesley and Anglicanism, see Frank Baker, *John Wesley and the Church of England* (London: Epworth Press, 1970). On Wesley, see Henry D. Rack, *Reasonable Enthusiast: John Wesley and the Rise of Methodism*, 2nd edn (Nashville: Abingdon Press, 1992). For a recent assessment, see Ryan Nicholas Danker, *Wesley and the Anglicans: Political Division in Early Evangelicalism* (Downers Grove, IL: InterVarsity Press, 2016).
33 Jones, *George Horne*, p. 207.
34 William Jones, 'A New Preface', in *Memoirs of the Life, Studies, and Writings, of the Right Reverend George Horne*, 2nd edn (London: J. Davis, 1799), p. ii.
35 Bristol, Reference Library, Catcott Correspondence, B 26063, George Horne to Catcott Junior, 19 October 1761, fo. 55.
36 Jones, *George Horne*, pp. 56.
37 Bristol, Reference Library, Catcott Correspondence, B 26063, George Horne to Catcott Junior, 19 October 1761, fo. 55.
38 Gurses, 'Hutchinsonian Defence', pp. 410–11.
39 Jones, *George Horne*, p. 74.
40 *Ibid.*, pp. 325 and 335, respectively. On Horsley, see F. C. Mather, *High Church Prophet: Bishop Samuel Horsley (1733–1806) and the Caroline Tradition in the Later Georgian Church* (Oxford: Clarendon Press, 1992).
41 Jones, *George Horne*, pp. 60–1.
42 *Ibid.*, p. 94.

Relational Reading and Imagined Religious Community in Catherine Livingston's Evangelical Spirituality

RACHEL COPE, BRIGHAM YOUNG UNIVERSITY

Abstract

Although Catherine Livingston Garrettson (1752–1849) initially encountered feelings of isolation upon converting to Methodism, she discovered that the written word allowed her to engage in relational rather than solitary religious experiences. Over time, the written word helped her create a web of meaningful ties with imagined and actual kin and motivated her to form, develop and foster additional relationships in multiple contexts. Garrettson's story thus demonstrates the need to consider how the real and imagined communities encountered through reading and constructed through writing have played a role in the spiritual development of early American women. Indeed, women's experiences serve not simply to explain aspects of American social development, but to illuminate their broader world of connections – familial, religious, social and literary.

Keywords: print culture; women; religion; conversion; imagined community; reading

Following a powerful conversion experience in October 1787, Catherine Livingston (1752–1849) withdrew socially from unbelieving family members and friends. In this seemingly isolated state, she immersed herself in a world of texts. On 9 December 1787, for example, she recalled:

> I read St Pauls advise to Timothy to stand fast in the faith whereunto he was called ... Read in the Old Testament, that lively emblem of our Blessed Lord in the Brazen Serpent that was lifted up in the wilderness ... I took up Mr Westlys Journal and found great satisfaction in reading the experience of some great Christians of Germany. Their great tryals, enabled me to lift up my Heart with gratitude to God ... After this I read with much satisfaction Mr. Doddri[d]ge's charge to Mr. Jennings. After this, I turned over to his proof of the New Testament being written by divine inspiration.[1]

This impressive summation is far more than a reading list. In addition to capturing the variety of Livingston's reading practices, it introduces us to the early formation of her textual community – an imagined community that 'connected authors, publishers, texts, and readers in an interlocking "web of relationships"'.[2] The Bible, theological works, devotional literature, sermons, hymns and personal manuscripts written by deceased relatives invited Livingston to participate in powerful fictive conversations about religious experience, doctrine and practice. Despite initial feelings of isolation upon becoming a Methodist, she soon discovered that the written word allowed her to engage in relational rather than solitary religious experiences.

Kinship and friendships, both real and imagined, shaped Livingston's sense of self in ways that scholarly accounts of early American religious life do not sufficiently consider. While scholars such as Patricia Bonomi and Mechal Sobel emphasise the religious and social development of individuals – the emerging 'individualistic and egocentric' nature of religious conversion and the evolution from a 'we-self' to a 'me-self' – Livingston, like so many other women, thought of her life in the context of a shared identity incompatible with our modern, liberal emphasis on the individual.[3] In emphasising a relational self, rather than the classical liberal self, I build upon the work of Barbara Clark Smith, drawing her emphasis on a relational, networked self from the political realm into the ecclesiastical.[4] In Livingston's personal writings – thousands of pages of spiritual diaries, written between 1787 and 1849, as well as correspondence written to family members and friends – she augments familial and spiritual networks with imaginative ties to lives both fictive and historic, writing these lives together. Historical analyses often rely on sources emphasising real space, which include the political, the economic and the ecclesiastical, at the expense of sources that construct imagined space, such as reading, writing and ritual. However, the latter are essential for understanding religious experience, particularly for marginalised groups excluded from the physical spaces monopolised by ministers and other authority figures. I draw upon such sources in my work in order to demonstrate that women's experiences serve not simply to explain aspects of American social development, but to illuminate their broader world of connections – familial, religious, social and literary. Recovering this networked sense of a religious self not only restores our awareness of the imagined communities central to early American religious life; it also offers a model for conceptualising the modern religious self, in an age when imagined social media communities play a greater role in shaping religious beliefs and behaviours than face-to-face interactions with clergy or other congregants.

While my larger project considers the various types of community formation that Livingston engaged in, this article focuses on the imagined communities that grew out of her reading of religious texts. Several thinkers have influenced my use of the term 'imagined community'. Although Benedict Anderson coined the term to frame discussions about nationalism, a number of literary scholars have broadened the scope of his argument and applied it to the formation of imagined literary communities.[5] For example, Michael Cohen's recent work applies the idea of imagined community to the reading of poetry, arguing for the 'variety of social relations that poetry made possible'.[6] Texts, he contends, 'positioned people within densely complex webs of relation'.[7] Other scholars such as Heather Blair and Edward Soja have added nuance to Anderson's work by creating additional social categories to explain how topics such as religious pilgrimage can fit within the constructs of imagined community. By arguing for the importance of 'real space' (what we can see and touch), 'imagined space' (what and how we think of the world) and real-and-imagined space (the convergence of the real and the imagined), Blair creates room for religious subjects.[8] Building upon the work of these scholars, I contend that historians need to consider how the real and imagined communities encountered through reading and constructed through writing have played a role in the spiritual development of eighteenth-century Evangelical women.[9]

Reading Practices

Although many historians of religion have considered why women write, and have shown a particular interest in their commitment to the genre of life writing, an exploration of women's reading practices, and the larger implications those practices have had on their spiritual development, has been largely overlooked.[10] Reading offers an expansive and representative way to examine the development of women's spiritual and intellectual lives in the context of relationships. Reading religious texts heightened Livingston's sense of relationship with the divine and opened up a world where fellow believers from both sides of the Atlantic, living and dead, could commune with one another in intellectual and spiritual ways. This exchange of ideas not only gave her access to great theological and literary minds, but also offered a space in which she could grapple with and challenge doctrines and practices that did not align with her own spiritual consciousness. The fictive conversations she engaged in, with text, author and reader, allowed her to be expansive in her thought – deep engagement with texts freed her from the narrow confines of religious instruction available in the Hudson River Valley area of New York at the time and gave her room to discover and articulate her own interpretations and understandings of Church teachings, through the words she recorded in her diaries and letters, thus allowing for a negotiation of religious authority.

Livingston also had opportunities to engage with manuscript texts written by deceased family members; through such means she became familiar with the religious commitment, practices and belief of her ancestors – a familiarity that allowed her to shape, imagine and embrace a sense of her spiritual genealogy. By reading the words written by her progenitors, she discovered the religious roots she longed to find.[11] She learned, for example, that her deceased father had 'besought heaven for thy [God's] childrens best interests'.[12] These deeply personal yet ethereal encounters with kin who had passed on ultimately allowed her to develop greater compassion for and a desire to heal relationships with her living family members. The act of reading enabled her to connect with the dead as well as the living, and helped her embrace the past as she grappled with her present circumstances – she came to long for reconciliation with her mother and her siblings, for example, rather than accepting the separation that emerged as she assumed a different religious identity. Ultimately, the countless hours Livingston devoted to reading, and writing about the things she read, nurtured her spiritual growth and helped her develop a sense of belonging to a larger spiritual community that transcended time and space.

As someone whose personal and social development had been shaped by her reading practices throughout childhood, Livingston was drawn to acts of spiritual literacy as an adult seeking religion. This appetite for reading prepared her for her introduction to Methodism and its place within a transatlantic Evangelical community drawn together, in part, through shared textual engagement. Upon receiving John Wesley's writings from her mother's housekeeper – a woman whose spiritual literacy was likely a product of Wesley's efforts to encourage spiritual and textual kinship across class lines – Livingston discovered in Methodism a theology and reading practice that resonated with her.[13] Her later declaration that Wesley's writings 'opened to me the way to get religion and the only way to keep it when attained' suggests that she found doctrinal truth in his words, and that she relied upon such texts to develop and maintain her commitment to her new-found faith since she lacked access to a local Methodist community at the time. Livingston's subsequent diary entries make it clear that Wesley's discussion of the possibility of holiness, perfection and unity with the divine piqued her curiosity – indeed, she wrote extensively about these topics until her death at the age of 96. Specifically, Wesley's words expanded her understanding of conversion to include sanctification as well as justification, a theological topic that became the overarching theme of her spiritual diaries, as suggested by the following passage: 'I find myself more than ever engaged for Sanctification. I desire to rest in nothing short of this great privilege. I want to serve my God with a perfect heart and a willing mind. I have long seen a great beauty in this doctrine and long to bear witness to the truth of it.'[14] Wesley's declaration that 'the gospel of Christ knows of no religion, but social; no holiness but social holiness' underscored to Livingston the importance of relationships, human-to-human as well as human to divine, in shaping personal spirituality and enabling sanctification.[15] A relationship with God, she noted, allowed her to 'lose sight of my little self; and make nearer Aproaches [sic] to him, each day, each hour that I lived'. On this particular occasion, such approaches came as she 'read another most charming Sermon' written by another believer.[16] Christian fellowship in all its varieties, Livingston discovered, served as an essential part of the sanctification process and, since actual fellowship was not available to her immediately following her conversion, textual engagement became spiritually essential. Reading functioned as an act of spiritual *and* social communion because it fostered ties between saints committed to the cultivating of sanctified lives.

The first indication that Livingston recognised the importance of fictive ties came when she declared Wesley her 'spiritual father' – a role he assumed, and sought, with men and women within the transatlantic Methodist community.[17] While reading his words, Livingston entered an imaginary conversation with a figure who understood her spiritual needs, ideas and feelings. He became to her a father, a mentor, a spiritual guide. Upon learning that he had passed away, Livingston recorded the following prayer in her diary, 'Lord grant that tho' dead he may still speak.'[18] By developing a textual relationship with Wesley, Livingston discovered a spiritual home – an imagined space that provided her with opportunities to connect to a community of fellow believers at a time when she felt emotionally and spiritually isolated from her consanguineal kin. As she continued to read from the works Wesley wrote, and from material composed by other religious writers, some of which Wesley actively promoted, she became a part of an imagined conversation that connected her not only to Wesley, but to a vast Christian community and, eventually, back to her own family. The printed word reduced geographic distance, transcended the divine between heaven and earth, and created space for the family of God to form meaningful relationships with their extensive spiritual kin.

Wesley's emphasis on shared textual practices – he encouraged all of his followers to read the many works he authored, including sermons, essays and letters, while also providing suggested reading lists for them – spoke to Livingston's sensibilities, making space for her to actively participate in her religion, even when separated from fellow believers.[19] Convinced that regular textual engagement could foster spiritual edification and growth, and that memoirs and conversion narratives could serve as models of interpersonal piety, Wesley made theological and devotional literature written by authors from a vast array of Christian traditions affordable and readily available.[20] Over the course of time, for example, he authored, edited, abridged and published countless titles – eventually, 1,500 imprints would bear his name.[21] As a part of his impressive output, Wesley published inexpensive edited works of authors from a number of religious traditions, including Catholics, Lutherans, Scots Presbyterians, Puritans and Anglicans. He also reproduced a number of works by American theologians like Jonathan Edwards, which he edited heavily to fit within his Arminian views.[22] Wesley's emphasis on informal canons of text encouraged fellow believers to establish a textual community, thus shifting the centre of religion beyond the local congregation and into an expansive, imaginative realm accessible to all believers. This space was utilised by women and other marginalised groups to create a community beyond the congregation, thus enabling them to engage in acts of spiritual development not readily available to them through traditional ecclesiastical structures.[23] For Livingston, books abated some of the loneliness she felt in the literal spaces of home and community by allowing her to become a part of a network bound together through literary practices encouraged by Wesley and influenced by her own theological curiosities. Reading and writing, she explained, made her feel 'more composed', indeed, more connected.[24] Reading from a wide range of Christian books allowed her to participate in intimate conversations about religious subjects that mattered to her. Books, and the relationships books fostered, both literal relationships formed between those sharing, exchanging and discussing texts, and the imagined relationships formed between reader and author, or between reader and reader, were of immediate import to Livingston's spiritual journey as a Methodist and to her growing commitment to, and reliance on, Christian community.

Reading and Imagined Community

After embracing Methodism, Livingston, like others drawn to the tradition, often engaged in hours of private devotional reading, meditation and prayer, activities she carefully detailed in her spiritual diary in an effort to capture the imagined conversations in which she participated. Specifically, devotional literature, sermons, theological works, scripture and family manuscripts, such as diaries and letters, consumed her attention. 'I read in St. Luke, that we ought always to pray, and not to faint', she explained on one occasion. Capturing the sense of connection she felt with the antagonists in that story, she continued, 'I cried out with the blind man in the same Chap: Lord make me to receive sight from thy hand.'[25] For Livingston, religious texts created and fostered significant and meaningful relationships with the divine, as well as the living and with the dead. Reading the Bible, for example, enabled the relationship with God that she had been seeking and hoping to nurture. 'I sought my God in his Word, and found him every Where present', she declared.[26] Reading scripture bridged the gap between divine and mortal and, Livingston explained, helped her approach him daily.[27]

The depth and breadth of the texts she read also helped her discover her own voice and encouraged her to develop her own theological interpretations. Her deep commitment to conversational, interactive reading is captured in a diary entry composed on 31 December 1787: 'I read this day St. John Eps. To the well beloved Gaius, of whom he speaks with great Esteem and love. I then read Witsius on the Person of the Surety. This is the most improving Chapter, particularly as its references to Holy Writ is so satisfactory; and brings much Glory to God.'[28] Longing to encounter the God Herman Witsius described, Livingston figuratively engaged this author in a discussion about what it meant to experience divine communion. 'I have found myself much strengthened and delighted by this days reading', she concluded. '''Tis my prayer to the Supreme, to open the eyes of my understanding, that I may be able to comprehend the great, and Glorious Mystery of Mans redemption.'[29] Livingston came to view God as 'my Benefactor; and my friend', and, ultimately, as a being with whom she could have a deeply personal relationship.[30] Her reading practices seem to have involved the body as well as the soul; she engaged her entire self in the transcendent act of reading. For Livingston, this included reading methods that combined the intellectual and the spiritual. She engaged with the texts she read critically, while also abiding in reverence as she pored over their words. Although she did not agree with everything she read, she found a means to spiritual growth in each text. After finishing a treatise on justification written by Witsius, for example, she described the receipt of 'Health, and Grace, from above'. She continued: 'I hope to improve [spiritually] from the writings of this Great and Good man.'[31] Her diaries suggest that total communion with the divine involved more than just learning about Him, but actually allowed her to bask in his presence and experience His love and mercy in an almost tangible, albeit figurative, way.[32] An active rather than a passive reader, Livingston fully engaged in fictive conversations with the authors whose work she read and became entirely committed to worshipping and uniting with the divine. She found 'much confidence and refreshment' in the written word.[33]

As a new convert, Livingston continued to read an array of texts, specifically devouring the works of St Augustine, John Wesley and Phillip Doddridge. These Christian authors not only invited her into God's presence – they invited all readers to form a spiritual community that could dwell in God's presence together. From Wesley's journal, for example, she learned of the powerful religious experiences that he had observed among the Moravians in Germany.[34] His notion that fellowship should unite all Christians, even despite differences, seems to have settled upon Livingston as she read his words.[35] 'Their great tryals', she noted, 'enabled me to lift up my Heart with gratitude to God; for his great mercies [also] bestowed on me so unworthy as I find myself.'[36] Livingston, through Wesley, felt a sense of connection to Moravian spirituality. As time went on, Livingston's fictive conversations, through reading, cultivated her desire for fellowship with other living and breathing Christians. As she reflected upon the 'exalted friendship' and 'charity' expressed in Paul's 'tender' letter to Philemon, and commented on the 'Prophitess [sic] Miriam' leading the children of Israel to victory, her growing interest in relationships becomes increasingly evident. Reading from official and unofficial Christian canons, Livingston began to see herself as belonging to an expansive network of religious kin. Her spiritual pilgrimage resembled the pilgrimages made by those she read about – she, too, could 'throw my soul and body at the feet of Christ my Redeemer, Father, Friend in the fulest [sic] confident of his support, here and forever'. Reading helped her recognise that she had embarked on the same journey as her imagined Christian friends.[37]

Being a part of a community of writers and readers gave Livingston and other eighteenth-century American women the space to develop their own thoughts and interpretations of religious ideas that contested the ministerial prerogatives of men.[38] In her letters and diaries, she engaged in lively discussions and debates about religious doctrine, practice and experience, debates she likely felt unable to begin in her local meetinghouse. She read theological works critically; while she gleaned meaning from the work of Witsius, who remained one of her favourite authors for years, she also disagreed with his strong Calvinist views and thus challenged several of his theological observations in her diary. 'I think him right in some of his positions but extremely erronious in others', she declared.[39] For example, as an Arminian, Livingston quite emphatically challenged Witsius's views on the doctrine of election, noting that she was 'fully convinced by the Word of God' – or, her own reading and interpretation of the Bible – 'that those who indure to the End, are the Elect'. Evidence that one could fall from grace, she contended, is found in the 'instance of Judas'. But Livingston also agreed with many of Witsius's observations, noting that another part of his work is 'beautifully proved by the Old, and New Testament'.[40] As Livingston's spiritual diaries demonstrate, reading served as a space where she could think outside of the views promulgated by theologians and other male figures. In short, reading allowed her to develop her own views rather than being forced to conform to formal authority. And having a diary outlet served, in part, to mitigate and abet the effects of public powerlessness. As a reader who inhabited an imagined religious community, she could enter into discussion and debate with the author rather than simply accepting what the author had to say. Reading relationships thus offered Livingston a theological community where she could enact and understand spiritual experience and divine presence, while also inviting her to become a part of sacred narrative.

As a part of her devotional exercises, Livingston also recorded and reflected upon hymns throughout the pages of her diary – texts that captured the unfolding of the Christian journey towards holiness. She was particularly drawn to those written by Isaac Watts and John Wesley – noting that their hymns 'showed my wants, and What I ought to pray for'.[41] Livingston, like other Christians, found spiritual guidance while reading hymns and she quoted from them, at length, in her diaries. The vast appeal of hymnody can be explained, in part, by the fact that the messages laced throughout hymns, and the words used to convey their messages, had universal appeal. Livingston's affinity for Charles Wesley's 'Love Divine, All Loves Excelling', for example, likely centres on a message that captures the all-encompassing nature of God's love, and the gift of salvation he offers to his children. The terms 'us' and 'we', as used throughout the hymn, convey the idea of a salvific spiritual community.[42] All are invited to participate together. Hymns crossed class and denominational lines, thus giving them the powerful capacity to foster community. Indeed, Candy Gunther Brown argues, 'hymns extended the reach of the evangelical textual community'.[43] They infused spiritual power into a variety of contexts, thus sacralising daily and ordinary experiences and encouraging spiritual intimacy among believers who felt committed to attaining a sanctified state.

Reading and Kinship

In addition to reading from printed materials that connected her to a world of fictive kin, Livingston also read from family manuscripts – a reading practice that helped her feel connected to the spiritual lives of her ancestors. She read, for example, Dutch sermons translated by 'Grand papa' as well as pious letters from her grandfather's copybook. Seeing the level of religious commitment demonstrated by her own family members comforted Livingston, and helped her desire and form a spiritual relationship with the deceased. Religious community, she discovered, fostered networks of relationships that transcended time and space.

Livingston further highlighted her desire to foster kinship ties with those deceased and living when she wrote about receiving from 'Mama a large bundle of letters from the Best of Fathers, and the worthiest of Men'. As she pored over the words her deceased father had written, she felt that they 'lifted my soul above the world, and filled my heart with gratitude to the most beloved, the most respectable of Characters, a father in heaven'.[44] The Father in heaven to which Livingston refers is not the divine father she calls by the same name – but rather a recognition that her mortal father was also in heaven, watching over her, and communicating with her through the powerful manuscripts that he had left behind. Delighted by this idea, she observed in her diary, 'After the duties of the morning I gathered my sisters and read my Fathers letters. What a St. and Christian did I find him.'[45] Feeling a deep sense of connection to her father – a spiritual connection that could transcend the divide between heaven and earth, Livingston invited her sisters into a space of Christian fellowship. She shared their father's words with them, hoping that they, too, could sense his presence – she wanted them to experience the powerful connection that she felt, and thus become a part of the spiritual community to which she had been drawn. The separation she felt from her family, living and dead, dissipated as she came to know more about her ancestors' religious lives. Her budding awareness of their spiritual pilgrimages initiated her desire to share the gospel with her living family members, rather than merely isolating herself from them. She devoted the remainder of her life to doing just that.

Conclusion

Through the written word, Livingston created a powerful network of imagined spiritual ties. Reading, praying, writing, and later dreaming and envisioning, became relational acts that allowed her to encounter a divine presence and to feel connected to Christians, living and dead, on both sides of the Atlantic. Indeed, Diane Lobody notes that the reading Livingston engaged in, among other things, fostered 'immediate experience', serving as one way she encountered God. Reading provided a quiet, liminal space, where deeply personal relationships could be formed – it not only helped Livingston unite with the divine, but helped her create a network of ties with other readers. Simultaneously, the material she read shaped how she viewed God and Christ in the context of friendship, and how she viewed the nature of spiritual kinship in both fictive and literal ways. Livingston's spiritual growth was not individual; it involved a growth in relationship.[46] Reading served as one means of expanding her opportunities for, and allowing her recognition of, such growth. It would, in turn, cultivate visions, experiences through which she gained a sense of a mediating and friendly Trinity. The act of reading and forming fictive ties, then, helped Livingston recognise the need for additional spiritual relationships – relationships she developed and fostered over the course of her long life, often through ongoing religious correspondence – deep spiritual engagement that enabled a 'union of spirits' despite geographic distance.[47] Ever aware of the need to nurture souls, Livingston also prayed for and dreamed about the living as well as the dead. Of one deceased friend, she recalled the following after waking from a dream: 'My soul was powerfully united to her, and blessed be God, I felt as if we should be united eternally.'[48] Spiritual friendships, Livingston believed, had eternal implications. Relationships bridged the gap between heaven and earth.

Detailed attention to Catherine Livingston's life illuminates our need to look beyond our modern, liberal emphasis on the individual, and to instead consider women's lives as they understood them – through the lens of a composite, connected self. Livingston's story reveals the importance of community by demonstrating that personal spiritual development was not an isolated event but rather a 'growth in relationship' that developed within various forms of real and imagined communities over time. For Livingston, as for other women, reading and writing served as powerful relational acts that allowed her to encounter the transcendent and develop a sense of connection with Christians, living and dead, on both sides of the Atlantic. Furthermore, active engagement with print and manuscript texts enabled her to reflect upon and develop her own interpretations of religious belief and practice, and to become a conversation partner with prophets, theologians, devotional writers and her own deceased family members. Ultimately, the act of reading created a quiet, liminal space, where Livingston formed deeply personal spiritual networks.[49] The written word helped her create a web of meaningful ties with imagined and temporal kin and motivated her to form, develop and foster additional relationships in multiple contexts over the course of her long life. By understanding the relational complexities of the spiritual self, we not only discern the important role that community played in early American religious life; we also discover a parallel for the modern religious self.

Notes

1 Madison, New Jersey, United Methodist Archives and History Center, Drew University (hereafter UMAHC), Garrettson Family Papers, 1080-5-2: 1, Catherine Livingston Garrettson Diary, 9 December 1787. For further information on Livingston's readings see 1 Corinthians 16:13; Numbers 21:9; John Wesley, *The Journal of the Reverend John Wesley, A.M.*, ed. John Emory (New York: T. Mason and G. Lane, 1837), pp. 76–109; Andrew Kippis, *Biographia Britannica: Or the Lives of the most Eminent Persons who have Flourished in Great-Britain and Ireland* (London: Strahan, 1793), p. 273.
2 Candy Gunther Brown, *The Word in the World: Evangelical Writing, Publishing, and Reading in America, 1789–1880* (Chapel Hill: University of North Carolina Press, 2004), pp. 9–10.
3 See Patricia Bonomi, *Under the Cope of Heaven: Religion, Society, and Politics in Colonial America* (Oxford: Oxford University Press, 2003), p. 159; and Mechel Sobel, *Teach Me Dreams: The Search for the Self in the Revolutionary Era* (Princeton: Princeton University Press, 2000), p. 19. In her work, Bonomi considers the ways in which the Great Awakening elevated the individual; similarly, Sobel considers the effect of dreams on the shaping and reshaping of religious identity, a shift from a collective to an individualised self. Bonomi, *Under the Cope of Heaven*, pp. 159–60; Sobel, *Teach Me Dreams*, pp. 17–54. Note that my use of the term liberalism in this context is not in reference to liberalism in the eighteenth century, but rather, our modern, liberal emphasis on the individual as the basic unit of society.
4 Barbara Clark Smith, *The Freedoms We Lost: Consent and Resistance in Revolutionary America* (New York: New Press, 2010). In her monograph, Clark Smith argues that a number of Americans had more freedoms prior to the revolution than they did two decades later.
5 Benedict Anderson, *Imagined Communities: Reflections on the Origin and Spread of Nationalism* (London: Verso, 1991).
6 Michael Cohen, *The Social Lives of Poems in Nineteenth-Century America* (Philadelphia: University of Pennsylvania Press, 2015), p. 4.
7 Cohen, *The Social Lives of Poems*, p. 7.
8 Heather Blair, *Real and Imagined: The Peak of Gold in Heian Japan* (Cambridge, MA: Harvard University Press, 2015). See also Edward Soja, *Third Space: Journeys to Los Angeles and Other Real-and-Imagined Places* (Cambridge: Blackwell, 1996); and Henri Lefebvre, *The Production of Space* (Oxford: Blackwell, 1991).
9 In my research, the term spiritual is used to refer to the ethereal and the religious. The ethereal is essential for understanding imagined space; within Livingston's writings, my use of ethereal almost always describes religious characteristics, such as a sense of connection to the transcendent, feelings of holiness, and so on.
10 See, for example, Mary McCartin Wearn (ed.), *Nineteenth-Century American Women Write Religion: Lived Theologies and Literature* (Farnham: Ashgate, 2014); Rebecca Styler,

Literary Theology by Women Writers of the Nineteenth Century (Farnham: Ashgate, 2010); Cynthis Scheinberg, *Women's Poetry and Religion in Victorian England: Jewish Identity and Christian Culture* (Cambridge: Cambridge University Press, 2002); F. Elizabeth Gray, *Christian and Lyric Tradition in Victorian Women's Poetry* (New York: Routledge, 2010); D. Cook and A. Culley (eds), *Women's Life Writing, 1700–1850: Gender, Genre, and Authorship* (New York: Palgrave Macmillan, 2012); Linda H. Peterson, *Traditions of Victorian Women's Biography: The Poetics and Politics of Life Writing* (Charlottesville: University Press of Virginia, 1999).

11 For a discussion about the meaning and implications of the genealogical imagination, see Eviatar Zerubavel, *Ancestors and Relatives: Genealogy, Identity, and Community* (Oxford: Oxford University Press, 2012). See also Alondra Nelson, *The Social Life of DNA: Race, Reparations, and Reconciliation After the Genome* (Boston: Beacon Press, 2016).

12 UMAHC, Garrettson Family Papers, 1080-5-2: 4, Catherine Livingston Garrettson Diary, 26 May 1788.

13 In her autobiography, Catherine Livingston Garrettson recounts the story about her mother's servant sharing John Wesley's writings with her. See UMAHC, Garrettson Family Papers, 1080-5-2: 41, Catherine Livingston Garrettson Autobiographical Sketch. On Methodist reading practices, see Vicki Tolar Burton, *Spiritual Literacy in John Wesley's Methodism: Reading, Writing, and Speaking to Believe* (Waco, TX: Baylor University Press, 2008); Isabel Rivers, *Vanity Fair and the Celestial City: Dissenting, Methodist, and Evangelical Literary Culture in England, 1720–1800* (Oxford: Oxford University Press, 2018); D. Bruce Hindmarsh, *The Spirit of Early Evangelicalism: True Religion in a Modern World* (Oxford: Oxford University Press, 2018). See also Phyllis Mack, *Heart Religion in the British Enlightenment: Gender and Emotions in Early Methodism* (Cambridge: Cambridge University Press, 2008).

14 UMAHC, Garrettson Family Papers, 1080-5-2: 5, Catherine Livingston Garrettson Diary, 1 December 1791.

15 John Wesley, *Hymns and Sacred Poems* (London: William Strahan, 1739). For a discussion about different interpretations of this quote, see Andrew C. Thompson, 'From Societies to Society: The Shift from Holiness to Justice in the Wesleyan Tradition', *Methodist Review*, 3 (2011), 141–72.

16 UMAHC, Garrettson Family Papers, 1080-5-2: 1, Catherine Livingston Garrettson Diary, 30 November 1787.

17 UMAHC, Garrettson Family Papers, 1080-5-2: 41, Catherine Livingston Garrettson Autobiographical Sketch. Anna M. Lawrence, *One Family Under God: Love, Belonging and Authority in Early Transatlantic Methodism* (Philadelphia: University of Pennsylvania Press, 2011), p. 171. Livingston also mourns Wesley's death in her diary on 15 April 1791, declaring that she is relating the 'death of my Father in Christ'. UMAHC, Garrettson Family Papers, 1080-5-2: 5, Catherine Livingston Garrettson Diary, 15 April 1791. Anna Lawrence explains that 'Wesley continued to be an almost mythical figure in American Methodism', *One Family Under God*, p. 216.

18 UMAHC, Garrettson Family Papers, 1080-5-2: 5, Catherine Livingston Garrettson Diary, 15 April 1791.

19 For a discussion of Methodist reading practices, see Tolar Burton, *Spiritual Literacy in John Wesley's Methodism*, pp. 233–63.
20 Jonathan M. Yeager, *Jonathan Edwards and Transatlantic Print Culture* (Oxford: Oxford University Press, 2016), pp. 92–3.
21 *Ibid.*
22 *Ibid.*
23 See, for example, Tolar Burton, *Spiritual Literacy in John Wesley's Methodism*, pp. 151–96; and Kevin J. Hayes, *A Colonial Woman's Bookshelf* (Knoxville: University of Tennessee Press, 1996).
24 UMAHC, Garrettson Family Papers, 1080-5-2: 3, Catherine Livingston Garrettson Diary, 22 April 1788.
25 *Ibid.*, 14 March 1788.
26 UMAHC, Garrettson Family Papers, 1080-5-2: 1, Catherine Livingston Garrettson Diary, 28 November 1787.
27 *Ibid.*, 30 November 1787.
28 UMAHC, Garrettson Family Papers, 1080-5-2: 1, Catherine Livingston Garrettson Diary, 31 December 1787. Herman Witsius (1636–1708) was a Dutch Reformed theologian.
29 UMAHC, Garrettson Family Papers, 1080-5-2: 2, Catherine Livingston Garrettson Diary, 31 January 1788.
30 UMAHC, Garrettson Family Papers, 1080-5-2: 1, Catherine Livingston Garrettson Diary, 30 November 1787.
31 UMAHC, Garrettson Family Papers, 1080-5-2: 3, Catherine Livingston Garrettson Diary, 22 March 1788.
32 Robert Orsi, *History and Presence* (Cambridge, MA: The Belknap Press of Harvard University Press, 2016).
33 UMAHC, Garrettson Family Papers, 1080-5-2: 2, Catherine Livingston Garrettson Diary, 28 January 1788.
34 *The Journal of the Reverend John Wesley*, ed. Emory, pp. 76–109.
35 UMAHC, Garrettson Family Papers, 1080-5-2: 1, Catherine Livingston Garrettson Diary, 9 December 1787.
36 *Ibid.*
37 UMAHC, Garrettson Family Papers, 1080-5-2: 4, Catherine Livingston Garrettson Diary, 4 May 1788.
38 Other examples include Sarah Osborne and Priscilla Carter. See Catherine A. Brekus, *Sarah Osborne's World: The Rise of Evangelical Christianity in Early America* (New Haven, CT: Yale University Press, 2013); Hayes, *A Colonial Woman's Bookshelf*.
39 UMAHC, Garrettson Family Papers, 1080-5-2: 2, Catherine Livingston Garrettson Diary, 12 January 1788.
40 UMAHC, Garrettson Family Papers, 1080-5-2: 1, Catherine Livingston Garrettson Diary, 23 December 1787.
41 *Ibid.*
42 Charles Wesley, 'Hymn 385 – Love Divine, All Loves Excelling', *A Collection of Hymns, For the Use of the People Called Methodists* (London: J. Rouche, 1779), p. 368. UMAHC,

Garrettson Family Papers, 1080-5-2: 3, Catherine Livingston Garrettson Diary, 25 April 1788.
43 Brown, *The Word in the World*, pp. 191–2.
44 UMAHC, Garrettson Family Papers, 108-5-2: 4, Catherine Livingston Garrettson Diary, 26 May 1788.
45 *Ibid.*
46 Diane Helen Lobody, 'Lost in the Ocean of Love: The Mystical Writings of Catherine Livingston Garrettson' (PhD dissertation, Drew University, 1990), p. 107.
47 UMAHC, Garrettson Family Papers, Catherine Livingston Garrettson Diary, 1 December 1825.
48 UMAHC, Garrettson Family Papers, 1080-5-2: 7, Catherine Livingston Garrettson Diary, 22 May 1810.
49 Cohen, *The Social Lives of Poems*, p. 7.

Disappearing Women: The Gendered Politics of Publication of Mary Fletcher's Auto/Biography

CAROL BLESSING, POINT LOMA NAZARENE UNIVERSITY

Abstract
This article focuses on the representation of Methodist preacher Mary Bosanquet Fletcher (1739–1815) in her biography by the Revd Henry Moore. His omissions and commentary served to neutralise some of her more radical ideas and early feminism, which can be discovered by reading her manuscript journals, as well as the manuscript correspondence between Mary Tooth, keeper of Mary Fletcher's papers, and Henry Moore. The product of archival research in the Methodist collections at the John Rylands Library in Manchester, this article owes a great debt to archivists Dr Peter Nockles and Dr Gareth Lloyd.

Keywords: women's preaching; Methodism; Madeley, Shropshire; Mary Bosanquet Fletcher; Mary Tooth; autobiography

Mary Bosanquet Fletcher (1739–1815), a wealthy, independent and outspoken British woman of Huguenot extraction, worked tirelessly within Methodist circles before, during and after her three-year marriage from 1782 to 1785 to Anglican priest and Methodist leader, the Revd John Fletcher (1729–85), whom John Wesley had appointed his successor to lead the Methodist movement. As the younger, unmarried Mary Bosanquet, her letters and journals detailed her conversion and lifetime devotion to the Methodist movement, the renunciation of her wealthy family's lifestyle, her desire to care for female children in need of a home, and her calling to ministry, whatever that meant for her as a woman before women were ordained in such roles. She was the most famous member of early Methodism's cadre of remarkable women who actively participated in the movement through various forms of public speaking, writing and/or financial support; in fact, she inspired and mentored other women of her time.

The Life of Mary Fletcher: Autobiography or Biography?

Mary Bosanquet Fletcher's enduring legacy rests primarily on her autobiography, or biography, *The Life of Mary Fletcher*, published in multiple nineteenth-century editions. In *The Autobiographical Subject: Gender and Ideology in Eighteenth-Century England*, Felicity Nussbaum cited Bosanquet Fletcher's work in the Methodist movement, but did not discuss her autobiography, perhaps because it is erroneously regarded as a biography by Revd Henry Moore, rather than a first-person life story compiled by Bosanquet Fletcher herself.[1] Indeed, it was in many ways shaped by its editor, Moore, who did not present an unexpurgated version of Bosanquet Fletcher's manuscripts. His omissions and commentary neutralised her more radical proto-feminist ideas and can be discovered only through reading her manuscript journals, as well as the manuscript correspondence between Mary Tooth (1778–1843), who was the keeper of Bosanquet Fletcher's papers, and Moore.

Notably, Moore radically censored Bosanquet Fletcher's fully developed apologia for women's preaching. While his editorial role necessitated judicious cutting to control the length of publication, comparing Bosanquet Fletcher's manuscripts to Moore's published version demonstrates how the editor shaped his female subject and lessened both her and her assistant's more outspoken roles and views of women in ministry. Moore also omitted the fundamental role that Mary Tooth, Bosanquet Fletcher's adopted daughter, scribe and successive leader of Methodist class meetings in the Shropshire area, played in archiving Fletcher's manuscripts and holding Moore accountable for their publication, despite Tooth's attempted intervention in the publication process to present more of Bosanquet Fletcher's radical role in early Methodist ministry.[2]

Moore opened his 1817 work *The Life of Mrs. Mary Fletcher, Consort and Relict of The Rev. John Fletcher* with the following account regarding how he had come to edit her manuscripts into a published life story.[3] He wrote:

> A short time after I was appointed to the Birmingham District, the papers of the late Mrs Fletcher were put into my hands. I was informed at the same time, that the venerable person whose life was recorded in them, had mentioned me as one that she wished should prepare and publish her papers; and that an application to that effect would have been made to me before that time; but that the distance of my former appointment had prevented it, Mrs Fletcher having laid an injunction on her friend, to whom, by will, she had committed them, not to give them absolutely into the hands of any person whatsoever.[4]

The friend to whom Moore referred is of course Mary Tooth, the anonymous woman who made possible not only the *Life of Mary Fletcher* in 1817 and subsequent editions, but also the Fletcher-Tooth Collection in the Methodist Archives and Research Centre at the John Rylands Library and, indeed, much of our knowledge about the Methodist movement in Madeley, Shropshire. One of Tooth's early notes, repeated in two draft letters for Mary Fletcher, was, 'My Dear Mrs Fletcher desires me to be her scribe & write while she dictates.' This note was possibly written not only for informational purposes, but to show her delight in her new position which became her lifelong vocation.[5]

Mary Bosanquet Fletcher's Ministry as Recorded and Archived by Mary Tooth

Although John Fletcher's early death thwarted Wesley's plan for his succession to leadership, his widow continued to coordinate the Methodist movement in Madeley, Shropshire. Until her death in 1815, Mary Fletcher led class meetings, counselled parishioners in person and through letters, held love feasts, scheduled circuit preachers, and essentially functioned as a preacher herself. In an 1820 draft letter to an unknown recipient who enquired about Fletcher's denominational loyalties, Mary Tooth wrote the following description of Bosanquet Fletcher's religious involvement, both active membership in the local Anglican Church and vocational activities within the Methodist movement:

> She was from an early period of life both a member of the Church of England & of the Methodist Society. From the age of twelve when she received her first ticket from Mr Wesley to the day of her translation to glory she always received her ticket at the quarterly visitation. Her stated engagements in the city of Madeley was as follows, at 9 o'clock on the Sabbath morning she met a class which ended when the Church bells began to ring. Which service she attended when her health would admit. Before the afternoon service in the church she had a public meeting in which she expounded the scriptures, concluding as in the morning when the bell began for the church service. At 6 in the evening was a prayer meeting after which she had a society meeting. On Monday evening at 7 o'clock she again expounded the scriptures & on Tuesday morning met a class, in the evening the Methodist preachers preached & on Wednesday Morning she met another class. These meetings was regularly attended every week, others that she had was once a fortnight, & some once a month. I should have said the Preachers came to Madeley only once a fortnight & on the Tuesday they were not at her house she met some persons in class which she had invited to come & spend that hour at her room, & from that meeting have come several most useful class teachers & local preachers.[6]

Throughout her life, Mary Fletcher kept extensive journals, copies of her correspondence, and transcriptions of her Sunday night sermons, which she called 'Watch-Words', and employed Tooth as archivist of her papers, showing Fletcher's intention to produce a carefully crafted autobiographical work. Towards the end of her life, in her journal, Fletcher expressed concern that her writings be misinterpreted or reflect negatively on the Methodist movement:

> I have had some trials with regard to our affairs. But I have a full confidence all shall end well. We have had for 30 years a oneness of people but now there is a separation from the desire of the minister – it hurts me. Yet I believe the Lord will make all well; I here declare I have been joined to the people united to Mr Wesley for above three score year & I trust to die among them as yet the life of true religion is among them & the work increases. If my papers fall into any hands [I] entreat there Jesus may never be defeated.[7]

She considered it crucial to control how and by whom her 'papers', that is her draft of her autobiography, would be printed to accurately (according to her own constructions of people and events) represent her late spouse, John Fletcher, the Methodist movement in Madeley, and herself as a woman in ministry.

In one of Mary Tooth's letters, she stated that Fletcher had, in fact, wanted Tooth to edit and publish the work herself; Tooth felt inadequate for the task, but Fletcher tried to persuade her by reminding her that God would enable her. However, Tooth did not go further than to give her word that she would take charge of her papers and use the utmost care in determining who was worthy of them.[8] One of Tooth's draft letters states:

With regard to my dear departed friend's Life & every other manuscript she had, they are all in my hands, for me to do whatever I may judge best with them, her love to & confidence in me was unbounded, the former of these can never be erased while memory last, & I trust a gracious God will preserve me from abusing the latter. On the very day before she died, she expressed her compleat satisfaction in having left her writings entirely to my disposal. I consider them an important deposit.[9]

Mary Tooth Requests Henry Moore's Assistance in Publishing the *Life of Mary Fletcher*

Tooth recognised the need for Methodist male ministerial authority to authorise Mary Fletcher's lifework. Conscientiously fulfilling her charge as keeper of Fletcher's manuscripts, Tooth turned down Joseph Benson's offer to edit the work[10] and ultimately sought out Henry Moore, John Wesley's scribe, Methodist preacher, twice president of the Wesleyan Conference, and noted biographer who, with Thomas Coke, had already published *The Life of the Rev. John Wesley* in 1792,[11] to publish Fletcher's papers, a decision apparently aligned with her mentor's wishes. In an undated letter to a Miss Thomas, Mary Tooth wrote: 'I am at present corresponding with Mr H. Moore on the subject but whether he will be the Editor or not, is not at present determined. I am daily giving the matter into the hands of my dear heavenly father.'[12] Henry Moore's 26 September 1816 reply to Tooth stated: 'I have received the Life & Journals of your excellent Friend . . . I cannot express the admiration of it as I could wish, especially in this short letter. It describes "the simple life divine", which men are so aware to receive, and in comparison of which even what is prized among many in Religion, is wood, hay, and stubble.'[13] Moore took the editorial responsibility, as Tooth thanked him on 23 December 1816 for his acceptance of the task:

> I am much obliged by your kind letter the contents of it was very pleasing. It would have been a painful circumstance to have had the Life of my dear Friend printed without the concurance [sic] of that Body of men whom I do truly love & revere (many of them for their own sake & all of them) for their work's sake, but I trust all is now going on in a right track & that the result will prove divine wisdom had ordered the affair. Am fully satisfied now the whole is left in your hands.[14]

In an 1818 letter to Tooth, Mary Whittingham, Mary Fletcher's niece, reinforced Tooth's decision, as she noted that Fletcher had spoken favourably of Moore being the future publisher of her work: 'I much appreciate of its being done by Mr Moore [the bio] as he was the person my dear Aunt approved. You appear to me to have done your duty to her memory, and your attention to the publishing of her life is greatly to my satisfaction.'[15]

Moore, however, did not mention Tooth in his preface as the source of the biography. Nor did he relate Tooth's work in carefully writing, copying and filing letters, journals and other accounts, providing the primary documentation of the lives of Mary Fletcher, Sarah Ryan and herself, as well as material on John Fletcher, and making suggestions and corrections to the biography. All the editions of the *Life* credited Moore solely with the work, though in actuality it was a joint effort with Tooth. While Moore included Tooth's narrative of Mary Fletcher's death as an epilogue, he otherwise erased her from printed history. In fact, he excised portions of Fletcher's journals that discuss how valuable Tooth's help had been to her. These omitted excerpts in Fletcher's manuscript journals can be seen crossed out in pencil:

> Aug 1 1802 – I find Miss Tooth a very great help & a faithful diligent assistant. She is truly a gift of God that I could not do without – how true is that now 'no manner of thing that is good shall be withheld.' Nov 13 1802 – True, I have a good deal to do, much writing on my hand, & many things to attend too for the poor as physick clothes & c, and as my health is short all motion, this would be difficult without my dear Sally who was as my right hand on all these occasions?, but I was not permitted to feel this want, as the Lord who never fail me gave Mary Tooth to me as an assistant, & her a capacity to take off several burdens.[16]

Mary Tooth's letters to Moore further show her working actively with him to try to shape the account of her beloved Mary Fletcher in a positive manner, and most importantly, to have her presented as a female preacher. Fletcher willed her papers to Tooth to get them published, no doubt knowing that latter's diligence would make her an apt steward for her legacy. Fletcher's draft letter of 6 December 1805 to an unknown recipient shows her as already contemplating her own death ten years ahead of her passing, expecting Tooth to coordinate the care of her papers with the Methodist Connexion. Her detailed, explicit instructions follow:

> Both age & illness calls on me to look for a remove perhaps [sudden] – & I would wish to show my love & respect to the Connexion I have more then half a century been united with.
>
> Therefore for the Bennefit of the Conference I desire my papers (viz according to a paper of Contents included) but I desire to have some opinion better then my own whether they are thought proper to be presented or not. For that purpose I here fix on you if you think well to reject them for the press I beg you to accept the included ten pound notwithstanding my advantage that may accrue as a Member of Conference.
>
> A thought strikes my mind perhaps the best mode of printing them might be in numbers suppose the Life in four parts is now divided – then the journals; & S. Ryans Life diary & Letters after in the Same manner. If the Watchwords as wee call them – on the names of Christ & the Church are thought worthy any them I could wish them added to the little tract called my Soul's Legacy to the dear people of Madeley. They were wrote as a subject for meditation one each fortnight when we had our local meeting ... They will all be left in the hands of Miss M. T. who will deliver them to you. One disadvantage is, I have for many years been scarce able to write any thing twice over ... [the work] is mostly from my rough draft (but I had it done to render it up [unreadable section]) & there wrote chiefly for my own use just as the thoughts occur.) However, I have neither strength nor time to make them shorter you will therefore find them pretty bulky.

The Life of S. Ryan I hope will not be altered in any thing for I know all I have said to be truth & far short of what might have been said. <u>Mine</u> is made up of ingratitude & mercys, but the latter has been so great that (tho I have often thought of Pruning it) on consideration I believe is my duty to declare the long suffering & loving kindness of the Lord, that others might avoid my sins & be incouraged by my favours[?] & now my adorable Saviour I commit the whole to thee if this Soul mite do any good let it be preserved – if not may it be sunk in oblivion – I have no interest but thy Glory.[17]

Mary Tooth's Attempts to Include Mary Bosanquet Fletcher's Complete Apologia for Women Preaching

A pertinent file of Henry Moore's letters located outside of the Fletcher-Tooth Collection contains ten letters in dialogue with Tooth regarding the publishing process of Mary Fletcher's *Life*. Moore initially expressed great enthusiasm about the papers and the project; he opined that the life 'needs but little correction or abridgment', and reiterated his desire to consult Tooth on all issues of importance.[18] Moore also pressed the Methodist book steward to allow him to have the work published locally and in two volumes, as well as to produce a lower-cost one-volume edition to be given to a poorer audience, according to Tooth's wishes.[19] However, on one major issue he and Tooth parted ways. Tooth was particularly concerned with presenting Fletcher as a legitimate, groundbreaking female speaker/preacher, one whose ministerial experience and theology enabled her to write what she regarded as a clear apologia for women's preaching, as documented in correspondence with Henry Moore and his wife Mary Ann Moore. On 22 December 1817, Tooth began a letter topic which she continued for several months: 'Dear Brother – Am sorry to trouble you (that have so many daily) with a letter from me, but receiving a letter on Saturday enquiring among other things, Why Mrs Fletcher's letter to Mr Wesley on Women's speaking with his answer, was not inserted in her life? I thought I had better sent it you, tho' it may be too late, as possibly you have concluded the work by this time.'[20]

Subsequent letters from Tooth on the same topic highlight her resolve: Fletcher's complete letter to Wesley must be a part of Fletcher's biography. She wrote again: 'Have this moment received yours, & hasten to send you the remaining part of my dear Mrs Fletchers letter, & Mr Wesley's reply. The last sentence I copied was Deborah's going with Barak.' She proceeds, 'ob. but all these were Extraordinary calls, sure you will not say, yours is an Extraordinary call?'[21] Tooth proceeded to recopy the lengthy letter.[22] The document in question was a deliberately developed, carefully argued version of the oft-quoted correspondence with Wesley, who had responded on 13 June 1771 with this reply concerning her work:

> MY DEAR SISTER, – I think the strength of the cause rests there – on your having an *extraordinary* call. So I am persuaded has every one of our lay preachers; otherwise I could not countenance his preaching at all. It is plain to me that the whole work of God termed Methodism is an extraordinary dispensation of His providence.

Therefore I do not wonder if several things occur therein which do not fall under the ordinary rules of discipline. St. Paul's ordinary rule was, 'I permit not a woman to speak in the congregation.' Yet in extraordinary cases he made a few exceptions; at Corinth in particular. – I am, my dear sister,

Your affectionate brother.[23]

While Wesley's letter at first seemed to give positive encouragement for Bosanquet's preaching, it also raised the issue of the double standard to which Wesley held: a woman's preaching was anomalous, not a practice he wanted to institute or reinforce. Nonetheless, Wesley clearly felt Bosanquet a gifted woman, one whom he approved to marry his intended successor John Fletcher. Later, however, Wesley would write a letter to George Robinson to censure females' speaking, saying, 'I desire Mr Peacock to put a final stop to the preaching of women in his circuit. If it were suffered, it would grow, and we know not where it would end.'[24] Even so, despite Wesley's reservations, women's preaching not only continued but grew exponentially.

The letter Tooth wanted to include in the biography was Mary Fletcher's 1771 detailed apologia for women's speaking. In his 1993 volume, *She Offered Them Christ: the Legacy of Women Preachers in Early Methodism*, which included a transcribed, shorter version of the letter, Paul Chilcote noted that the print version first appeared in Zachariah Taft's 1820 *The Scripture Doctrine of Women's Preaching: Stated and Examined*.[25] However, Taft's was actually a much-abridged version. Taft stated in his volume that this is 'part of Miss B.'s letter, and part of his [John Wesley's] answer, regarding an extraordinary call, are as follows', as he printed the exchange to show Wesley's somewhat grudging acceptance of Mary Bosanquet's speaking as an extraordinary call in the extraordinary Methodist movement.[26] Chilcote's book, *John Wesley and the Women Preachers of Early Methodism*, however, does include a modernised and regularised transcription of the longer letter, with a note that it was taken from the copy at Duke University, and states that the original manuscript is unknown.[27] I located several copies of the original in Tooth's hand in the Fletcher-Tooth Archives. The version Tooth presented is similar, but not identical to the one Chilcote reproduced, but it is very different from that published in Moore's *Life of Mary Fletcher*. The letter in the John Rylands Library is significantly longer, more developed in its arguments, and more inclusive of important contexts, condemning the notion that all men are free to pursue ministry no matter how little qualified, while women are limited to an exceptional call which is even then viewed with apprehension and limited in scope.

Forty-six years after it was written, Tooth recognised that this was a key work in documenting Fletcher's motivations for her ministry as well as a justification for other female preachers to follow. The multiple times Tooth recopied the letter demonstrate her understanding of the document's importance not only for posterity, but for her own ministry as a female. Chilcote surmised that Moore did not know of the complete letter, but Moore's manuscript correspondence shows otherwise, as this article records Tooth's unhappily unsuccessful persistence in trying to have

Moore publish the entirety of it.[28] The complete letter, as heavily edited by Moore, who excised about two-thirds of its content, aptly exemplifies the gendered politics of representing both Fletcher and Tooth.[29]

Moore removed much of Fletcher's experiential documentation of her preaching work, beginning with weekly prayer meetings that she led with helper Sarah Ryan, which had grown into meetings held three to four times weekly in Yorkshire, reaching, as she estimated, hundreds of people. Though supported by a Mr Oliver, other male preachers castigated her work as unscriptural female teaching; nonetheless, Fletcher continued to preach in private houses, as well as more public spaces, explaining that because of 'the Zeal of the people they have given out the meeting in a Preaching-house because they had no private house that would hold the people nor one half quarter of them. When we came & I saw hundreds of carnal were there, my heart yearned over them & I feared my Master should say "their blood will I require of you".'[30] Moore also excised the bulk of Fletcher's reasoning and scriptural interpretation to justify women preachers. She answered the argument that some 'improper' women might try to speak with a deft reply: 'This I acknowledge I have feared, but the same might be said of every Preacher that comes out, will not some improper man follow him?' Fletcher continued with the dialogical form, circling back to her divine calling as ultimate justification. 'Ob. But if an improper man comes out the church has proven to stop his mouth but you wont let your mouth be stopped. An. Yes, on the same condition I will, you would not say to him, no man must speak therefore be silent, but only you are not the proper man, now allowing women may speak prove to me it is not my personal call & I will both lovingly & cheerfully obey.'[31]

Not only did Moore omit much of Fletcher's apologia for women's preaching, but he provided his own sheepish explanation for Fletcher's activities for her preaching through his commentary entitled 'A Review of Her Character';[32] this commentary was added to the second edition, two-volume set of Mary Fletcher's *Life*. Seeking to control the perception of his subject by rendering her more acceptable to wider audiences, Moore actually undermined Fletcher's work. The gendered power struggle is obvious; Tooth's determination to present Fletcher as the strong outspoken woman who had mentored her and provided a model of a woman in ministry is overcome by Moore's unchallenged position of ministerial authority and access to publishing. By rewriting the epistolary exchange between the then Mary Bosanquet and John Wesley, Moore literally edited out a portion of her life, as he asserted, when introducing her activities, in the *Life of Mrs. Fletcher*:

> I am sensible that I here tread on tender ground. The question of the lawfulness, or even of the expediency of Female preaching, will recur to every sensible and pious reader; – especially as Mrs Fletcher lived and died a Member of the Church of England, and of the Methodist Society, neither of which sanctions a Female Ministry. But I cannot but think that much that has been said on this question, especially since the days of George Fox (when the Ministry of Females received a regular establishment in his Community) may be spared on this occasion ... Mr Wesley, who never sanctioned a regular Ministry of that kind, permitted, and it

may be said, encouraged her Christian efforts in that way. Her conflicts were very great concerning her call in that respect; and the taunts which she had to endure from men, were very painful. These she at length embodied in a letter to Mr Wesley, declaring her willingness to abide by his decision; and that she would gladly resist this impression, if the Lord should so direct her by him. Mr Wesley, who well knew her simplicity, godly sincerity, and admirable understanding, replied, – 'That he considered it to be an extraordinary call, – That he also looked upon the whole work of God, termed Methodism, to be an extraordinary dispensation. Therefore,' says he, 'I do not wonder if several things occur therein, which do not fall under ordinary Rules of Discipline. St. Paul's ordinary Rule was not to permit a woman to speak in the congregation; yet in extraordinary cases he made a few exceptions.' – Mrs Fletcher thanked God for this answer, and continued her labours of love to the close of her life.[33]

Although hesitant to admit what these 'labours of love' entailed, Moore knew that both Fletcher and Tooth had stretched Wesley's ideas regarding women in ministry, acknowledging the criticisms that Fletcher faced. Fletcher's mysticism was also a controversial issue; she catalogued her numerous dreams and visions, many of her dead husband speaking to her, in her journals, a subject dealt with at length by Phyllis Mack.[34] Moore's annotated and crossed-through manuscripts of Fletcher's *Life* show his edits of numerous portions of Fletcher's more mystical experiences, including some of her dreams and waking visions, though he did include a section entitled 'Her Thoughts on Communion with Happy Spirits'. A note in Moore's hand and signed 'Ed.' on the reverse side of Fletcher's journal account of helping heal a young girl by recommending a 'common' medicine revealed the way in which Fletcher's work was regarded, as a special outpouring of the Spirit, rather than as a precedent for continued practice:

> As it was in the days of the Personal Ministry of the Son of God, so it is in His Spirit's Gospel day – He hides those things from the wise and prudent, and revealeth them unto Babes – the weary and heavy laden – who believe. Matthew XI.25–30 How easy it is to forget this? How hard to keep it in remembrance, and to allow it its due weight! Did ever any man, since the days of St. Paul, more fully or more constantly, appreciate this than Mr Wesley? It was the Principle that governed, and directed, his whole life and labour; and on which account he denominated the fruit of those labours – 'The Work of God.' A Work which He began, supported, and prospered; and in respect to which Mr Wesley, notwithstanding his unparalleled activity, always considered himself as a mere passive instrument. Ed.[35]

Henry Moore's Caution in Advocating for Women's Preaching

Henry Moore's editing decisions, however chauvinistic they may seem today, were most likely done with good intent. In producing his version of Fletcher's life, Moore exercised caution to allow the volume to be published and record Madeley's Methodist practice for posterity; he was no doubt wary of ostracising Methodist officials and reducing the audience for what became in some ways his book, if he included the extent of Fletcher's work and her lengthy justification for women's preaching. In 1803, the Methodist Conference had censured women's preaching, though Fletcher, Tooth, Mary Taft and other women within the Methodist movement clearly violated the injunction, which follows:

> Of Women Preaching
>
> Ques. SHOULD women be permitted to preach among us?
>
> Ansr. We are of the opinion that in general they ought not.
>
> Because a vast majority of our people are opposed to it.
>
> Because their preaching does not at all seem necessary;
>
> there being a sufficiency of Preachers, whom God has accredited, to supply all places in our connexion with regular preaching. But if any woman among us think she has an extraordinary call from God to speak in public (and we are sure it must be an extraordinary call that can authorise it,) we are of the opinion she should in general address her own sex, and those only. And, upon this condition alone, should any woman be permitted to preach in any part of our connexion; and, when so permitted, it should be under the following regulations. 1. They shall not preach in the Circuit where they preside, until they have obtained the approbation of the Superintendent and a Quarterly Meeting. 2. Before they go into any Circuit to preach, they shall have a written invitation from the Superintendent of such Circuit, and a recommendatory note from the Superintendent of their own Circuit.[36]

Other letters exchanged between Tooth and the Moores show Tooth's concern for the progress of the printing, the distribution of the books and other content issues of Fletcher's biography. Mary Ann Moore answered Tooth on 1 March 1818 regarding the omission of Sarah Lawrence's life and other details:

> In regard to those papers you call the Legacy, as Mr Moore hopes he may be able to come, he thinks it may be time enough to examine them then, it will also give a little time for the Life to have full affect, and render a further publication more acceptable perhaps. How could, any person say the account of Sarah Lawrence is left out, everything respecting her is put in as full as could be done with propriety, but it was Mrs Fletcher's Life which is given, not hers, moreover there had been a printed account of her already, I think my dear friend on a reappraisal you will be satisfied it is just as it should be and that Mr Moore has left nothing out that Mrs Fletcher put in, the two mistakes which you mention, if you write to Mr Blanchard, and state them, they will be altered in the next.[37]

Mary Tooth's Enduring Significance

Mary Tooth became Fletcher's heir apparent after the deaths of Fletcher's other helpers and female preachers-in-training Sarah Ryan and Sarah Lawrence. Tooth not only acted as scribe for some of the letters, as her handwriting was superior to Fletcher's often illegible hand, but as a careful copyist of letters written and received, sermons by both Fletchers, works of John Wesley, accounts of other conversions and 'happy deaths', dues records, and more. She was also a carefully organised archivist of the multitudinous papers that fill the forty-four boxes of the Fletcher-Tooth Collection in the John Rylands Library. Tooth also continued to coordinate much of the circuit preachers in Madeley's Methodist movement, as well as meet classes and respond to other speaking engagements herself, carrying on for twenty-eight years following Fletcher's death, with the blessing of her spiritual mother, who wrote on 1 June 1808:

> I see death as near & find it on my heart to pray for & take thought of the work of God here. O my Saviour cause it to increase abundantly – keep away stumbling blocks come power of the Spirit in a peculiar manner on my dear husbands orphans. I would wish Miss Tooth to remain in Madeley if a way should be made for her – & that she might be able to take in the preachers. There is nowhere I can see so likely & proper – & I think it would be the most comfortable to them. All is in the hand of the Lord. She has the Cause of God truly at heart & if her health is spared will I believe be very usefull in speaking & meeting the people.[38]

In an 1817 letter to her sister Rosamund, Tooth discussed checking proof sheets of the second volume of Fletcher's *Life*, and the popularity of the previous volume: 'but have not yet read all I've got, but am well satisfied with all I have read, am fully persuaded prayer is answered in this thing also, for surely the Lord has gone before & evidently done what will be most for his own glory. There is not a single copy left at London unsold, but they are going about another edition immediately however I hope I have secure as many as will supply those that I promised at Madeley.'[39] Tooth had carried out as well as possible the final wish of her adopted mother, incomplete as the work was regarding Fletcher's important letter to Wesley.

Tooth's speaking ministry far outlasted Fletcher's, documented by her journals and letters. For example, her 1824 journal recorded her leading a Methodist love feast without male authority: 'Dec 7th this evening the Lovefeast was held in my upper room neither of our Preachers could make it convenient to attend but glory be to a Triune God Jesus was present to break the bread of life to all our waiting souls'.[40] In an 1828 letter, she wrote of not only being asked to speak in a small room at the Dudley Chapel in London, which overflowed with listeners, but being requested to return a second night to the chapel itself. She comments that she has even won over former naysayers who had been opposed to female preaching:

> There was [sic] fresh solicitations for me to take then an appointment ... at Dudley Chapel the next evening this I repeatedly refused but at length Mr Goward said if I would only do what I find I cou'd at the time ... He declared he never asked a female in his life before to take his work & when he had had opportunity so to do never felt in the least inclined to it ... Mr Neath joined him saying I have gone beyond you Brother Goward for I have been an opposer of women speaking However I did not at last consent only sayed I wou'd pray that the Lord wou'd shew me the thing proceeded from himself & if he wou'd be with me I shou'd satisfy me of my call to it. They prayed & I prayed & in the morning I awoke with a commission from the Lord. Viz. Go in this they might have not known I sent thee. I felt from that moment a willingness to go to that great Chapel which is twice the size of Madeley Church.[41]

Towards her later years, Tooth encountered difficulties in Madeley, as her ministry was perceived as conflicting with the official Methodist chapel constructed in the area. Portions of a letter dated 5 November 1833 from John Radford show criticisms of her vicarage barn meetings at the same time as the services in the new chapel, as the Methodist movement sought to stabilise itself into a more conventional denomination.[42]

Prized by Fletcher for her devoted love, faithfulness and usefulness, Tooth is primarily remembered by posterity as Fletcher's secretary, a role that is often devalued because it is primarily gendered female. Epistolary writings were considered an appropriate women's genre; without them, however, the Methodist movement of Shropshire and beyond would have been weakened and short-lived. Both of the Marys' ministry included letters not only of information but also of comfort, exhortation and teaching. Tooth's worth extends far beyond a trivial secretarial position, for without her, we would have little knowledge of the Methodist movement within Madeley in the late eighteenth and earlier nineteenth centuries. She served as the sole archivist for the Methodist movement in Madeley and environs as well as of the Fletcher library, with her name inscribed in most of its volumes. In addition to her scribal strengths, Tooth also followed in the footsteps of her spiritual mother in coordinating circuit preachers, leading class meetings, collecting dues, and even preaching. This was ongoing until at least 1832, when Henrietta Roberts enquired of Tooth, 'We have heard that you have lost the Barn as a preaching house. I long to hear that you go on. Have you got a chapel or are you preaching in your upper room?'[43]

The depth and importance of Mary Tooth's roles are little acknowledged in Henry Moore's volume. Tooth proved a strong advocate for Mary Fletcher's preaching, though she was unsuccessful at persuading Moore to publish in its entirety the strongest apologia for women's preaching since Quaker co-founder Margaret Fell Fox's 1666 *Womens Speaking Justified, Proved and Allowed of by the Scriptures*.[44] Thanks to her letters and preservation of Fletcher's papers, however, Tooth has preserved the unexpurgated version of this work for us today; this example highlights the necessity of archival research, especially in earlier eras when the politics of publication required male editing of a female's work for the sake of conventionality.

Notes

1. Felicity A. Nussbaum, *The Autobiographical Subject: Gender and Ideology in Eighteenth-Century England* (Baltimore: Johns Hopkins University Press, 1989), pp. 174–5.
2. For more on Mary Tooth's ministry in Madeley, see Carol Blessing, '"Oh That the Mantle May Rest on Me!": The Ministry of Mary Tooth', in Geordan Hammond and Peter S. Forsaith (eds), *Religion, Gender, and Industry: Exploring Church and Methodism in a Local Setting* (Eugene, OR: Pickwick Publications, 2011), pp. 156–72.
3. Henry Moore, *The Life of Mrs. Mary Fletcher, Consort and Relict of The Rev. John Fletcher*, 2 vols (Birmingham: J. Peart and Son, 1817).
4. *Ibid.*, vol. 1, p. v.

5 Manchester, John Rylands Library, Methodist Archives and Research Centre, Fletcher-Tooth Collection (hereafter JRL, MARC, FTC), MAM Fl 13/1/49 and MAM Fl 13/1/59.
6 JRL, MARC, FTC: MAM Fl 34/9/16.
7 JRL, MARC, FTC: MAM Fl 8/3, journal entry for 3 August 1815.
8 JRL, MARC, FTC: MAM Fl 3/9/7.
9 JRL, MARC, FTC: MAM Fl 3/9/5.
10 JRL, MARC, FTC: MAM Fl 3/9/9.
11 Thomas Coke and Henry Moore, *The Life of the Rev. John Wesley* (London: G. Paramore, 1792).
12 JRL, MARC, FTC: MAM Fl 34/2/13.
13 JRL, MARC, FTC: PLP 77/4/5.
14 *Ibid.*
15 JRL, MARC, FTC: MAM Fl 7/17/6.
16 JRL, MARC, FTC: MAM Fl 40/3/243; MARC, FTC: MAM Fl 40/3/248.
17 JRL, MARC, FTC: MAM Fl 37/5/8.
18 JRL, MARC, FTC: PLP 77/4/5; MARC: PLP 77/4/8.
19 *Ibid.*
20 JRL, MARC, FTC: MAM Fl 34/5/6.
21 JRL, MARC, FTC: MAM Fl 34/5/5.
22 JRL, MARC, FTC: MAM Fl 34/5/1.
23 John Wesley to Mary Bosanquet, 13 June 1771, *The Letters of the Rev. John Wesley, A. M.*, ed. John Telford, 8 vols (London: Epworth Press, 1960 [1931]), vol. 5, p. 257.
24 John Wesley to George Robinson, 25 March 1780, *ibid.*, vol. 7, p. 9.
25 Paul W. Chilcote, *She Offered Them Christ: The Legacy of Women Preachers in Early Methodism* (Nashville: Abingdon Press, 1993), pp. 78–9.
26 Zechariah Taft, *The Scripture Doctrine of Women's Preaching: Stated and Examined* (York: R. and J. Richardson, 1820), pp. 19–20.
27 Paul W. Chilcote, *John Wesley and Women Preachers of Early Methodism* (Metuchen, NJ: Scarecrow Press, 1991), pp. 299–304.
28 Chilcote, *She Offered Them Christ*, p. 137.
29 The complete letter, as copied by Mary Tooth, is JRL, MARC, FTC: MAM Fl 34/5/1.
30 *Ibid.*
31 *Ibid.*
32 Moore, *The Life of Mrs. Mary Fletcher*, vol. 1, pp. 293–95.
33 *Ibid.*, pp. 296–7.
34 Phyllis Mack, *Heart Religion in the British Enlightenment: Gender and Emotion in Early Methodism* (Cambridge: Cambridge University Press, 2008), pp. 219–60.
35 JRL, MARC, FTC: MAM Fl 22/4/64.
36 Philip Garrett, *A Digest of the Methodist Conferences, from the first, held in London by the Late Rev. John Wesley, A.M. in the year 1744, to the year 1826*, vol. 2 (Halifax: Thomas Walker, 1827), p. 188.
37 JRL, MARC, FTC: MAM Fl 5/5/4.
38 JRL, MARC, FTC: MAM Fl 8/1.
39 JRL, MARC, FTC: MAM Fl 34/7/11.

40 JRL, MARC, FTC: MAM Fl 14/E.
41 JRL, MARC, FTC: MAM FL 34/8/7.
42 JRL, MARC, FTC: MAM Fl 6/2/19.
43 JRL, MARC, FTC: MAM Fl 6/8/11.
44 Margaret Askew Fell Fox, *Womens Speaking Justified, Proved and Allowed of by the Scriptures* (London, 1667).

Seductive Splendour and Caricatured Simplicity: Catholicism and Nonconformity in Nineteenth-Century 'Jewish Conversion' Novels

ANDREW CROME, MANCHESTER METROPOLITAN UNIVERSITY

Abstract

This article examines English Evangelical novels focused on the conversion of Jewish characters, published from the 1820s to the 1850s. It concentrates particularly on the way these novels emphasised the importance of the Church of England in constructing national and religious identity, and used Jewish conversion as a way to critique Catholicism and Nonconformity. Jewish worship, rabbinic authority and Talmudic devotion were linked to Roman Catholic attitudes towards priesthood and tradition, while Jews were also portrayed as victims of a persecuting Roman Church. Nonconformity was criticised for disordered worship and confusing Jews with its attacks on respectable Anglicanism. As a national religion, novelists therefore imagined that Jews would be saved by a national church, and often linked this to concepts of a national restoration to Palestine. This article develops and complicates understandings of Evangelical views of Jews in the nineteenth century, and their links to 'writing the nation' in popular literature.

Keywords: Jews; Jewish conversion; Charlotte Elizabeth Tonna; Catholicism; Nonconformity; Evangelicalism

At an early point in Charlotte Elizabeth Tonna's *Judah's Lion*, the impetuous Alick Cohen refuses to kneel before the host during a Maltese Corpus Christi procession. An altercation follows, which draws praise from a local rabbi and a Protestant missionary. While each admire Alick for his zeal against idolatry, the incident leads to a disagreement. As the missionary tells the rabbi: 'you with your Talmud are as far astray from the law of Moses as the poor Papist with his wafer-god is from the gospel of Christ'.[1]

This comparison was not unusual. Historians have noted that Protestant polemic against Judaism often paralleled devotion to the Talmud and rabbis with Catholic devotion to the priesthood and tradition.[2] These connections helped Protestant writers put an 'alien' faith in terms readers might understand, and take advantage of knowledge of anti-Catholic discourse to score polemical points. Yet critiques of Judaism did not simply repeat attacks on Catholicism. Their criticism combined hope for Jewish conversion to Protestantism with a 'pure' biblical faith. Biblical commentaries, prophetic exegesis, polemic and missionary periodicals all contained conversion narratives to encourage British Protestants. A number of Evangelical writers also produced novels dealing with Jewish conversion from the 1820s to the 1850s. These presented conversion as a rejection of tradition and repudiation of Catholic idolatry that demonstrated Protestant superiority. However, these conversions were denominationally specific. They repeatedly affirmed the superiority of the

Church of England, and in projecting a future Jewish homeland and national church in Palestine, the importance of ecclesiastical establishment. The narratives sidelined Nonconformists alongside Catholics, with dissent often referred to obliquely as a deterrent to Jewish conversion. This article examines these tropes, suggesting ways that authors used Jewish characters to explore concerns within British Evangelicalism, projecting an image of a unified, national church as the carrier of Christianity. It, therefore, builds on existing work on the way Protestants linked Judaism with Catholicism, extending it by arguing explicitly for the importance of denominational identity in the novels. Conversion novels show how popular Evangelical literature sought not simply to write the nation, but to contribute to a distinctive Anglican identity that brought the Church of England into alliance with converted Israel.

'Jewish Conversion' Novels

Active interest in Jewish conversion developed in England during the early nineteenth century. Its best-known manifestation, the foundation of the London Society for Promoting Christianity amongst the Jews in 1809, was part of the proliferation of missionary movements in the first decades of the 1800s. Better known as the 'London Jews' Society' (hereafter LJS), it was originally founded on a non-denominational basis. Arguments about the consecration of the Society's chapel, combined with the necessity of a bailout by wealthy lawyer Lewis Way, led to its reconstitution along Anglican lines in 1815. The LJS succeeded in gaining large subscriptions and funded missionary work in Britain, Europe and Asia by the mid-century. Its effectiveness in terms of conversions remained small, particularly at home, where it was often criticised by Jews for its aims and methods.[3] Continued interest in Jews was further fuelled by the growing popularity of millennialism among Evangelicals.[4]

Alongside proofs that Jesus was the prophesied messiah and model prayers for potential converts, the Society's publications often included conversion narratives.[5] Whether from the Society's missionaries, excerpted from eighteenth-century English texts, or reprinted from contemporary European sources, they were a common feature of its periodical publications. Readers of the June 1816 edition of *The Jewish Expositor and Friend of Israel* were treated to a Polish rabbi's conversion narrative, followed by descriptions of oral testimony from London converts.[6] Most of these conversions were drawn-out processes marked by doubt, fear of persecution, and a slow dawning of salvation.[7] While some accounts featured an initial conversion to Catholicism followed by a later shift to Protestant belief,[8] others emphasised an open repudiation of Rome. Many missionaries were convinced that the Roman Church's 'idolatry' was the key impediment to Jewish conversion,[9] and that Rome's historic persecution of Jews turned them against Christ.[10]

Protestantism was the logical corrective to this, with its focus on the scriptures and condemnation of images in worship. Yet it was specifically Anglicanism, with its liturgy and structure, that the LJS believed was the most attractive form of faith to Jews. As the introduction to a collection of LJS hymns noted, 'in the ritual and worship of our venerable church, there is so much which seems peculiarly adapted to promote the edification of the descendants of Abraham, that we might almost be induced to suppose that the founders had even anticipated their accession to it'.[11] This implied that Nonconformist worship was alien to Jews, if not worse. When the missionary Joseph Wolff defended himself from Catholic attacks in 1828, he vehemently denied links to nonconformity: 'I dislike the Church discipline of the Wesleyan Methodists more than I do that of the Church of Rome.'[12]

Conversion to Anglicanism therefore allowed Jews to associate themselves with the English establishment. This tied Jewish conversion into debates on national identity in the period.[13] Works about conversion appeared against a background of disputes regarding Church establishment and the political nation: from the repeal of the Test and Corporation Acts and Catholic emancipation, to the furore surrounding the Tractarian movement and Nonconformist campaigns against tithes and Church rates. Hovering over all of this, from the 1830s onwards, was the question of Jewish emancipation – when might Jews be permitted to enter Parliament?[14] Conversionist works were, therefore, about more than just Jewish conversion. They also served to comment upon a range of issues of interest to English Christians.

Alongside memoirs, tracts and handbooks, conversionists published a number of novels discussing Jewish conversion. These were written almost exclusively by Anglican Evangelicals, although they were read and known more widely: for example, Disraeli's *Tancred* (1847) and George Eliot's *Daniel Deronda* (1876) parodied particular staple elements of the pious stories.[15] While Evangelicals had initially been suspicious of fiction as a means of communicating gospel truth, this faded in the 1830s and 1840s as authors displayed a willingness to adopt the style of a *roman à thèse*.[16] Consequently, these novels were explicit about their didactic and improving purpose.[17] The conversion novel, which Rachel Howard places in a wider genre of 'moral-domestic fiction', could focus on nominal Protestants, Catholics, missionary converts or Jews.[18] Jewish conversion novels appeared throughout the early nineteenth century, many directly citing the LJS's activities as their inspiration.[19]

Early examples included Charlotte Anley's *Miriam* (1826), about the conversion of a rich Jewish girl in Westmorland, and Revd Charles William Chalken's anonymously published *The Hebrew* (1828).[20] Amelia Bristow, a convert from Judaism herself,[21] published a trilogy of novels: *Sophia de Lissau* (1826), *Emma de Lissau* (1828) and *The Orphans of Lissau* (1830). These dealt with the conversions of Polish Jewish émigrés in the eighteenth century. Some authors produced numerous works. Osborn W. Trenery Heighway published 'genuine' conversion narratives including *Leila Ada, The Jewish Convert* (1852), its sequel *Children of Abraham, or Sketches of Jewish Converts* (1857), and *Adeline: Or, Mysteries, Romance, and Realities of Jewish Life* (1854). The two most influential conversion novels were written by important Evangelical writers. Charlotte Elizabeth Tonna has attracted increasing critical attention in recent years for her work as editor of the *Christian Lady's Magazine* and her social reform fiction.[22] *Judah's Lion*, first published serially in 1841,[23] told the story of urbane young Jew Alick Cohen's conversion to a form of Jewish Anglicanism during a journey to Palestine. Annie Webb first published *Naomi, Or the Last Days of Jerusalem* in 1840. The book spun its conversion narrative around Josephus's descriptions of Jerusalem's destruction, and was immediately popular. By 1860, it had gone through seventeen editions, and remained in print until 1899.[24] Its popularity led Webb to write other novels on Jewish history (e.g. *Benaiah* [1865]) and contemporary Jewish conversion (e.g. *Julamerk* [1849]).

While these novels were popular enough to go through a number of editions, it is unlikely that many Jews were reading them. The books appeared from publishers used to dealing with works for the Evangelical market, such as Seeley, Burnside and Seeley, or John Hatchard and Son. They were advertised in the mainstream press, as well as in Evangelical publications, and often reviewed by missionary journals and denominational periodicals. While authors hoped that Jewish readers would engage with the novels, it was recognised that their principle aim was to instruct Christians in how to view, evangelise and pray for the Jewish people. The *Eclectic Review*'s comments on *Judah's Lion*, for example, hoped that 'in an age of awakening sympathy and interest towards the Israelitish race, the volume deserves, and we hope may obtain, a wide circulation'.[25] The novels therefore often included passing references to recent events involving Jews (for example, the Damascus Affair or controversy surrounding the Jerusalem bishopric) in order to argue for their timeliness. As Webb noted in her introduction to *Naomi*, 'The signs of the present times point strongly towards the Holy Land and the once glorious city of Jerusalem; and the eyes of many (both Jews and Gentiles) are turned thither in anxious expectation of the approaching fulfilment of those promises of favour and restoration which are so strikingly set forth in Scripture.'[26]

The novels were generally priced for the higher end of the market; particularly in the 1820s and 1830s, novels were too costly to consider distributing at reduced cost. Anley's *Miriam*, for example, appeared first in octavo priced at 16*s.* 6*d.* in 1826, with the duodecimo edition a more affordable 7*s.* 6*d.* three years later. In 1830, readers could own the two-volume edition of *Emma de Lissau* for 12*s.*, or the third edition of *Sophia de Lissau* for 5*s.*[27] Prices fell during the 1840s and 1850s, as technology improved and incomes rose.[28] *Judah's Lion* cost just 4*s.* in 1842; the twelfth edition of Webb's substantial *Naomi*, published in 1854, cost 7*s.* 6*d.* in octavo.[29] The novels were profitable, as both the number of editions, and authors' own comments, suggest. Anley's appeal to the Royal Literary Fund for charity in 1851 rued her failure to recognise her work's commercial appeal: 'unfortunately little discerning of the popularity with which the latter [*Miriam*] has, especially, been favoured, I sold its copyright for a sum'.[30]

Didacticism in the novels could suggest their authors' discomfort at writing fiction. Plots often acted as a way to set up discussions, allowing Christians to correct Jewish errors. Sometimes, as in *Miriam*, the potential convert debated with Christian ministers to remove their doubts, allowing the cleric to share large portions of Evangelical theology.[31] In other instances, such as *Emma de Lissau*, set piece disputations took place between the eponymous convert and rabbis.[32] In extreme cases, this led to the near total absence of plot in favour of dialogue disputation.[33]

Some novels falsely claimed to be genuine conversion stories. Bristow's *Sophia de Lissau* stated that it was an 'authentic' narrative, written 'to convey an outline of the domestic and religious habits of the Jews'.[34] Heighway protested that he had 'nowhere written one word, look, or expression which is not most exact truth' in *Leila Ada*.[35] That said, he was later sued by his publishers for inventing fictional converts.[36] Another technique was to incorporate historical figures into the novel. Webb's *Julamerk* wove in genuine stories of suffering and persecution in her attempt to promote Christian charity towards the Nestorians, whom she believed to be descended from the lost tribes of Israel. This theory was propagated by American missionary Asahel Grant, who also appeared as a character in the novel.[37] Footnotes directed readers to sources detailing the persecutions. More imaginatively, the novels often blended with historical fiction. Bristow's *Emma de Lissau*, for example, had her characters meet a dull Tom Paine in revolutionary France.

The novels often drew from popular secular genres. *Naomi* was an example of romantic historical fiction, weaving its conversion story around both Josephus's account of the city's fall and its heroine's love life. *Leila Ada* was part conversion narrative, part European travelogue, while *Adeline* dabbled in broad comedy, with questionable success.[38] Several novels used tropes from popular Gothic or adventure fiction, including the kidnapping and confinement of young women, shadowy conspiracies and battle scenes. Tonna disavowed fiction after the adventurous elements of *Judah's Lion* excited her to such an extent that they took on a life of their own.[39]

Jews and Catholics

As Nadia Valman noted, conversion novels were permeated with 'virulent anti-Catholicism'.[40] This was often direct. *Julamerk*, for example, paralleled Nestorian Christian hero Isaac with the attempt of the Roman Church to undermine his faith. His 'cheerful and earnest piety' compared positively to the 'dull and spiritless' devotion of the monks.[41] Alick's reaction to Catholicism in *Judah's Lion*, even before his conversion, was to view it as 'a system that falsely usurps the name of Christianity'.[42] In Bristow's work, it was a faith associated with 'seductive splendour ... well adapted to the mind of man in his natural state'.[43]

Catholicism was inherently threatening to Jews, both in terms of its 'idolatrous' worship, and owing to the persecutions it had orchestrated. Jewish characters commonly condemned these elements of the faith, and authors compared Jews positively to Catholics when discussing their rejection of idolatry.[44] At the start of novels, Jewish characters often wrongly equated Protestant worship with Catholic superstition. In *Julamerk*, the future convert Zoraide's family rejected Christianity due to its 'ignorance and superstition' after witnessing Catholic worship. Isaac, the novel's Christian hero, corrected Zoraide: 'Those who belong to the Greek and Romish churches are, undoubtedly, holding a sadly corrupted faith ... But, believe me, the fault is not in our blessed religion as it was taught by the Redeemer and his apostles.'[45] In *Adeline*, the Jewish heroine and her lover visited St Paul's Cathedral, comparing it to 'our own glorious temple'. They bemoaned the way in which Catholics corrupted such buildings: 'in front of that altar they place a semicircle of burning lamps, or else great wax candles, arranged in trinities, as they say. These throw a pale, unsteady light upon an image of the cross and a man upon it. Just fancy it here, and away goes the poetry.'[46] Anglicanism was marked not just by pure worship, but also by good taste.

Catholic history of persecuting Jews was another common theme. Rabbi Selig in *Emma de Lissau* discussed Christianity with Emma, revealing that his distrust of Christians came from 'hardships endured by the Jews on the continent, particularly in Roman Catholic districts'.[47] Anticipating the 1858–59 Mortara affair, Selig's infant siblings were secretly baptised by Catholics and: 'as they were now received into the bosom of the Church, their Jewish relatives had no longer any claim on them!'[48] Later, Emma travelled to Rome, where she saw at first hand the effect of Catholic persecution. Bristow established a contrast along both national and religious lines: 'But never had she, a native of happy England, that favoured land of gospel light and generous toleration, imagined even in her gloomiest moments, a state of mental debasement and servile misery, so completely revolting, as that now presented to her view in the Ghetto of Rome.'[49] In *Adeline*, the benevolent Mr Cohen was moved by tales of Jewish suffering in Poland: 'The Roman Catholics are foremost in the persecution ... infatuated people, headed by their priests.'[50] The Jewish patriot Da Costa in *Judah's Lion* recalled being attacked by monks who 'not only avowed but gloried in the persecutions and massacres of their church'.[51]

Many of the more ghastly examples of persecution drew from both anti-Catholic polemic and tropes of Gothic fiction, a genre that often invoked the anti-Semitic persecution of the Spanish Inquisition.[52] Jesuits were particular targets.[53] In *Adeline*, after converting the young Jew Eva St Maur, Jesuit Father Barrett planned to steal her away to marry her, before claiming her fortune and becoming the *cicisbeo* of a Tuscan countess.[54] In *Judah's Lion*, Da Costa and Alick searched for a young Jew kidnapped by monks and hidden in a monastery dungeon.[55] *Julamerk*'s Jesuit Geronimo was a figure described in explicitly Gothic terms, working from his 'gloomy and solitary cell' to enact his 'deep-laid scheme ... or revenge for its failure'.[56]

The novels also set up structural parallels between Judaism and Catholicism. Despite their differences, there were a number of reasons to link them. Superficially, both were 'foreign' faiths opposed to Anglicanism (and, thus, Englishness). Discussions of civil disabilities and the extension of political rights in the state also often brought up discussion of Judaism together with Catholicism.[57] David Feldman has noted that comparisons between Jewish and Catholic beliefs were rhetorically powerful, and (Protestants hoped) would help drive internal Jewish reform and eventual conversion.[58] For example, the most influential critique of Judaism, Hebraist and LJS missionary Alexander McCaul's *Old Paths* (1837), made clear a distinction between the mass of Jews (who were praised), and rabbis (who were linked to despotism and Catholicism).[59] Notions of Catholic conspiracies, persecutions and plotters might also suggest links to Judaism. As Carol Margaret Davison has argued, plots centred on secret societies often raised fears of a vast Jewish conspiracy tied to the Illuminati, Freemasons and others 'behind' the French Revolution.[60]

The most popular way of making this connection was by comparing Jewish devotion to the Talmud and rabbis to the Catholic emphasis upon tradition and the priesthood.[61] As Joseph Wolff lamented, 'as the Church of Judea began to neglect the commandments of God ... in like manner, the Church of Rome neglected and perverted the pure word of the Gospel, and substituted for it cunningly devised fables ... and just as the Rabbis of old attributed to themselves *infallibility*, so the doctors of the Church of Rome do the same'.[62]

Conversion awakened Jews to these resemblances. At times, converts directly confronted priests about them. In *Emma de Lissau* the eponymous heroine told Father Dermot 'that she thought there was a great affinity between Judaism and the Romish religion, in many respects. Nor did she fail, among other allusions, to compare the Jewish presiding Rabbi, in some measure, with the sovereign Pontiff at Rome.'[63] In *Judah's Lion*, Alick's aversion to 'the idolatrous errors of Popery' prepared him to renounce his Judaism. As he demolished Catholic arguments with scripture, the missionary Mrs Ryan 'took occasion by this to show him how similarly unfounded and unscriptural were the doctrines and traditions of the Talmudists'.[64] When, in the same novel, Rabbi Ben-Melchor accused Mr Ryan of promoting idolatry, he responded with fury: 'You perfectly know that the religion of these people [Catholics] is not my religion, but that it much more resembles your's [sic].'[65] Heighway made the charge that, like Catholics, Jews 'have introduced an enormous rival to divine revelation' in the oral law.[66] Failure to perceive these similarities could be disastrous. Raphael, the hero of *Orphans of Lissau*, chose to consult Catholic monks rather than flee to Amsterdam or London on his conversion: 'He knew not how little the Roman priests differ from the Jewish Rabbis ... the dogmas of both rest upon legends and traditions, and neither of them take the written word in its purity, as the guide of their ceremonies.'[67]

Similarities could also be more subtle. In *Naomi*, Webb engaged in a description of Temple worship that directly recalled Catholicism. The service was marked by 'imposing magnificence, the glittering fold and jewelled dresses of the priests ... clouds of incense ... splendid altars ... ordained to impress the senses'. In comparison, the early Christians made 'no prostrations ... no outward gestures or vehement excitement' and worshipped in a building marked by its 'simplicity'.[68]

Structural comparisons between the faiths also appeared. The *Lissau* novels drew clear thematic parallels between Judaism and Catholicism. When the matriarch Anna discussed Sophia's education with Rabbi Colmar, she refused to allow her daughter a Bible. Although 'divinely inspired', she told Sophia, 'it is more particularly from the Oral Law you are to deduce your daily practice; – indeed, without the Oral Law to explain many points, the Bible would be almost useless'.[69] This parallels a discussion in *Emma de Lissau* in which the heroine's fellow convert Catherine Levy turned from her Evangelical faith towards Catholicism: 'Holy Mother Church allows not her children to use their own weak judgment, on a volume so mysterious, so difficult to understand ... Pray how *can we* pretend to decide on the real meaning of every dark passage we meet within it?'[70]

The temptation of Catholicism was always a danger in Bristow's eyes. Supposed Catholic hatred of Jews, therefore, combined with an awareness of the Church's attractions. This came across most clearly in *Emma de Lissau*, where Emma encountered her Catholic double, Victorine Anschel. Victorine, the daughter of a rabbi, was preparing for a life as a nun, and travelled to Rome with Emma and her father. On the journey, the two women acknowledged the genuine nature of the other's faith, and shared reflections on the number of superficial believers in both of their traditions. Subsequently, Emma was aided by Madame Dupont, who gave her a locket 'blessed by the Pope' to protect her on the voyage back to England. Although she viewed the gift as the 'bigotry of the kind-hearted giver', when subsequently saved from shipwreck she remembered the 'assertions respecting its talismanic virtues'.[71]

While these elements of the Roman faith attracted Emma, Bristow reminded readers of the realities that lurked behind them. Victorine's faith was 'quiet' as opposed to Emma's public testimony; her future in the convent described in Gothic terms as 'desolate . . . a living tomb'. Their journey to Rome ended in Emma seeing the horrors of the ghetto first-hand. On her return to England, Emma passed on Dupont's locket to a young Catholic girl. While for the Jewish convert the locket returned to being a 'curious work of art', for the Catholic 'it was an inestimable relic'.[72] Protestant rationality ultimately won out over idolatry and superstition.

Whereas Jews relied on the Talmud, converts relied exclusively on scripture.[73] Asher Mordecai, the hero of *The Hebrew*, converted after stealing a New Testament and reading it in romantic mountain solitude.[74] When Miriam debated with the Anglican minister Mr Howard, she brought the Talmud as her 'talisman . . . [it] seemed to defy, if size and beauty of covering could do so, every attack against its boasted truth'. Howard, who used only a pocket Bible, nonetheless prevailed.[75] In *Leila Ada*, rabbis questioned the heroine surrounded by the Talmud, commentaries and Maimonides' *Guide for the Perplexed*; yet 'Leila had only the Bible.'[76] Burstein is right to highlight that this proliferation of texts is an attempt by Jewish characters to 'conceal from themselves their essential lack of significance'.[77] More than this, it provides a coded critique of both Catholicism and liberal theological trends in Protestantism. The true believer relied on scripture, not on commentaries, academics or priests.

Interrogation scenes, such as in *Leila Ada*, further recalled images of Catholic inquisitorial practices. Although Jews were victims of Catholic persecution, the novels emphasised the similarities between persecuting rabbis and overbearing priests. As Bristow noted of Raphael in *Orphans*: 'the Synagogue that he had quitted, and the Church he was now a member of, were but too closely assimilated in their discipline and customs. Equally intolerant and bigoted, excommunicating and anathematising all who differed from them – equally exclusive in their creed – equally rigorous in their dealings with apostates – equally devoted to an endless round of carnal ceremonies, the invention of man.'[78] Again bearing similarities to Jesuits in Gothic literature, rabbis in the novels were involved in nefarious schemes to de-convert those who turned to Christianity.[79] Jewish heroines saw spaces they presumed as homes or sanctuaries converted into prisons. Emma de Lissau was kidnapped, imprisoned and hidden away by her mother.[80] Leila Ada was sent to her zealous uncle's house and subjected to violent questioning and cursing by rabbis.[81] On her conversion, Naomi was locked in her room while her father called down curses on her. The Talmud, like Catholic jurists, justified violence against both Jewish converts and all gentiles alike in the eyes of many novelists. Several drew on the historic charge that the Talmud supposedly called for the death of gentiles.[82] While Christian missionaries in Tonna's work acknowledged that no Jew actually sought to kill gentiles, they instead used the charge to show that Jews were therefore disobedient to the Talmud itself.[83]

These links between Judaism and Catholicism reveal the ambiguous nature of Protestant views towards Jews in the nineteenth century. Jews were potentially threatening in their foreignness and shared attributes with Catholicism. At the same time, they served both to justify Protestant belief, and to provide further rhetorical ammunition against Catholicism.

Nonconformity

All Protestant denominations could be fertile ground for interest in both Jewish conversion and anti-Catholicism. Despite this, while Nonconformists were willing participants in the battle against popery, they were often fighting the Church of England over issues such as church rates, tithes and burials. Establishment remained a continual bugbear, and in one sense made Nonconformists a natural ally with Catholics when they campaigned against civil disabilities. These issues often limited Protestant cooperation, even when sharing broad theological agreement. The LJS's false start as a non-denominational group illustrates the sort of problems that could derail joint Anglican and Nonconformist missionary work.[84] As John Wolffe and D. G. Paz have both shown, popular anti-Catholicism often fractured over issues of establishment and church–state relations. While the pan-Protestant meeting to discuss a unified response against Sir Robert Peel's 1845 Maynooth grant attracted over 1,000 delegates from across the country and the denominational spectrum, a number of Dissenters seceded when it refused to discuss establishment.[85] Likewise, responses to the 1850 'Papal Aggression' that began as displays of Protestant unity often ended in squabbling and splits.[86]

Elisabeth Jay noted that the majority of Evangelical novels were written by middle-class Anglicans.[87] The same holds true for the conversion novels. It is therefore unsurprising that the novels were solidly Anglican in their ecclesiology. The Christians that Jews encountered in them were invariably associated with the established church. When Nonconformity appeared, it was usually as a passing critique from non-Christian characters, drawing attention to the excesses of behaviour that were not acceptable within the theologically sound and respectable world of Anglicanism. Uncomfortable hints in the novels also suggested that the practice of Nonconformity contributed to Jewish reluctance to convert. For example, Tonna discussed the barriers that denominational confusion presented to conversion. Although complaining about the idolatry he found among Christians in the Holy Land, the Jewish patriot

Da Costa also cited disagreement among Protestants as a reason for rejecting Christianity: 'You know what a jumble there is in London: Churchmen, Presbyterians, Baptists, and some fifty more who agree in nothing but eschewing image-worship and deifying the Nazarene.'[88]

The novels highlighted the advantages of specifically Anglican Christianity, particularly social benefits. Alick's father, who harboured ambitions for his son in English society, was alarmed by the warnings of the ship's schoolmaster that Alick was being seduced into Methodism: 'not merely from the religion of his fathers, but to join a sect so extremely bigoted, narrow-minded, and despised by all sensible people, as to become a scoff among respectable Christians'.[89] An association with Evangelicalism, in whatever form, was socially unacceptable for Mr Cohen.

A similar social fear haunted characters in *Miriam*. Although Anley was possibly a Quaker herself, the novel found no place for Nonconformity in its idyllic Westmorland setting.[90] The parish minister Mr Howard was a dedicated and kind Evangelical, and the Anglican Church was at the centre of village life. Whereas the Stuart family, who first attract Miriam to Christianity, were Presbyterian, their Scottish heritage ensured connection to an established church. The widowed Helen Stuart was a wife of the manse, while her oldest son entered the kirk as a minister. Characters were keen to disavow any connection to the perceived excesses of Nonconformity. Miriam's father feared that Mrs Stuart was 'one of those always singing psalms, and talking of her own cursed creed', but was reassured by his gardener that she was respectable.[91] When the wayward Edith Stuart repented after an affair, she expressed the strength of her regret by invoking Nonconformity: 'what would I not give to be the very being I have so often spurned and derided – a child of God – a *methodist* [sic], any thing to be but safe within the fold of heaven'.[92] *Leila Ada* therefore emphasised the blessing converts found in the Book of Common Prayer. After Leila's death the Anglican funeral service, rather than scripture, was the impetus for her father's conversion: 'It made him weep – he prayed – and a ray of divine comfort illuminated his soul.'[93]

While characters in *Adeline* praised the beauty and propriety of St Paul's in comparison to the extravagance of Catholicism, Heighway simultaneously condemned the austerity of Nonconformity. Describing Mr Cohen's private synagogue, the author applauded the tasteful decoration and aesthetic:

> Beautiful exceedingly are these little temples. For ourselves – we can never think of them save with feelings of deep delight. That caricatured simplicity – that palpable, undisguised meanness – which so frequently characterise the house of God amongst Christians, and especially dissenting congregations – as if, although nothing is too good or too beautiful for their own house, anything is good enough for His – this, we say, is not known here. Elegance, grandeur, harmony, and chasteness, mingling in a thousand forms of perfect loveliness, mark the disposition within them.[94]

In the same way that Isaac earlier criticised Catholic decoration for removing the poetry from devotion through over-elaboration of the worship space, so Nonconformity did the same through a false humility. Simplicity was a cover for stinginess.

It is important to consider why the novelists highlighted the Anglican nature of the conversions of their Jewish characters. As Howard has suggested, conversion novels were preoccupied with writing the nation and establishing the boundaries of acceptable belonging within it. They therefore constructed stable others in Jews and Catholics against whom to define national identity.[95] While this is borne out to some extent, the position nonetheless needs nuancing with reference beyond a generalised Protestant identity towards a specifically Anglican one. Incorporation of Jews within the established church dealt with authors' national anxiety on several levels. First, it served to demonstrate that God worked primarily through national churches, thus helping to legitimise the nation state from the Bible.[96] Anglicanism and Presbyterianism structured society in England and Scotland respectively in *Miriam*.[97] In *Julamerk*, Zoraide's journey to conversion began when she heard a debate between a rabbi and the Anglican bishop of Jerusalem's chaplain.[98] In *Judah's Lion*, England's authority was bound up with the influence of its established church in the Holy Land. As the LJS argued, the liturgy of the Church of England seemed particularly suited to Jewish sensibilities. Imagined as a national body themselves, it logically followed that as Jews converted they would pledge their support to a national church.

Second, the link dealt both with concerns over Jewish assimilation and incorporation into English identity, and with the troubling connection between Judaism and Catholicism. In the same way that Judaism often seemed to be a national faith without a national territory, refusing assimilation, so Catholicism 'was a religion without a country'.[99] Conversion in the novels dealt with this by incorporating Jews within the English church and nation (as in Bristow's work), or by emphasising their continued separation as a unique nation with a future in Palestine. Here, Jews retained their nationhood, but affirmed their distinction from Catholicism by safely linking territorial possession to their national church. Like the Church of England, they once more became an established faith with a national territory attached. This drew on a popular providential view among Evangelical Anglicans that saw both the Church of England and state security as linked to the nation's positive treatment of Jews.[100]

Some of the novels, particularly *Judah's Lion* and *Naomi*, demonstrated what Donald Lewis has described as a 'teaching of esteem' towards Jews.[101] Where Burstein read these works as suggesting a 'historical emptiness' to Judaism, it is important to stress that they emphasised a continued, distinctive Jewish identity and the Christian duty to support this.[102] As Alick stated at the conclusion of *Judah's Lion*: 'I love England, I desire to see her noble lion supreme among the nations; and to insure this, I would see him ever closely allied to the Lion of Judah.'[103] Webb's preface to *Naomi* introduced her novel of Jerusalem's fall with a statement on its future restoration: 'The signs of the present times point strongly towards the Holy Land and the once glorious city of Jerusalem ... [God who] made them a mark for the scorn and reproach of the Gentile nations, can as easily gather them together and bring them again into their own land.'[104] A national return to Palestine echoed through the novels as true Jewish national feeling that transcended Englishness. As Adeline told her lover Isaac:

> You are a noble-minded Jew, Isaac; be a patriot Jew too. We are now fighting in a moral struggle for our country, not where we have lived and breathed alone – not that land which we have loved because in it we first saw the soft spring time, the beauty of summer skies, the brightness of heaven and the gladness of earth – but the land for which we have longed for which we have hoped and suffered – for which our souls have burned, and our hearts have beat in unison with the hearts of thousands of heroic breasts – that land for which we have lived, for which we have prayed – of which we honour the mighty exiles live, of which we love the illustrious dead.[105]

This also disarmed tensions surrounding Jewish Messianism. In *Miriam*, the heroine's father Imlah was obsessed in his youth with restoring his people to Palestine, sentiments he attempted to relive through his daughter.[106] This appeared threatening; Imlah's 'mad enthusiasm' inspired 'passionate hatred against every class of Christian people',[107] while Miriam's imagination of the messiah's coming looked forward to the day when Jews would 'wave the banners of our faith amidst the bleeding heaps of those detested Christians!'[108] Conversion did not destroy these hopes, but redirected them. Miriam learned of the messiah's love rather than his judgement, while Imlah's final conversion to the established church fulfilled his dream of Jewish restoration as an Anglican. He became a missionary 'preaching the glad tidings of salvation to unbelievers in Syria, Palestine and Turkey'. As he had always wished, 'he died in the Holy Land'.[109] There was no restoration by independent political means, rather through association with England and its national church.

Conclusion

The presentation of Catholicism and Nonconformity within these novels offers a glimpse into the complexities of English attitudes towards Jews and Jewishness in the nineteenth century. Examining the books through this lens supports existing work on Evangelical linkage of Judaism and Catholicism, but also complicates it. Jews were like Catholics in their dependence on tradition and human authority, and unlike them in their repudiation of idolatry. They could be simultaneously both persecuted victims and inquisitors. However, Christian identity was equally complex in the novels. As well as critique of nominal Christians, they promoted a specifically Anglican form of faith as the type of Protestantism to win Jews to Christ. These conversions set Jews clearly apart from Catholics and affirmed the importance of establishment and God's preference for national churches. In terms of social respectability, liturgical practice and the interests of unity, the Church of England could appeal to Jews in ways impossible for Nonconformity. These appeals were also prophetic, linking the established church's destiny to the future restoration of Anglicanised Jews to Palestine and ensuring the Church's place in God's providential plan. These links were not progressive, and often (as in Tonna's work) directly denied the possibility or desirability of assimilation into English society.

The way in which the novels expressed these views suggests the complexity of tracking what supporting and 'loving' Jews actually meant for Evangelicals in the first half of the nineteenth century. An end to persecution combined with a denial of 'true' Englishness; deep emotional connections to Jews with fear and hatred of Catholicism; condemnation of the Talmud and synagogue service with distrust of the 'meanness' of Nonconformist worship. The implications of what it meant to 'remember God's ancient people with love and compassion'[110] go far beyond missionary history, affecting church controversy, intra-Protestant relations, popular literature and anti-Catholic tension.

This suggests important caveats for historians working on both British Jewish history and in the field of church history. As has long been recognised, works about Jews were not necessarily concerned with Judaism; texts often used Jews as a foil for other debates.[111] Historians approaching Christian texts from a background in Jewish history must therefore be sensitive to the complexities of intra-Evangelical debate within Evangelical works dealing with Jews. While anti-Catholicism could unite Evangelicals across the denominational spectrum, as Gareth Atkins has recently shown, there continued to be a subtle yet powerful discourse that equated Anglicanism with 'real' Evangelicalism.[112] Jewish converts (fictional and real) could be used to subtly make this point.

At the same time, there must also be a resistance to going too far in the opposite direction. These texts might have been concerned with intra-Christian disputes, national identity, eschatology and geopolitics. Yet, at times, this can be pushed so far as to suggest that they were therefore entirely unconcerned with 'real' Jews and Judaism.[113] Aside from the difficulty of discussing the 'reality' of novelistic depictions, this approach wrongly downplays a genuine desire in many of the novels to instruct readers about Jewish life, culture and practice. The fact that this came with a conversionist bent should not be surprising given that Evangelicals desired to convert all people; they viewed this, as the Rubinsteins point out, as an 'act of kindness'.[114] Neither should the fact that we find such presentations distasteful lead us to downplay the genuineness of Evangelical concern for Jews. To acknowledge that there was genuine concern implies neither our agreement over the form it took, nor that we hold their descriptions accurate. Acknowledging that Evangelicals were concerned with denominational disputes and national identity when writing about Jews does not therefore preclude genuine interest in Jewish culture as well. As with contemporary historians, so nineteenth-century Evangelicals could write with multiple motives, aims, concerns and (unconscious?) biases all working together at once. Monocausal explanations are neat and appealing, but seldom reflect the messiness of human motivations.

Continued exploration of these novels, and similar missionary ephemera surrounding Jewish conversion, will open new windows into both perceptions of Judaism in nineteenth-century England, and Evangelicalism's self-understanding and positioning within denominational structures. Similar research on missionary novels more generally would present opportunities for interesting comparisons with how Muslims, Native American faiths and the beliefs of South Asia were perceived and linked into denominational arguments. The 'great and interesting cause'[115] remains a fruitful subject of study for historians across a range of disciplines.

Notes

Thanks to Donald M. Lewis for helpful comments on an earlier version of this article. This article draws on research funded by the Jewish Historical Society of England.

1. Charlotte Tonna, *Judah's Lion*, 3rd edn (London: Seeley, Burnside, and Seeley, 1847), p. 61.
2. E.g. Miriam Elizabeth Burstein, 'Protestants against the Jewish and Catholic Family, *c.* 1829 to *c.* 1860', *Victorian Literature and Culture*, 31:1 (2003), 333–57; David Feldman, 'Popery, Rabbinism, and Reform: Evangelicals and Jews in Early Victorian England', in Diana Wood (ed.), *Christianity and Judaism*, Studies in Church History, 29 (Oxford: Blackwell, 1992), pp. 379–86.
3. Michael Ragussis, *Figures of Conversion: 'The Jewish Question' and English National Identity* (Durham, NC: Duke University Press, 1995), pp. 17–22.
4. See Martin Spence, *Heaven on Earth: Reimagining Time and Eternity in Nineteenth-Century British Evangelicalism* (Eugene, OR: Pickwick Publications, 2015).
5. E.g. *Helps to Self-Examination and Prayers on Different Subjections, for the Use of Humble-Minded and Inquiring Jews* (London: A. Macintosh, 1819).
6. *Jewish Expositor and Friend of Israel*, 1:6 (July 1816), 208–39.
7. This was the most common Anglican model, and one way of drawing a distinction against 'enthusiastic' conversions among Nonconformists. See Elisabeth Jay, *The Religion of the Heart: Anglican Evangelicalism and the Nineteenth-Century Novel* (Oxford: Clarendon, 1979), pp. 59–65.
8. The most famous case was Joseph Wolff (1795–1862), who studied at Rome and later became a monk in Fribourg. In 1819 he moved to London and converted to Anglicanism, before serving as a missionary in Asia in the 1840s.
9. E.g. *Jewish Expositor*, 3:11 (1818), 410–17; *Jewish Expositor*, 14:1 (1829), 6, or the LJS tract *Two Letters from a Merchant in London to his Friend in Amsterdam* (London: B. Goakman, 1819).
10. E.g. *Jewish Expositor*, 13:11 (1828), 414–16; *Jewish Expositor*, 14:4 (1829), 134–7.
11. Reprinted in *Jewish Expositor*, 1:4 (1816), 148.
12. *Jewish Expositor*, 14:2 (1829), 63.
13. See Andrew Crome, *Christian Zionism and English National Identity, 1600–1850* (Basingstoke: Palgrave Macmillan, 2018); Heidi Kaufman, *English Origins, Jewish Discourse, and the Nineteenth-Century British Novel: Reflections on a Nested Nation* (University Park: Pennsylvania State University Press, 2009); Ragussis, *Figures of Conversion*; Nadia Valman, *The Jewess in Nineteenth-Century Literary Culture* (Cambridge: Cambridge University Press, 2007).
14. See Ragussis, *Figures of Conversion*, pp. 22–6.

15 See Jay, *Religion of the Heart*, pp. 46–50 on the dominance of Anglican authors, and Ragussis, *Figures of Conversion* on links to *Tancred* and *Deronda*.
16 Jay, *Religion of the Heart*, pp. 195–201.
17 See the introduction to Annie Webb's *Julamerk: A Tale of the Nestorians* (London: Simpkin, Marshall & Co., 1852), pp. i–iv, where she claims the novel aims to encourage Christian charity towards the Nestorians.
18 Rachel Howard, 'Domesticating the Novel: Moral-Domestic Fiction, 1820–1834' (PhD thesis, Cardiff University, 2007).
19 E.g. Amelia Bristow, *The Orphans of Lissau and Other Interesting Narratives* (London: T. Gardiner and Son, 1830), p. 1; Annie Webb, *Naomi: The Last Days of Jerusalem*, 12th edn (London: Arthur Hall, Virtue & Co., 1854), 'Preface'.
20 Chalken wrote to William Blackwood about publication from 1826 to 1828. Although he claimed his sister wrote the novel, Blackwood and his reviewers attributed it to Chalken. See Edinburgh, National Library of Scotland, MS 4020, fol. 84.
21 Howard, 'Domesticating the Novel', pp. 200–5.
22 E.g. Ella Dzelzainis, 'Charlotte Elizabeth Tonna, Pre-Millenarianism, and the Formation of the Ten Hours Campaign', *Victorian Literature and Culture*, 31:1 (2003), 181–91; Joanne Nystrom Janssen, '"Embodying Facts": Anxiety About Fiction in the *Christian Lady's Magazine* and Charlotte Elizabeth Tonna's Social Problem Novels', *Victorian Periodicals Review*, 44:4 (2011), 327–53; Hilary L. Rubinstein, 'A Pioneering Philosemite: Charlotte Elizabeth Tonna (1790–1846) and the Jews', *Jewish Historical Studies*, 35 (1996–98), 103–18.
23 Published serially in the *Christian Lady's Magazine*; published as a novel in late 1842.
24 Joseph Shadur, *Young Travelers to Jerusalem: An Annotated Survey of American and English Juvenile Literature on the Holy Land, 1785–1940* (Ramat Gan: Ingeborg Rennert Center for Jerusalem Studies, 1999), pp. 78–81.
25 *The Eclectic Review*, n.s. 14:7 [78] (July 1843), p. 114.
26 Webb, *Naomi*, 'Preface'.
27 Prices taken from advertisements in the *Morning Chronicle*, 11 April 1826 and 9 July 1829 respectively, reproduced at 'British Fiction, 1800–1829', www.british-fiction.cf.ac.uk/titleDetails.asp?title=1826A002 (accessed 10 August 2020); and from the *Morning Chronicle*, 24 May 1830.
28 Simon Eliot, 'From Few and Expensive to Many and Cheap: The British Book Market 1800–90', in Simon Eliot and Jonathan Rose (eds), *A Companion to the History of the Book*, 2 vols, 2nd edn (Chichester: Wiley, 2020), vol. 1, pp. 471–84.
29 Prices from *Southampton Herald*, 24 December 1842 and *A Catalogue of Amusing and Instructive Works for the Young* (London: Arthur Hall, Virtue & Co., 1854), n.p.
30 London, British Library, RLF 1261/2, Anley to Trustees of Royal Literary Fund, 12 February 1851.
31 Charlotte Anley, *Miriam: Or, The Power of Truth*, 2nd edn (London: John Hatchard and Son, 1829), pp. 108–46. Several sections provide readers with a summary of Thomas Scott's commentary.
32 Amelia Bristow, *Emma de Lissau: A Narrative of Striking Vicissitudes and Peculiar Trials*, 4th edn (London: T. Stevenson, 1837), e.g. pp. 89–100, 235–42.

33 Ragussis, *Figures of Conversion*, p. 16.
34 Bristow, *Sophia de Lissau*, p. iv. Nonetheless, in the sequel Bristow admits that 'many persons consider the narrative of Sophia an ingenious fiction' (*Emma de Lissau*, pp. 248–9).
35 Osborn W. Trenery Heighway, *Leila Ada, The Jewish Convert: An Authentic Memoir* (London: Partridge, Oakley, & Co., 1854), p. xv.
36 Valman, *Jewess*, pp. 66–7.
37 Asahel Grant, *The Nestorians; or, The Lost Tribes* (London: John Murray, 1841).
38 Osborn W. Trenery Heighway, *Adeline: Or, Mysteries, Romance and Realities of Jewish Life*, 2 vols (London: Partridge, Oakey, & Co., 1854). As *The Athenaeum* commented witheringly in their review, 'we will spare our readers the comedy' (May 1854), 651–2.
39 Lewis Hippolytus Joseph Tonna, *A Memoir of Charlotte Elizabeth* (New York: M. W. Dodd, 1848), pp. 11–14.
40 Valman, *Jewess*, p. 56.
41 Webb, *Julamerk*, p. 34.
42 Tonna, *Judah's Lion*, p. 59.
43 Bristow, *Emma de Lissau*, p. 298.
44 Burstein, 'Protestants', 344.
45 Webb, *Julamerk*, p. 55.
46 Heighway, *Adeline*, vol. 1, p. 35.
47 Bristow, *Emma de Lissau*, p. 236.
48 *Ibid*., p. 238.
49 *Ibid*., p. 268.
50 Heighway, *Adeline*, vol. 1, p. 71.
51 Tonna, *Judah's Lion*, p. 256.
52 Ragussis, *Figures of Conversion*, pp. 127–73; Carol Margaret Davison, *Anti-Semitism and Gothic Literature* (Basingstoke: Palgrave Macmillan, 2004), pp. 77–81.
53 On the links between the Gothic and anti-Catholic novels, see Susan M. Griffin, *Anti-Catholicism and Nineteenth-Century Fiction* (Cambridge: Cambridge University Press, 2004), pp. 27–32.
54 A *cicisbeo* is a companion or lover. Heighway, *Adeline*, vol. 1, pp. 300–31.
55 Tonna, *Judah's Lion*, pp. 356–62.
56 Webb, *Julamerk*, p. 42.
57 Michael Wheeler, *The Old Enemies: Catholic and Protestant in Nineteenth-Century English Culture* (Cambridge: Cambridge University Press, 2006), pp. 31–3.
58 Feldman, 'Popery', pp. 379–86.
59 David B. Ruderman, 'Towards a Preliminary Portrait of an Evangelical Missionary to the Jews: The Many Faces of Alexander McCaul (1799–1863)', *Jewish Historical Studies*, 47:1 (2015), 62–5.
60 Davison, *Anti-Semitism*, pp. 55–86.
61 Burstein, 'Protestants', 339.
62 Joseph Wolff, *Joseph Wolff's Appeal to his Brethren, the Jews of Great Britain* (London: A. Macintosh, 1826), p. 26 (original emphasis).
63 Bristow, *Emma de Lissau*, p. 318.

64 Tonna, *Judah's Lion*, p. 133.
65 *Ibid.*, p. 164.
66 Heighway, *Leila Ada*, p. 10.
67 Bristow, *Orphans of Lissau*, p. 84.
68 Webb, *Naomi*, p. 132. On this, see Valman, *Jewess*, p. 70.
69 Bristow, *Sophia de Lissau*, p. 73.
70 *Ibid.*, p. 176.
71 *Ibid.*, pp. 282, 288.
72 *Ibid.*, p. 330.
73 Tonna, *Judah's Lion*, p. 217.
74 [C. W. Chalken], *The Hebrew, A Sketch in the Nineteenth Century* (Edinburgh: W. Blackwood, 1828), pp. 55–9.
75 Anley, *Miriam*, pp. 125–6.
76 Heighway, *Leila Ada*, p. 178.
77 Burstein, 'Protestants', 339; See also Ragussis, *Figures of Conversion*, pp. 39–40.
78 Bristow, *Orphans of Lissau*, p. 103.
79 Ragussis, *Figures of Conversion*, pp. 34–6.
80 Bristow, *Emma de Lissau*, pp. 89–140.
81 Heighway, *Leila Ada*, pp. 141–95.
82 On this, see François Soyer, 'Emotion and the Popularization of Anti-Jewish Discourse in Early Modern Europe', in Christian von Scheve, Anna Lea Berg, Meike Haken, Nur Yasemin Ural (eds), *Affect and Emotion in Multi-Religious Secular Society* (Abingdon: Routledge, 2020), pp. 33–50.
83 Tonna, *Judah's Lion*, pp. 332–6.
84 Recalling reactions to the Society's financial crisis that caused the split, Charles Simeon remarked sardonically 'The dissenting part of the managers then took to the long boat, and the Churchmen set to work at the pumps.' Quoted in W. T. Gidney, *The History of the London Society from Promoting Christianity Amongst Jews* (London: London Society, 1908), p. 47.
85 John Wolffe, *The Protestant Crusade in Great Britain, 1829–1860* (Oxford: Clarendon, 1991), pp. 198–205.
86 D. G. Paz, *Popular Anti-Catholicism in Mid-Victorian England* (Stanford: Stanford University Press, 1992), pp. 184–90.
87 Jay, *Religion of the Heart*, pp. 46–50.
88 Tonna, *Judah's Lion*, p. 357.
89 *Ibid.*, pp. 44–5.
90 Anley is best known for investigating conditions in Australia on behalf of Elizabeth Fry. See Charlotte Anley, *The Prisoners of Australia: A Narrative* (London: J. Hatchard and Son, 1841), p. 7. While this has led to the assumption that she was a Quaker, this does not necessarily follow. Her later novel *Earlswood* (London: Thomas Hatchard, 1855) was about Tractarianism and a defence of the Anglican Church, significantly described by her as 'our blessed Anglican *Protestant* Church' (p. 542).
91 Anley, *Miriam*, p. 33.
92 *Ibid.*, p. 177.

93 Heighway, *Leila Ada*, p. 263.
94 Heighway, *Adeline*, vol. 1, p. 219.
95 Howard, 'Domesticating the Novel', 161–229.
96 Spence, *Heaven on Earth*, pp. 154–7.
97 Anley, *Miriam*, pp. 335–6, where the Stuarts and Mr Howard praise the oversight of the established churches in helping keep the Sabbath in both Westmorland and Scotland.
98 Webb, *Julamerk*, pp. 58–9.
99 Zygmunt Bauman argued that one of the key reasons for post-Enlightenment ambiguity over Jews was their identification as a nation without a national territory. 'Allosemitism: Premodern, Modern, Postmodern', in Bryan Cheyette and Laura Marcus (eds), *Modernity, Culture and 'The Jew'* (Cambridge: Polity, 1998), pp. 143–56; Griffin, *Anti-Catholicism*, p. 4.
100 Crome, *Christian Zionism*, pp. 24–7.
101 Donald M. Lewis, *The Origins of Christian Zionism: Lord Shaftesbury and Evangelical Support for a Jewish Homeland* (Cambridge: Cambridge University Press, 2010), pp. 63–5.
102 Miriam Elizabeth Burstein, '"Not the Superiority of Belief, but Superiority of True Devotion": Grace Aguilar's *Histories of the Spirit*', in Brenda Ayres (ed.), *Silent Voices: Forgotten Novels by Victorian Women Writers* (Westport: Praeger, 2003), p. 7.
103 Tonna, *Judah's Lion*, p. 445.
104 Webb, *Naomi*, 'Preface'. In the updated preface to the seventeenth edition, Webb wrote that her confidence in restoration had been vindicated. Quoting the paragraph cited here, she wrote 'how much more emphatically may the same assertion now be made!' *Ibid.*, p. iii.
105 Heighway, *Adeline*, vol. 1, pp. 235–6.
106 Imlah promises Miriam to the Continental Jewish leader Menasseh ben Israel in marriage (Anley, *Miriam*, pp. 85–6): the name derives from the Amsterdam rabbi who pushed for Jewish readmission to England in the 1650s.
107 *Ibid.*, p. 4.
108 *Ibid.*, p. 11.
109 *Ibid.*, p. 383. Similarly, in *The Hebrew*, Asher ends his days working in 'a great and interesting cause; – namely, the progress of Christianity among his Jewish brethren' ([Chalken], *The Hebrew*, p. 216).
110 Anley, *Miriam*, p. 388.
111 Eliane Glaser, *Judaism without Jews: Philosemitism and Christian Polemic in Early Modern England* (London: Palgrave, 2007); Ragussis, *Figures of Conversion*.
112 Gareth Atkins, *Converting Britannia: Evangelicals and British Public Life, 1770–1840* (Woodbridge: Boydell, 2019), pp. 106–18.
113 For example, Eitan Bar-Yosef, *The Holy Land in English Culture, 1799–1917* (Oxford: Oxford University Press, 2005).
114 William D. Rubinstein and Hilary L. Rubinstein, *Philosemitism: Admiration and Support in the English Speaking World for Jews, 1840–1939* (Basingstoke: Macmillan, 1999), p. 133.
115 *The Hebrew*, p. 216.

The Spirituality of the Wesleyan Methodists of Brunswick Chapel, Leeds, in the Victorian Era

DAVID BEBBINGTON, UNIVERSITY OF STIRLING

Abstract

The spirituality of Brunswick Chapel, Leeds, in the Victorian era illustrates the legacy of John Wesley when Wesleyan Methodism was a power in the land. The priorities were conversion, turning to Christ in repentance and faith, the Bible as the source of divine instruction, the cross as the way in which salvation was achieved and activism as the proper human response. These features were prominent in the whole of the broader Evangelical movement which Wesley inaugurated. There was concern with death, and especially last words, in providing evidence of the assurance on which Wesley insisted and which was cultivated in the class meetings he began. Prayer, Charles Wesley's hymns and sermons loomed large. Men and women had their own channels for the expression of piety, but some avenues, especially in Sunday school teaching, were open to either sex. Some still professed Wesley's sublime doctrine of entire sanctification. Towards the end of the period there were signs that the tradition was decaying, with the spirituality becoming shallower, but for the bulk of the period the tradition was flourishing.

Keywords: spirituality; Wesleyans; Methodists; Leeds; Victorians

The Wesleyan Methodist Connexion was the second largest Protestant body in England during the Victorian period. In 1851, the year of the only religious census of the century, it attracted as large a proportion as 5.1 per cent of the population to worship.[1] Methodism had mushroomed since the Evangelical Revival of the previous century and Wesleyans – those who adhered to the organisation created by John Wesley – formed by far its largest sector. Their spirituality was still largely moulded by the teaching of their founder. Wesley had proclaimed the imperative of the new birth, an experience of conversion to open an authentic Christian life, but had also differentiated himself from other Evangelicals by repudiating Calvinism. A person did not have to be a member of a predetermined elect to become a true disciple, for anyone could believe and be saved. Also unlike Calvinists, Wesley held that real Christians could fall away from the faith. All believers had to guard against lapsing into a condition that would debar them from heaven. On the other hand, those who had been justified by faith could go on to a more advanced form of holiness. This 'entire sanctification' delivered them from sin while still on earth. The spirituality of Wesleyans was framed by the obligation of conversion, the ability of all to come to Christ, the avoidance of backsliding, and the call to entire sanctification.

Although Wesley's own convictions have been analysed at length, the way in which his spiritual legacy developed in later years when his followers had expanded to form a vast community has been far less studied. Earlier works were broad surveys. A chapter of Gordon Wakefield's *Methodist Devotion* (1966), a book which pioneered the investigation of the history of Methodist spirituality, is helpfully allocated to the nineteenth century.[2] The official four-volume history of British Methodism published a couple of decades later contains two relevant articles, one exploring early Victorian Methodist spirituality and worship and the other examining Wesleyan developments down to 1902.[3] Michael Watts, in the second volume of *The Dissenters* (1995), incorporated a section on the central experience of conversion, but his material conflates Wesleyans with other denominations outside the Church of England.[4]

More recent writing goes into greater detail. Linda Wilson has scrutinised a sample of obituaries from denominational magazines in a book which, while focusing on the spirituality of Nonconformist women, also examines the experience of their male counterparts. Wesleyans are distinguished from others for statistical analysis, but the latest cohort is from 1870–72.[5] An article and a book have concentrated on accounts of death. Henry Rack has written on Evangelical deathbed piety, dealing largely with Methodists, and Mary Riso has examined Evangelical Nonconformist obituaries with statistical care, distinguishing those relating to Wesleyans, though again not going beyond the 1870s.[6] I have examined the development of entire sanctification among Methodists during the nineteenth century elsewhere.[7] These writings shed much light on Methodist spiritual lives, but they all attempt to cover the whole country. Most individuals selected for commemoration in national sources were regarded as particularly notable for their piety, so that the syntheses of their experience in the secondary works risk emphasising the outstanding at the expense of the ordinary. A local study is more likely to reflect the realities of Wesleyan spirituality. That is what is offered here.

The place for examination is the Wesleyan congregation of Brunswick Chapel, Leeds. As the flourishing heart of the woollen textile industry, Leeds was the largest centre of population in the West Riding of Yorkshire. It was also a bastion of Methodism, with many woollen merchants and associated manufacturers lending their patronage to the movement. As Walter Farquhar Hook wrote about the town on becoming vicar of Leeds in 1837, 'The *de facto* established religion is Methodism.'[8] In 1851 there were ten Wesleyan places of worship in the town, six of them claiming over 1,000 attendances on census Sunday.

Brunswick Chapel, with the second highest total after the town-centre congregation, had nearly 2,000 attendances.[9] It had been built on the northern edge of Leeds in 1825 to cater for the inhabitants of the adjacent Georgian terraces without excluding the poorer folk who lived nearby. The chapel boasted a fine classical stone exterior, an interior enriched with polished mahogany and a vast organ dominating the sanctuary.[10] The erection of the organ, demanded by a majority of the first trustees in 1826, had occasioned a crisis in the whole connexion. There was stiff resistance from most of the local preachers who resented this symbol of popish affectation. The will of the leading trustees was enforced by the denominational authorities, overriding proper procedures, and the outcome was a sizeable secession from Wesleyanism to form the 'Protestant Methodists'.[11] For all its desire to show its standing in the world, Brunswick maintained a vigorous outreach to the less well-to-do in its vicinity, establishing branch Sunday schools which sometimes grew into parallel congregations. Brunswick Chapel, together with its satellite organisations, was an agency for the rich and the poor.

All these people, at least in theory, had their spiritual experience recorded for posterity. From 1873, the circuit, the bureaucratic tier in Methodism above the congregations, required the writing of an obituary for every member. All Methodists belonged to a class, usually a group of around twelve, though sometimes much larger, which met weekly for mutual religious support. The expected pattern of class meetings, apart from hymn-singing and prayer, was for the members to recount their struggles and triumphs of the previous week. At Brunswick, from the 1870s until the First World War, when the reporting system broke down, the class leader was expected to summarise the life of each member in a statement to the quarterly meeting of the circuit, which was subsequently recorded in a book. This volume, containing 270 entries relating to Brunswick and its satellites, survives among the copious records of the Brunswick circuit.[12] In practice many members escaped the net, but a large number did have their spiritual lives, extending back to the early Victorian years and in some cases even earlier, documented in the book. In a few cases ministers or relatives contributed the memoirs, but most entries were written by the leaders and so dwelt on what the subjects had described in class. The models were the obituaries in the monthly *Methodist Magazine*, and indeed in one case the Brunswick account was abridged from a memoir in the magazine written by the superintendent minister of the circuit.[13] As a result, the pattern is stylised, with similar experiences recorded and phrases often repeated. It can be questioned how far the memoirs accurately reflect reality, but even when they say almost as much about the expectations of the writers as about the experiences of the subjects, they lay bare the substance of denominational culture. The very formulae show the nature of Wesleyan spirituality.[14]

Evangelical Basics

One point around which most of the obituaries are organised is conversion. The phraseology is varied, but the meaning is the change in life at the time of becoming a Christian. Several subjects were 'soundly converted';[15] others were 'led into the way of peace' or 'led into the joy of salvation';[16] one 'gave her heart to God', another 'experienced a change of heart';[17] a man 'found peace', a woman was granted 'spiritual illumination'.[18] All these forms of expression, together with many others, were designed to indicate that the person had entered on Christian pilgrimage. Many conversions came in two stages, with conviction of sin preceding the discovery of gospel freedom. Thus Rebecca Todd, who attended a cottage prayer meeting in 1870, was 'awakened to her need, and led to seek a sense of the pardon of God'.[19]

There were occasional instances where the standard type of conversion seems to have had no place, but these cases caused obituarists some discomfort. Margaret Crowther, who was brought up as an Anglican for the first thirty years of her life, had passed through no such decisive experience, but her class leader explained that she could be supposed to have had an imperceptible transition from childish innocence to conscious acceptance by God.[20] Normally, however, the time of conversion could be pinpointed. 'On Sunday Nov 17 1872', it was said of Richard Bells, 'he sought & found the Salvation which is by grace through faith in our Lord Jesus Xt.'[21] And the effects of a change of direction were palpable. As Robert Hudson, a stalwart of the congregation in later life, put it of himself, 'when he turned round, he turned completely round and never looked back'; and Zerubbabel Barraclough, another holder of many chapel positions of responsibility, 'never got away from the simple fervour of his conversion, it gave a rich glow to the whole of his Christian life'.[22] Conversion was the supreme moment cherished in a believer's memory.

A second feature commonly found in the memoirs preserved in the circuit collection is an emphasis on the Bible, which could play a part in conversion. Urged by his wife to read the scriptures, Thomas Wood concluded at the age of 58 that 'if the Bible is right, I am wrong' and soon found salvation.[23] The good book became the lodestar of many a Wesleyan. William Coates, for instance, had 'a deep reverence for the Word of God, & it was manifest that he searched the Scriptures with serious attention, for his mind was largely stored with God's word which he made the great rule of life'.[24] Dedicated Bible reading was recorded of many of the subjects. The result was that Jabez Layton was never at a loss for texts and Jane Kettlewell used to remind her household each evening in the language of scripture that they could cast all their care upon the Lord 'for He careth for you'.[25] One member of Roscoe Place, a branch of Brunswick, served for twenty-three years as a Bible woman, going round poorer neighbourhoods selling the scriptures from door to door.[26] A particularly prominent member of the same branch, a prosperous oil merchant named Benjamin Threlfall Vickers, placed absolute faith in the Word of God. 'He believed every promise', according to his obituary, 'was for him'.[27] A Bible could achieve iconic status. A friend asked to receive Eliza Ann Dixon's companion Bible after her death because it had done so much for her; and the Wesleyan wife of a sergeant-major who had changed residence eleven times on different postings before reaching Brunswick sold everything during the moves except the Bible she had acquired on her marriage.[28] The scriptures played a major determinative and symbolic role in the religion of the Brunswickers.

A further element in many spiritual biographies, in the third place, was the cross. In general doctrine did not loom large, but the atoning death of Christ was an exception. The reason is that it was the crucifixion that reconciled God to humanity and so secured the salvation of penitent sinners. By contrast the resurrection is nowhere mentioned in the obituaries, for the cross possessed unique soteriological significance. The wife of John Whitehead, for example, 'relied entirely on the sacrifice of Christ as her only plea for salvation'.[29] A hymn declaring that God had been reconciled led Ann Wood 'to cast her soul by faith on the atonement of Christ'.[30] The atonement was likewise said to be a favourite theme of Dr Rossvally, a colourful converted German Jew.[31] The context in which the cross most frequently appears in the obituaries is the approach of death. Thus the last connected utterance of a young man of 24 was the passage from the Old Testament most commonly applied to the atonement, 'He was wounded for our transgressions, He was bruised for our iniquities.'[32]

In their last days, Margaret Stoney spoke of 'the sufficiency of the atonement' and Thomas Norris cried out 'Victory! Victory! through the blood of the Lamb.'[33] Even more dramatically Thomas Groundwell, a former Sunday school superintendent and class leader, raised his hand on his deathbed, pointed with his finger and when his daughter asked what he saw, he replied simply, 'Calvary'. 'That', according to his obituarist, 'was his last word'.[34] Again, as a visitor to an assiduous local preacher leant over him to repeat the hymn 'Rock of Ages' by Augustus Toplady, saying 'In my hands no price I bring, simply to thy cross ...', the dying man took up the words, 'I cling', 'I cling'.[35] And similarly, shortly before the death of William Bilborough, his class leader 'found him clinging to the Cross'.[36] The cross was a repeated theme of the memoirs.

So was activism, a desire to be up and doing which attracted high praise from the compilers of the biographies. 'Her life', it was said of a class leader, 'was one of constant activities in the service of her family & of others.'[37] Methodism offered an enormous range of opportunities for laypeople. Lay preachers took far more services than ordained ministers, women could perform many of the chapel tasks and there were recognised channels through which young people could show their zeal. Most obvious was the 'earnestness in trying to win souls for Christ' celebrated in the life of Jane Graham.[38] Prayer leaders were appointed to take charge of evangelistic cottage meetings and tract distributors were commissioned to circulate the written word. Beyond directly gospel efforts, activities such as hospital visiting, relieving the poor and temperance lecturing were equally approved. Sometimes members exceeded their strength in their busyness. William Henry Rishton, who threw himself into the Young Men's Christian Association and distribution of the evangelistic *British Workman* newspaper, made himself seriously ill in 1875 through intense work as secretary to an interdenominational Leeds mission and died at the age of 47 two years later.[39]

Administrative jobs, too, were available in abundance. John Stocks was described as 'of retiring disposition', yet he served Brunswick as society steward, chapel steward and trustee, offices of considerable responsibility.[40] It is true that some deceased members were labelled 'quiet', but even they were likely to be described by some such phrase as 'ever striving to help'.[41] Activism could not be divorced from the spirituality of the chapel. That is not surprising because, alongside the emphases on conversion, Bible and cross that have been noticed, it was one of the four qualities that have been seen as defining characteristics of the Evangelical movement of which Methodism formed a part.[42] The people of Victorian Brunswick expressed the perennial temper of Evangelicalism.

Common Themes

Other elements are almost constant features of the obituaries. The most consistently appearing topic, in fact, is death. The entries in the circuit book habitually dwell on the last days of their subjects, partly because those were closest in recollection but mainly because deathbed scenes demonstrated that the faith of Methodists sustained them to the end. Often there is a suggestion that the members were, as one memoir of a 77-year-old put it, 'ripening for eternity': their knowledge of God was not just steady but was advancing with their years.[43] As they grew older, in an age of rudimentary healthcare, most of the individuals entered a period, sometimes prolonged, of serious illness and acute suffering. Then faith provided much needed consolation. When affliction confined her to her home, Anne Hutchinson 'endured as seeing Him who is invisible'.[44] Likewise Annie Louisa Thompson showed 'cheerful constancy, quiet submission and calm trust in God in the midst of protracted pain'.[45]

Some Wesleyans, the obituarists admit, were not so tranquil. 'The enemy of souls', it was said of a former class leader, 'taking advantage of physical weakness grievously assaulted him'.[46] Another member had to wrestle in her final illness with 'the great adversary'.[47] The struggle, however, was depicted as always ending in victory. Last words were quoted to show that those on their deathbeds, free from doubt and fear, enjoyed peace, rest and 'a blessed hope of everlasting life'.[48] It was accepted practice for friends and relations to ply the dying with questions to elicit answers they could subsequently treasure. The favourite was to ask whether Jesus was precious.[49] The deathbed was a setting where those about to leave the world could still bear testimony to their faith.

Crucially, what they were expected to express was assurance. Wesley had maintained that a Christian must possess 'the witness of the Spirit'. Believers, in Wesley's view, are those who can sense the Holy Spirit communicating to their spirits that they are children of God. The Brunswick community remained aware of this legacy. John Bickers, long-term secretary of a branch Sunday school, believed in 'our Founder's teaching' not only about repentance and faith but also about the witness of the Spirit.[50] Repeatedly obituaries mention 'conscious . . . acceptance', 'clear assurance', 'felt . . . acceptance' and the like.[51] Two consecutive entries in the circuit book refer to the 'sterling piety' of the departed. One of them, Arthur Williamson, a promising young man who died at only 21, showed his piety by being 'always cheerful'; the other, Sarah Foster, an 84-year-old, displayed it through her 'unshaken confidence in Christ her Saviour'.[52] Cheerfulness and confidence were the expected outcomes of assurance. Timidity was a dubious sign, but it could be overcome by faith in God.[53]

Indifference to spiritual things was far more serious, betokening an actual fall from grace after which 'restoration to the favour of God' was required.[54] There were borderline cases. Sarah Hannah Fearnley, for instance, a schoolteacher who came to Leeds in 1880, was anxious to be right with God. Her conscientious class leader tried to point her towards a felt salvation, but she was plagued with 'doubt & fear'. After counselling in a mission in Leeds by the American evangelists Dwight L. Moody and Ira D. Sankey in 1883, Sarah reached 'the assurance of God's favor', but then again lapsed into a 'mental affliction' that took it away until her death at the age of 38 in 1885. Her class leader, faced with a case that did not fit the received categories, hoped that she had passed to a place where there is 'fullness of joy for evermore'.[55] Sarah

Fearnley, however, was exceptional. In most cases assurance was the foundation of a 'bright & happy' life.[56]

The weekly class meetings, where spiritual experience was recounted, are a prominent feature of the obituaries. Methodist membership was defined by holding a ticket for membership of a class, issued quarterly by a resident minister. The qualification for admission was a serious quest for true religion, not necessarily any profession of having found it. Often attenders were initially taken to class by a friend or relation, as was John Hutchinson, who was invited by a fellow warehouseman to attend a class belonging to Oxford Place, another Leeds Wesleyan chapel. It was only after he had been in class for a while that he 'gave himself fully to God'.[57] There was therefore a time when Hutchinson was a Methodist but not, according to the Methodist definition, a Christian. Once converted, however, members were expected to testify to the continuing vitality of their spiritual lives. John Whitehead, who gave generously to Brunswick funds, reportedly expressed at class meeting 'unbounded Faith in his Heavenly Father and unswerving Trust in Christ as his Saviour'.[58]

On occasion members could challenge the others in the group. Ann Blackburn, whose own experience was 'rich & clear', sometimes delivered impressive exhortations to her fellows; they were 'given in such a forcible manner as to be long remembered by them'.[59] Not all contributions were so edifying. Joseph Godley's experience was only 'generally satisfactory'; that of William Mackrell was only 'usually of a cheerful character'.[60] The class leaders were expected to turn the proceedings into profitable occasions. Elizabeth Ann Pierson, a South African who led a class at Brunswick for forty years until 1914, had an 'arresting personality' and so chapel members remembered 'the power she had over the minds and consciences of her classes'. Somebody has deleted in the draft of her obituary the words, 'Faults and failings she had, but', and so it is likely that the formidable Mrs Pierson could be domineering.[61] Not all were like that. Of Mary Crawford, a leader for over thirty years, it was written that 'She loved her members: and they in return loved her.'[62] In classes with such leadership, attenders found safe havens where problems could be broached and remedies canvassed. They were at the very core of Brunswick Wesleyanism.

Other aspects of the piety of the chapel were less distinctive to Methodism. The types and settings of prayer mentioned in the obituaries were similar to those found in other Evangelical denominations. There were prayer meetings after evening services designed primarily to encourage conversions. At the age of 19 in 1862, Sarah Milnes, who had started having 'serious impressions' some weeks before, could not resist going forward at a meeting after the Sunday evening sermon to kneel at the communion rail. 'The friends prayed with me & for me', she told a correspondent, and, though she left church dissatisfied, on returning home she felt a joyous sense of commitment.[63] Brunswick also had a prayer meeting on Friday evening apart from the midweek service on Wednesday.[64] There were further meetings for prayer early on Sunday mornings at Brunswick and the Roscoe Place branch, and there was yet another each weekday at 6 a.m., attended faithfully by Benjamin Randall Vickers, until, at last, he was the only one who came.[65] The prayer leaders who ran the numerous cottage meetings – in at least one case for about half a century – treated them (as the title of their office suggested) primarily as gatherings for prayer, though with singing and exhortation interspersed.[66]

As in other denominations, there were noted prayer warriors. Mary Cuttle was 'extraordinarily gifted in Prayer';[67] Jane Reynolds and her friends 'would stay up all night in earnest prayer to God that He would bless them in their efforts to extend his Kingdom'.[68] Such spirituality could exert a powerful influence. Mary Buck, a woman 'remarkable for the use of ejaculatory prayer' who 'constantly lived in the spirit of prayer', took her children aside to intercede for their individual conversion. It is no accident that one of her sons became a Wesleyan minister.[69] Prayer, especially with an eye to conversions, was a significant component in Brunswick life.

So was hymnody. Although hymn singing was general among Victorian Protestants, the compositions of Charles Wesley powerfully moulded the ethos of Methodism. Experience at Brunswick was regularly said to have been stated in terms of 'our hymns', 'our well known hymns' or 'old Methodist hymns'.[70] Sometimes writers of memoirs quote specific hymns by Charles Wesley. Henry Harrison was remembered for singing 'Jesu, lover of my soul' at class meeting and Charles Atkinson for quoting (appropriately, from his deathbed): 'Happy if with my latest breath I may but gasp His name' from 'Jesus, the name high over all'.[71] Regularly obituarists refer to the love of their subjects for hymns as well as for the Bible. The New Testament and hymn book used by John Wilton were 'simply worn out by constant use'.[72] With Eliza Ann Dixon, hymn singing was 'a very favourite employment'.[73] Mary Walker found quotations from hymns helpful 'when tempted to despondency' and for expressing the 'joy of conscious acceptance with God'.[74]

Hymns seem to have proved especially uplifting when death approached, as in the case of William Henry Rushton, who repeated many verses on the night of his passing.[75] Occasionally, compositions by other earlier writers are mentioned – Isaac Watts' 'I'll praise my Maker while I've Breath' and (again) Augustus Toplady's 'Rock of Ages' – and towards the end of the period a hymn by a contemporary, the American Fanny Crosby's 'Blessed Assurance', is quoted.[76] Nevertheless, the salience of hymnody in the obituary book is largely due to the legacy of Charles Wesley.

The worship at Brunswick was unusually dignified for a Wesleyan chapel. The magnificent organ which caused so much trouble at the opening of the chapel required a professional organist, who published his own collection of psalm tunes containing the *Te Deum* and *Benedicite*.[77] In addition there was a choir with paid soloists. One choir member composed tunes sung in the chapel's worship.[78] Several members especially enjoyed the services. Thomas Riley, for example, one of the more eminent figures who rose to become society and circuit steward, was 'a true lover of public worship'.[79] Something of the concern for high standards of music carried over into the branches, for the widow of George Penniston, a trustee, donated the entire cost of a new organ to the Roscoe Place Chapel, and John William Young, as organist and choirmaster at Lincoln Fields Sunday School and Society, raised subscriptions for an organ with three manuals, thirty-one stops and 1,288 pipes.[80] Brunswick held midweek services, appreciated by some, and either it or a satellite congregation provided the distinctively Methodist New Year's Eve watchnight services.[81]

What is almost entirely missing from the obituaries is Holy Communion. There is a single reference to one of the subjects being able, just before her death, to remain after the main service for the sacrament, but there is no hint of spiritual strength being gained from communion.[82] A couple of men are recorded as profiting from the lovefeasts where bread and water were passed round while individuals testified to their experiences, much as in class meetings.[83] It is clear that the Wesleyans of Brunswick were no sacramentalists. They were, however, lovers of preaching. Individuals are said to have been roused, awakened, convicted and converted under particular ministers. James Rayner displayed a 'love of the Sanctuary', but it was 'his attention to the preached word' that was specifically singled out as 'an inspiration to the Ministers'.[84] A remark about another man praised for his regular attendance, that 'it was not so much with him who the preacher was', indicates that the phenomenon of sermon-tasting must have been widespread.[85] Brunswickers liked a good sermon.

Gender Roles

Contemporary notions of appropriate gender roles naturally affected how the two sexes expressed their spirituality. Business was not the exclusive preserve of men, for widows like Mrs Scott and Mrs Oates, both dying in 1913, had been forced to take up gainful employment in order to bring up their families, showing 'devotion to duty & to God' in the process.[86] Yet work outside the home was largely a male province. The priority was making a good testimony. Edward Brown was 'a quiet and consistent Christian, witnessing a good confession for the Master before sceptics and infidels with whom he was brought into daily contact in one of the large workshops of Leeds'.[87] Again, on business journeys John Wilton 'used often to speak for God in the railway trains or to his customers'.[88] It was also imperative to show 'integrity & industry', as did William Hodgson, a coachbuilder employed at the same firm for over fifty years.[89]

Women, by contrast, presided over the home. 'The beauty of holiness' it was said of Mrs Hall, 'shone in her domestic life'.[90] The essential for a married woman was being, like Julia Schofield, 'a most devoted wife and mother'.[91] It was true of many, as it was of Elizabeth Wilkinson, that 'cleanliness and household order were part of her religion', and of many others, as it was of Eliza Oates, that her cast of mind was 'rather of the Martha than of the Mary kind'.[92] Female work was primarily located in the care of the household. Yet there were outlets for women that extended outside the home. Alongside a male equivalent, for instance, there was a Ladies' Juvenile Missionary Society which made collections for work at home and abroad. It was run by a committee and a secretary, for some time the unmarried Elizabeth Smith.[93] Some women organised mothers' meetings, speaking regularly themselves at what amounted to small single-sex church meetings midweek.[94] Women were also wholly responsible for the elaborate bazaars, large-scale sales of goods and crafts, that punctuated chapel life. There were long months of preparation, especially in weekly sewing meetings, where Maria Hudson, one of the regular devotees, was 'always employing her skilful fingers in working for Chapel or School Bazaars'.[95] There was no lack of opportunities for female Christian service.

Some spheres of ministry, however, were open to either sex. The most common was Sunday school teaching, which drew in a high proportion of Brunswick's young men and an even higher proportion of young women. Some began as younger teenagers, such as Mary Jane Crossby who started looking after a class at 15.[96] Exceptionally, George Thompson Dixon assumed responsibility in 1835 for what was called an ABC class in a branch school at the age of 10.[97] It was by no means an essential qualification to have professed conversion. Before his turning to God at 19, John Spink was active in the Brunswick Sunday School, and Abram Kirby long served as a teacher before finding his Saviour in his mid-forties.[98]

An instructor might continue for life, as did Mary Smith, who taught in the Little London and Lincoln Fields Sunday schools attached to Brunswick for half a century.[99] Female teachers could attain prominence, reading papers on methods at inter-congregational gatherings, as did Elizabeth Smith, who had charge of a young women's class at Brunswick. Nevertheless, there was a gendered dimension in Sunday schools because the organisers' posts of secretary and superintendent were restricted to men. Dixon worked his way up the Lincoln Fields classes until he was elected secretary in 1850 and superintendent in 1877,[100] but women could not do the same, even where the pupils were all girls. Other dimensions of service were filled by people of both sexes, but in practice more by women because men had other responsibilities during the working day. Thus Edwin Ball was 'ever ready to visit the sick',[101] but he never attained the distinguished record of some of the female members of Brunswick. Outstanding among them was Hannah Frost. At Lincoln Fields Chapel, Hannah ran a large weekly mothers' meeting, a senior girls' Sunday school class, and four class meetings, which at her death in 1904 included 120 individuals. She was the embodiment of Christian philanthropy in the deprived area of Newtown, where she was 'to be seen morning, noon, and night tramping, without regard to her own comfort or ease, from street to street'.[102] Women were often the public face of the church in areas of life where there was no gender bar.

Entire Sanctification

The crown of Methodist spirituality was Wesley's doctrine of entire sanctification. Its small number of exponents at Brunswick and its related causes were remarkable people. One stalwart, Benjamin Randall Vickers, had received entire sanctification shortly after his conversion as a teenager in 1812 but had lost it shortly afterwards. Although the obituary written by his son makes no claim that he recovered his former state, Vickers did show extraordinary dedication, giving generously to missions and spending whole days in fasting and prayer over important decisions.[103] William Coates, who seems to have had the same experience, saying in class that he could 'reckon himself dead ... unto sin', possessed an unusual reverence for the Bible and regularly attended early morning prayer meetings.[104] John Banks wrote in his journal in 1838, 'The blood of Jesus Christ cleanseth from all sin. And if I am not greatly mistaken it cleanseth me.' He proved to be a powerful local preacher and was 'mighty in prayer'.[105] Elizabeth Wardell found 'a deeper baptism of the Holy Spirit' and Mortimer Barraclough enjoyed 'life "more abundantly"', both becoming extremely effective soul winners, Elizabeth as a full-time home missionary and Mortimer as a persuasive local preacher.[106] Visits by Americans reinforced this current of holiness teaching. A mission at Brunswick by James Caughey in 1843 brought the blessing to individuals, including Robert Skilbeck, and the celebrated holiness teacher Phoebe Palmer spoke at Brunswick in 1862.[107] The greatest proponent, however, was Emma Graham, who 'lived in the profession of entire sanctification, exemplifying that doctrine in her daily life'. Emma was a superb class leader, showing tact in dealing with the problems of young people, served as a kindly district visitor and performed midnight rescue work among prostitutes. 'Her character', wrote her awed obituarist, 'reminds us of the Beatitudes'.[108] The account of Emma Graham's ministry was a striking advertisement for Wesley's teaching.

By the last years of the century, however, there were signs of decay in the pattern which Wesley had bequeathed. Rising respectability was taking its toll, so that Wesleyans felt reluctant to bare their souls in public, and alternative recreation facilities were becoming available, not least within the world of Nonconformity itself.[109] An obituarist lamented in 1895 that 'experimental Christian testimony' was rarer at class meetings than it used to be and in the following decade a member in her eighties 'knew the value of the class and could not understand why the present day members stood aloof'.[110] In his last years at the start of the twentieth century, a former society steward regretted that cottage meetings had been given up since they were a good training ground for young men.[111] Even conversion was described in milder terms or else, in many cases, omitted entirely from memoirs. At a time when those who were soon to enter the Wesleyan ministry were ceasing to profess a conversion experience, the people of Brunswick were becoming similarly hesitant.[112]

There can be no doubt that piety was in general shallower, with the last claimant of entire sanctification dying in 1900.[113] These symptoms in a particular locality confirm the diagnosis of Gordon Wakefield that by the opening of the First World War the Methodist class meeting was no longer a spiritual power.[114] Yet the spirituality of Brunswick Chapel down to 1900 illustrates the way in which Wesley's legacy was put into practice in the century after his own time. The priorities were conversion, Bible, cross and activism, as in the rest of the broader Evangelical movement which Wesley had helped to inaugurate. There was concern with death, and especially last words, in providing evidence of the assurance on which Wesley insisted and which was cultivated in the class meetings he began. Prayer, the hymns of Wesley's brother and sermons in the context of worship loomed large. Men and women had their own channels for the expression of piety, but some were open to either sex. A few individuals still professed Wesley's sublime doctrine of entire sanctification. Many in the reign of Victoria could have echoed what was attributed to Margaret Hewitt, converted in about 1837 and dying in 1881: 'Brunswick Chapel was to her, as it were, a heaven on earth.'[115]

Notes

1 David W. Bebbington, *Victorian Nonconformity* (Cambridge: Lutterworth Press, 2011), p. 11.
2 Gordon S. Wakefield, *Methodist Devotion: The Spiritual Life in the Methodist Tradition, 1791–1945* (London: Epworth Press, 1966).
3 Norman P. Goldhawk, 'The Methodist People in the Early Victorian Age: Spirituality and Worship', and Henry D. Rack, 'Wesleyan Methodism, 1849–1902', in Rupert Davies, A. Raymond George and Gordon Rupp (eds), *A History of the Methodist Church in Great Britain*, 4 vols (London: Epworth Press, 1965–88), vol. 2, pp. 113–42; vol. 3, pp. 119–66.
4 Michael R. Watts, *The Dissenters: Volume II, The Expansion of Evangelical Nonconformity* (Oxford: Clarendon Press, 1995), pp. 49–80.
5 Linda Wilson, *Constrained by Zeal: Female Spirituality amongst Nonconformists, 1825–1875* (Carlisle: Paternoster Press, 2000).
6 Henry D. Rack, 'Evangelical Endings: Death-Beds in Evangelical Biography', *Bulletin of the John Rylands University Library of Manchester*, 74:1 (1992), 39–56; Mary Riso, *The Narrative of a Good Death: The Evangelical Deathbed in Victorian England* (Farnham: Ashgate, 2015). See also David W. Bebbington, 'The Deathbed Piety of Victorian Evangelical Nonconformists', in John Coffey (ed.), *Heart Religion: Evangelical Piety in England and Ireland, 1690–1850* (Oxford: Oxford University Press, 2016), pp. 201–24, though this article does not isolate Wesleyans.
7 David Bebbington, 'Holiness in Nineteenth-Century Methodism', in William M. Jacob and Nigel Yates (eds), *Crown and Mitre: Religion and Society in Northern Europe since the Reformation* (Woodbridge: Boydell Press, 1993), pp. 161–75.
8 Walter Farquhar Hook to Samuel Wilberforce, July 1837, in William R. W. Stephens, *The Life and Letters of Walter Farquhar Hook, D.D., F.R.S.*, 2 vols (London: Richard Bentley & Son, 1878), vol. 1, p. 404.
9 Brian Greaves, 'Methodism in Yorkshire, 1740–1851' (PhD thesis, University of Liverpool, 1968), p. 104.
10 [Phoebe Palmer], *Four Years in the Old World*, 14th edn (New York: Foster & Palmer Jr, 1867), pp. 620–1.
11 David A. Gowland, *Methodist Secessions: The Origins of Free Methodism in Three Lancashire Towns* (Manchester: Chetham Society, 1979), pp. 6–8.
12 Leeds, West Yorkshire Joint Services Leeds Archives, Leeds Brunswick Circuit Quarterly Meeting Obituary Book, WYL 490/32 (hereafter OB). Entries relating to other chapels, not started from Brunswick though within the same circuit, have been excluded from consideration.
13 OB, John Banks, 23 February 1886. The obituary book is unpaginated and so reference is to names of subjects and dates of death, which are in roughly chronological order. Where no date of death is given, it is estimated with '*c.*'
14 It is so argued by Riso, *Narrative of a Good Death*, pp. 47–52.
15 OB, B. W. Chamberlin, 2 November 1910; Amelia Hornby, 3 April 1912; Walter Pitts, 6 March 1913.
16 OB, Henry Westmorland, 24 March 1898; Miss Redfern, 28 December 1899.

17 OB, Mary Cuttle, 7 July 1909; John William Wood, 9 July 1909.
18 OB, Joseph Wincup, 6 September 1889; Esther Sanderson, 2 September 1892.
19 OB, Rebecca Todd, 26 April 1873.
20 OB, Margaret Crowther, 24 August 1892.
21 OB, Richard Bells, 1 June 1874.
22 Leeds, West Yorkshire Joint Services Leeds Archives, Bundle of MS Obituaries, 1873–1917, WYL 490/258 (hereafter BO), Robert Hudson, 16 January 1913. This bundle contains drafts of obituaries that were not fully entered in the circuit record book as the system was breaking down. OB, Zerubbabel Barraclough, 21 March 1888.
23 OB, Thomas Wood, 1 December 1875.
24 OB, William Coates, 9 June 1879.
25 OB, Jabez Layton, 29 March 1895; Jane Kettlewell, *c.* December 1895.
26 OB, Jane Sparling, 14 December 1891.
27 BO, Benjamin Threlfall Vickers, 17 July 1917.
28 OB, Eliza Anne Dixon, 2 October 1893 (though no date given); Delilah Wills, 23 February 1895.
29 OB, Mrs John Whitehead, 11 July 1890.
30 OB, Ann Wood, 19 October 1886.
31 OB, Dr Rossvally, *c.* March 1893.
32 OB, Gustavus Fawcett, 8 October 1889.
33 OB, Margaret Stoney, 26 August 1875; Thomas Norris, 4 May 1883.
34 OB, Thomas Groundwell, 31 October 1876.
35 OB, John Cordukes, *c.* October 1889.
36 OB, William Bilborough, 19 November 1887.
37 BO, Mrs Amelia Hornby, 3 April 1912.
38 OB, Jane Graham, 15 May 1882.
39 OB, William Henry Rishton, 2 February 1877.
40 OB, John Stocks, 21 September 1876.
41 OB, Elizabeth Wood, 15 December 1911.
42 David W. Bebbington, *Evangelicalism in Modern Britain: A History from the 1740s to the 1980s* (London: Unwin Hyman, 1989), pp. 2–17.
43 OB, Thomas Belt, 17 January 1878.
44 OB, Ann Hutchinson, 4 December 1877.
45 OB, Annie Louisa Thompson, 23 January 1992.
46 OB, Charles Atkinson, 23 September 1882.
47 OB, Mrs Gibson, 21 August 1877.
48 OB, Mary Ann Ashworth, 19 October 1882.
49 OB, Joseph Bowser, *c.* July 1873; Mary Dixon, *c.* August 1874; John Kettlewell, 20 November 1875; H. B. Legg, 29 June 1881.
50 OB, John Bickers, 2 January 1900.
51 OB, Sarah Milnes, 9 May 1875; Mrs Hall, *c.* November 1877; Eliza Turner, 25 December 1885.
52 OB, Arthur Williamson, 28 October 1892; Sarah Foster, 22 October 1892.
53 OB, Elizabeth Atkinson, 29 November 1884.

54 OB, Mary Salter (? MS unclear), 8 February 1876.
55 OB, Sarah Hannah Fearnley, 23 June 1885.
56 OB, Sarah Ann Margaret Simpson, 9 May 1892.
57 OB, John Hutchinson, 11 March 1885.
58 OB, John Whitehead, 3 May 1898.
59 OB, Ann Blackburn, 2 January 1881.
60 OB, Joseph Godley, 9 October 1876; William Mackrell, 7 April 1891.
61 OB, Mrs Pierson, *c.* March 1914.
62 OB, Mrs Mary Crawford, 17 October 1889.
63 OB, Sarah Milnes, 9 May 1875.
64 OB, Isaac Rider Sunderland, 8 January 1897.
65 OB, William Coates, 9 June 1879; Thomas Belt, 17 January 1878; Benjamin Randall Vickers, 1 August 1881.
66 OB, Robert Skilbeck, 3 May 1880.
67 OB, Mary Cuttle, 7 July 1909.
68 OB, Mrs Jane Reynolds, 15 February 1887.
69 OB, Mary Buck, 19 June 1876.
70 OB, Fred Taylor, 18 July 1887; John Kettlewell, 20 November 1875; Thomas Sheers, 31 May 1896.
71 OB, Henry Harrison, 18 January 1889; Charles Atkinson, 23 September 1882.
72 OB, John Wilton, 5 March 1892.
73 OB, Eliza Ann Dixon, 2 October 1893 (though no date given).
74 OB, Mrs James Walker, 19 May 1874.
75 OB, William Henry Rishton, 2 February 1877.
76 OB, Charles Matthews, *c.* December 1911; George Smith, 26 February 1884; Mrs Ann Elizabeth Mortimer, 13 November 1910.
77 Edward Booth, *A Selection of the Most Approved Ancient and Modern Psalm Tunes, Arranged for the Piano Forte or Organ* (Leeds: J. Sykes, n.d.), nos 88, 89.
78 OB, Mr Thacker, 26 October 1903.
79 OB, Thomas Riley, 23 July 1874.
80 OB, Mrs Penniston, 27 January 1906; John William Young, 19 February 1912. James E. Ellison (ed.), *History of the Lincoln Fields Wesleyan Methodist Sunday School and Society (Brunswick Circuit, Leeds), 1830–1894* (Leeds: John Whitehead & Son, 1895), pp. 60–1.
81 OB, Esther Sanderson, 2 September 1892. BO, Edward Jarvis, 22 November 1913.
82 OB, Mary Cuttle, 7 July 1909.
83 OB, Benjamin Randall Vickers, 1 August 1881; Dr Rossvally, *c.* March 1893.
84 OB, James Rayner, 4 June 1898.
85 OB, William Coates, 9 June 1879.
86 BO, Mrs Scott, *c.* March 1913; Mrs C. Oates, *c.* March 1913 (quoted).
87 OB, Edward Brown, 28 July 1885.
88 OB, John Wilton, 5 March 1892.
89 OB, William Hodgson, 28 March 1883.
90 OB, Mrs Hall, *c.* November 1877.
91 OB, Julia Schofield, 6 October 1909.

92 OB, Eliza Oates, 21 November 1880.
93 OB, Elizabeth Smith, 20 June 1902.
94 OB, Helen Smith, 4 January 1893; Elizabeth Weston, 5 July 1898.
95 OB, Maria Hudson, 19 October 1883.
96 OB, Mary Jane Crossby, 13 April 1909.
97 OB, George Thompson Dixon, 27 October 1892.
98 OB, John Spink, 29 December 1882; Abram Kirby, 23 March 1876.
99 OB, Miss Mary Smith, 15 August 1900.
100 OB, George Thompson Dixon, 27 October 1892.
101 OB, Edwin Ball, 9 November 1892.
102 OB, Hannah Frost, 20 January 1904 (though no date given).
103 OB, Benjamin Randall Vickers, 1 August 1881.
104 OB, William Coates, 9 June 1879.
105 OB, John Banks, 23 February 1886.
106 OB, Elizabeth Wardell, *c.* September 1898; Mortimer Barraclough, 11 April 1900.
107 OB, Robert Skilbeck, 3 May 1880; [Palmer], *Four Years*, pp. 620–1.
108 OB, Emma Graham, 29 May 1892 (though no date given).
109 Hugh McLeod, '"Thews and Sinews": Nonconformity and Sport', in David Bebbington and Timothy Larsen (eds), *Modern Christianity and Cultural Aspirations* (London: Sheffield Academic Press, 2003), pp. 28–46.
110 OB, Richard Lodge, 22 November 1895; Sarah Stead, 23 May 1910.
111 BO, Robert Hudson, 16 January 1913.
112 Kenneth D. Brown, *A Social History of the Nonconformist Ministry in England and Wales, 1800–1930* (Oxford: Clarendon Press, 1988), p. 53.
113 OB, Mortimer Barraclough, 11 April 1900.
114 Wakefield, *Methodist Devotion*, p. 89.
115 OB, Margaret Hewitt, 12 February 1881.

Dissolving the 'Sacred Union'? The Disestablishment of the Church in Ireland

STEWART J. BROWN, UNIVERSITY OF EDINBURGH

Abstract

In 1869, Parliament disestablished the Church of Ireland, dissolving what Benjamin Disraeli called the 'sacred union' of church and state in Ireland. Disestablishment involved fundamental issues – the identity and purpose of the established church, the religious nature of the state, the morality of state appropriation of church property for secular uses, and the union of Ireland and Britain – and debate was carried on at a high intellectual level. With disestablishment, the Church of Ireland lost much of its property, but it recovered, now as an independent Episcopal church with a renewed mission. The idea of the United Kingdom as a semi-confessional Protestant state, however, was dealt a serious blow.

Keywords: United Church of England and Ireland; Act of Union; disestablishment; church and state

In July 1869, after some eighteen months of intense public debate, the United Kingdom Parliament passed the Act to disestablish and disendow the Protestant Church in Ireland. It was a highly contentious decision, seen as profoundly affecting not only Irish religious life, but the nature of the United Kingdom. As the London *Contemporary Review* observed in September 1869, 'whereever the English language was spoken, there was the Irish Church Bill discussed . . . It convulsed society and put each man at variance with his neighbour . . . It brought to the surface of society passions which it has been the policy of all modern governments as much as possible to keep under and suppress.'[1] According to Edinburgh's *Blackwood's Magazine* for February 1869, no question 'can more profoundly affect the fortunes and the future of the nation'.[2]

For many in the mid-Victorian United Kingdom, the state had a divinely ordained foundation, expressed through the religious establishment. They viewed the established churches as integral to the constitution, representing continuity with the past, giving a religious dimension to the state and elevating public life. The established churches were a recognition that a Christian state had a duty under God to provide religious instruction and observances for all inhabitants, and to pursue policies that reflected the divinely ordained moral law. The principle of established religion was expressed in the fifth clause of the Act of Union of 1800, which united the established churches of England and Ireland 'forever'. While the established Church in Ireland was a minority church, the established churches in most of the United Kingdom were large, influential and increasingly confident institutions, which were carrying on an effective home mission, taking a leading role in overseas missions, and representing the sense that the United Kingdom and its vast Empire had a higher, providential purpose. Irish disestablishment, the Conservative party leader, Benjamin Disraeli, wrote in March 1868, opposed this vital principle of established religion not only in Ireland but throughout the United Kingdom; it threatened to sever 'that sacred union between Church and State which has hitherto been the chief means of our civilisation and is the only security of our religious liberty'.[3] Nonetheless, in 1869, after a brief, but intense struggle, Parliament disestablished and disendowed the Irish Church.

This article explores the public discourse surrounding Parliament's decision to disestablish the Irish Church. The debates surrounding Irish disestablishment involved fundamentally conflicting conceptions not only of the Union between Britain and Ireland, but of the nature of the state and the role of religion in public life. The debates also involved property rights, including whether the state had the legal and moral authority to appropriate Church property and use it for secular purposes. The arguments were carried on at a high intellectual level in pamphlets, newspaper and journal articles, on the electoral hustings, and in both houses of Parliament. Irish disestablishment has been explored in valuable works by Edward Norman, Phillip Bell, Kevin Nowlan and Kenneth Milne.[4] In considering the debates over Irish disestablishment, this study gives particular attention to the relations of church and state, and to the Anglican conceptions of the state – drawing upon the path-breaking work of Peter Nockles on the politics of High Churchmanship.[5]

The Idea of an Established Church

The United Kingdom in the mid-nineteenth century was a semi-confessional state. The state maintained established churches to provide religious observances, religious instruction and pastoral care for the population and to represent a collective faith in God and divine providence – while at the same time extending freedom of worship and expression to other religious communities. There were two church establishments: the Episcopalian and Anglican United Church of England and Ireland, and the much smaller Presbyterian and Calvinist Church of Scotland. Both established churches ministered to the inhabitants of their respective countries through a parish system. The idea of an established church represented for many the higher purpose of the state, elevating it above a mere collection of competing interests and seeking to ensure that it expressed a moral conscience at home and overseas.

The established Churches in England and Scotland had experienced significant internal conflicts and external opposition during the 1830s and 1840s. Parliament imposed sweeping reforms on the Church of England between 1836 and 1840, and the Church was distracted by the theological controversies surrounding the Tractarian movement. The established Church of Scotland was deeply divided over issues relating to patronage, and suffered the loss of about a third of its ministers at the great Disruption of 1843.[6]

However, from about 1850, the English and Scottish establishments began recovering their influence and authority. The Church of England underwent a remarkable resurgence, associated with what Arthur Burns has termed a 'diocesan revival'.[7] The convocations of the provinces of Canterbury and York were restored in 1855 and 1861 respectively, giving clergy and laity a voice in Church governance, and over the next two decades most dioceses also began holding regular diocesan conferences. There was significant growth in the numbers of churches and clergy. Between 1835 and 1875, the Church of England consecrated 3,765 new or rebuilt churches, increasing its total number by 25 per cent; between 1835 and 1876, the Church of England was consecrating on average one new or rebuilt church every four days.[8] The overall number of Anglican clergy in England and Wales grew from 14,613 in 1841 to 19,336 in 1861.[9] The Church of England was also the major provider of primary education. By 1858, it maintained nearly 20,000 day-schools, and was educating almost 80 per cent of the children of England and Wales.[10] Almost every diocese had a teacher training college and schools inspectorate. In 1841, the Church of England formed the Colonial Bishoprics Fund to raise money to endow new bishoprics within the Empire. There were at this time ten colonial bishoprics. Over the next fifty years, the Fund endowed seventy-two additional colonial bishoprics, laying the foundation for the world Anglican Communion.[11] In Scotland, the established Church of Scotland also made a remarkable recovery after the Disruption of 1843. Between 1849 and 1874, the Scottish establishment increased the number of its endowed parish churches by 20 per cent, and grew increasingly active in education and home and overseas mission.[12] It was recovering its position as the church of the majority of the Scottish people.[13]

The established Church in Ireland could not claim similar growth, but it was steadily improving its pastoral care. The Church of Ireland in the mid-nineteenth century was governed by two archbishops, Armagh and Dublin, and ten bishops – with the archbishop of Armagh as primate. There were, according to the census conducted in Ireland in 1861, 693,357 adherents of the Church of Ireland, representing 11.9 per cent of the Irish population; this marked a slight increase from 1834, when the proportion had been 10.7 per cent. According to a royal commission report issued in 1867, the Church of Ireland included 1,518 parish livings, 1,509 parish incumbents and about 500 curates. Nearly 500 of these parishes were very small, with fewer than 100 Church of Ireland adherents, while 91 parishes had fewer than 20 Church adherents.[14] But pluralism and non-residence had been largely eliminated by the later 1830s, and the parish clergy now lived and worked among their parishioners, most in an exemplary manner. Parliament had abolished the Irish tithe in 1838, and the parish clergy were now supported by a tax on land (the tithe-rent), paid by the landowners. Although critics claimed it possessed vast wealth, the Church's revenues were in truth modest. The incomes of the Irish clergy were relatively low, with about 720 livings – almost half – valued at less than £200 per year, and 300 at less than £100 per year, although the low incomes were offset by substantial residence houses in most parishes, nearly 70 per cent of them built since 1800.[15] The Irish clergy were predominantly Low Church, or Evangelical; although, as Peter Nockles has shown, there was also a significant Irish High Church movement.[16]

The Irish Church was making the most of its resources amidst challenging circumstances. It had been forced to submit to reforms imposed by Parliament in the 1830s, including the suppression of ten bishoprics and a very significant reduction – over 25 per cent – in its income. Nonetheless, there had been growth in the number of its clergy, from about 1,200 in 1800 to about 2,200 in 1868, and in the number of churches from about 1,000 in 1800 to 1,579 in 1868.[17] Church of Ireland clergy bristled at the criticisms levelled at their minority status. They insisted that their claim to being a national church lay not in their numbers, but in the truth of their doctrines, the purity of their liturgy, the pastoral commitments of their clergy and the confidence of the state. The Church of Ireland maintained its parish structures, with its clergy offering public worship, sacraments, religious instruction and pastoral care to those who wished them, but not imposing their ministry on Catholics or Presbyterians. Many established clergymen and their families had demonstrated humanitarian commitment during the famine, working closely with Catholic priests on local relief committees, distributing relief to people of all denominations, visiting the sick and dying, and consoling the bereaved; some forty Church of Ireland clerics died of famine-related fever in 1847 alone.[18] However, the activities of the evangelical Irish Church Mission in the West of Ireland had led to greatly exaggerated allegations that the missions had used food to secure Catholic converts, and in the post-famine years these allegations overshadowed for Catholics the record of Protestant relief work.

The Call for Disestablishment

The call for disestablishment emerged at a time of renewed social unrest in Ireland. In the early 1860s, there were a series of poor harvests, combined with outbreaks of disease that devastated livestock and brought mass destitution. Many in Ireland feared a return of famine conditions, but the United Kingdom government refused any special relief measures. Irish distress and anger contributed to some popular support for the Fenian Brotherhood, a movement that had emerged in the late 1850s for achieving an independent Irish republic through physical force. In early 1864, the Fenians became increasingly prominent, recruiting by 1865 perhaps 50,000 oath-bound members, who marched and drilled, acquired some rifles, and cultivated relations with anti-British Irish expatriates overseas, and especially in America. There was an abortive Fenian rising in March 1867 in Ireland. While there was no real prospect of a successful rising, what R. V. Comerford described as the 'fenian fever' of 1865–67 made 'a major impact on the public mind' in Britain, as well as Ireland, and became a potent symbol of Irish discontent with the Union.[19]

In Ireland, Cardinal Paul Cullen, archbishop of Armagh and primate of the Irish Catholic Church, responded in part to the Fenian movement with the formation of a National Association of Ireland, aimed at pursuing constitutional means for the redress of the Irish grievances. Since becoming primate early in 1850, Cullen had worked with considerable political acumen to reform the post-famine Irish Catholic Church and make Catholicism a major force in shaping Irish national identity.[20] The National Association, popularly known as 'Cullen's Association', was inaugurated in December 1864 in Dublin. It embraced three main aims – land reform, state support for Catholic schools, and the disestablishment and disendowment of the Church in Ireland. In calling for disestablishment, the National Association entered into an alliance with the British Liberation Society – made up of Protestant Dissenters committed to ending the connection of church and state, nationalising the endowments of the established churches, and placing all churches on a voluntary basis. This alliance was surprising, given that most Protestant Dissenters were anti-Catholic, but at a pragmatic level the alliance made sense, reflecting a shared hostility to the Irish establishment.[21] Cullen was certainly hostile, describing the established Irish Church in December 1864 'as a badge of national servitude, offensive and degrading alike to all Irishmen'.[22]

The former Peelite Conservative politician William Ewart Gladstone was now emerging as the leading figure in the emerging Liberal Party. He underwent a fundamental change in his views on the established Church in Ireland during the mid-1860s. A High Church Anglican with Tractarian sympathies, Gladstone had been a prominent defender of the Irish establishment in the 1830s. But he gradually became convinced that the established Church in Ireland was indefensible and must be ended, a change of view he described in a pamphlet, *A Chapter of Autobiography*, published in the autumn of 1868.[23] He continued to support the established church principle in Britain, but no longer in Ireland, where he believed the United Church of England and Ireland could never be national and that its very existence served to alienate most Irish people from the Union. 'I started in life a believer in the Irish Church Establishment, and I spoke strongly for it more than thirty years ago', he informed the Quaker politician, John Bright, in December 1867. But now he believed it necessary 'to destroy the principle of State Establishment in Ireland' in order to bring justice to the country.[24]

His conversion to the Irish disestablishment also had an element of political pragmatism. The Liberals had been outmanoeuvred by Disraeli and the Conservatives over the second Reform Act of 1867, which had significantly expanded the franchise, and Disraeli was now prime minister. Gladstone viewed justice for Ireland, and especially Irish disestablishment, as a cause around which the new Liberal Party could rally. Whatever his political calculations, Gladstone's reputation as a devout High Churchman added credence to his view that the established Church in Ireland was indefensible.[25]

In December 1867, Gladstone became leader of the Liberal Party, and in March 1868, he introduced three resolutions in the House of Commons for the disestablishment of the Irish Church. 'This is a day of excitement – almost of exultation', he wrote to a friend. 'We have made a step, nay a stride . . . on the pathway of justice, and of peace, and of national honour and renown.'[26] In opposing Gladstone's resolutions, Disraeli appealed to the Coleridge vision of an established church as a national institution for the cultivation of the people. In language reminiscent of the Romanticism of his Young England period in the 1840s, Disraeli observed that 'Church property is the property of the people, set aside for a particular purpose – namely, their spiritual instruction'. He also appealed to the sacred union of church and state that he maintained formed the foundation of the United Kingdom. 'Government is to be not merely an affair of force', he insisted, 'but is to recognize its responsibility to the Divine Power . . . If Government is not divine, it is nothing. It is a mere affair of the police-office, of the tax-gatherer, of the guard-room.'[27] Disraeli was willing to accept further reform of the Irish established church, even another reduction in its size, but not its abolition.

After considerable debate, Gladstone's three resolutions on Irish disestablishment were passed with substantial majorities by the end of May. While the resolutions did not explicitly discuss the property of the Irish Church, it was clear that Gladstone's plan would strip it of nearly all its endowments. Significantly, the Irish Catholic bishops did not ask for the endowments of the Irish Protestant establishment; indeed, they insisted they would not accept the endowments if offered. They claimed to have no desire to enter into alliance with the United Kingdom state as Ireland's established church. The money, they said, should be used to benefit the Irish poor. After the passing of the resolutions, many Church of England clergy appeared to distance themselves from the Irish Church. 'Much wonder', observed the High Church *Christian Remembrancer* of July 1868, 'has been expressed at the seeming indifference of the English clergy' to the prospect of Irish disestablishment; it indicated that they did not want 'their own hard-earned progress in the cause of the Church to be imperilled by too cordial a sympathy with . . . the Irish Church'.[28]

His government's defeat over Gladstone's Irish disestablishment resolutions forced Disraeli to call a general election. Held in the autumn of 1868, it was the first conducted with the enlarged electorate created by the second Reform Act. The Liberal Party made Irish disestablishment its main electoral issue, and the Liberation Society (which had distributed over a million pamphlets on Irish disestablishment during the previous year) campaigned vigorously, with paid speakers giving over 500 lectures in support of disestablishment across the United Kingdom.[29] In November 1868, the Liberals were returned to government with a majority of 112 in the Commons. For Gladstone, the people had spoken, and the Irish Church would have to accept disestablishment. 'We are now', Richard Chenevix Trench, Protestant archbishop of Dublin, acknowledged on 21 November, 'to a great extent in the hands of our adversaries.'[30] Gladstone sought to meet with the Irish bishops to discuss the implementation of disestablishment and disendowment. But the Irish archbishops declined, claiming that they did not have the authority to make arrangements on behalf of the whole Irish Church. In truth, Trench confided to Bishop Samuel Wilberforce of Oxford on 5 January 1869, Irish Church clergy and lay members would feel 'slighted if not betrayed', were the details of disestablishment and disendowment to be agreed between Gladstone and the Irish bishops. It would appear as though 'we had helped him to sharpen the axe, adjust the block, and had pointed out the exact point in the neck of the Irish Church, where the head could with least trouble be separated from the body'.[31]

Instead, the two Irish archbishops asked Gladstone that the Irish Church Convocation, suspended since the early eighteenth century, be restored so that it could discuss the situation. (The convocations of Canterbury and York, which had also been suspended in the early eighteenth century, had been restored in 1855 and 1861 respectively.) Bringing together the bishops and representatives of the clergy and laity, the Irish Convocation would speak for the Irish Church as a whole. Gladstone responded on 14 January 1869 that he would only advise the Crown to restore the Irish Convocation if it promised to restrict its discussions to facilitating his government's disestablishment plans, but not if it intended to negotiate its fate.[32] The archbishops, not surprisingly, declined his terms. 'Archbishop Trench', Gladstone informed Bishop Wilberforce of Oxford, on 21 January 1869, 'seems to be a dreamer of dreams; and talks of negotiating at a time when all negotiations will have gone by. I must look, and the Government must look, to justify our measure in the eyes of those by whom it is supported, and who ... are *amply sufficient* to carry it.'[33] Gladstone proceeded to draft the disestablishment bill almost single-handedly, and introduced it in the Commons, in a masterly speech, on 1 March 1869.

To many, Gladstone seemed primarily concerned with rallying the Liberal Party after its election victory. 'The misery of this business', wrote the Church of England clergyman and historian, Joseph Blakesley, to Archbishop A. C. Tait in February 1869, 'is that the claims of party allegiances interfere with the dictates of right & reason'.[34] The whole plan for Irish disestablishment and disendowment had come with great rapidity, and seemed grossly unfair. In the 1830s, Parliament had imposed sweeping reforms on the Irish Church, abolishing nearly half its bishoprics, suppressing scores of parish livings, and depriving it of a quarter of its tithe income. The Irish Church had submitted to these reforms; it had made significant improvements in its organisation and clerical discipline; and it had carried on its work as an established church over the subsequent three decades. 'We are the Established Church', Trench had confidently proclaimed in 1865, 'because we are the Church which the State believes to be true'.[35] Yet within a few years of Trench's claim, the Church was being publicly vilified, denigrated as a 'badge of conquest', and treated in high political circles as a moral blight. 'All at once, and almost without notice', wrote a supporter of the Irish establishment in September 1868, 'the enemy is at our gates, and the assault is begun.'[36] The Church was given no opportunity to meet as a body to coordinate a collective response to disestablishment. Rather, efforts for Irish Church defence found expression in protest meetings, parliamentary speeches, pamphlets and newspaper and journal articles.

The Case for Irish Disestablishment

In this public debate, advocates of Irish disestablishment emphasised the theme of society advancing towards greater religious freedom and equality. Their main argument was that the minority Anglican Church in Ireland had no claim to be the national church of the Irish people. Nor would it ever become a national church because the very idea that, in the later nineteenth century, it should seek converts from the Catholic or Presbyterian communities was viewed as illiberal and unacceptable. There was no prospect of a state-supported mission to make the Irish Church truly national. This, in turn, meant that the Irish Church's endowments – which its critics claimed were the rightful possession of the Irish nation as a whole – were being used for the benefit of a small minority, and a minority that included some of the wealthiest, most privileged inhabitants of Ireland. 'It cannot be right', insisted Earl Russell in the House of Lords on 18 June 1869, 'that there should be an Established Church for one-eighth of the people of Ireland'. 'After the experience of three centuries', he added, 'it is quite time to give up this experiment.'[37]

While Gladstone was personally committed to preserving the established churches in Britain, many advocates of Irish disestablishment were religious voluntaries, embracing the separation of church and state as a matter of principle. They applauded how Gladstone's disestablishment plan, as it developed in late 1868 and early 1869, would make religion in Ireland voluntary – not only by appropriating the endowments of the established Church in Ireland, but also by ending the state subsidies to Maynooth College for the training of Catholic priests, and by abolishing the *regium donum*, state subsidies to the Irish Presbyterian ministers. While some Liberals would have preferred a policy of 'levelling up' all the Irish churches by providing increased state endowments for Irish Catholics and Presbyterians, Gladstone knew his British Nonconformist supporters would never approve increased endowments to the Catholic Church. His bill would achieve religious equality by ending all state-sanctioned Irish Church endowments. The money taken from the Irish churches would not go into the imperial coffers but to projects to help the Irish poor, including asylums for the mentally ill and specialised schools for children who were deaf or blind, or had learning disabilities.

Many supporters of disestablishment hoped religious voluntaryism in Ireland would become a precedent for the rest of the United Kingdom. 'I look upon it as an unreasonable doctrine', insisted the Duke of Argyll in the Lords, 'that every man should be called to pay for every other man's religion'. The spirit of the age was moving inevitably towards 'the principle of free and unendowed Churches' and he was confident that disestablishment 'will be looked back upon as one of the greatest triumphs of constitutional government'.[38]

Disestablishment, its supporters insisted, would also remove what was for Irish Catholics an historic grievance. In the past, the Irish established church had benefited from the anti-Catholic penal laws and the Protestant ascendancy. This meant that for Irish Catholics the established church was associated with subjugation and oppression; it was a badge of conquest and reminder of past wrongs. Many believed that the Protestant Church's property and endowments had been stolen from the Catholic Church by the English Crown at the Reformation. In introducing the disestablishment bill on 1 March 1869, Gladstone asserted that the Irish Church was 'the token and the symbol of ascendancy, and, so long as that Establishment lives, painful and bitter memories of ascendancy can never be effaced'.[39] There was no way that the minority Irish establishment would have lasted for three hundred years, insisted the leading Liberal, John Bright, on 19 March 1869 in the Commons, 'except by the power which founded it – namely, the power of conquest'.[40] By removing this symbol of past wrongs, disestablishment would be a major step towards ending social unrest in Ireland, diminishing Fenian support and securing Catholic loyalty to the United Kingdom state. It would also lead to more equal relations between all the churches in Ireland – Protestant, Presbyterian and Catholic – ushering in a new era of religious peace and toleration. Supporters of Irish disestablishment emphasised how the people of the United Kingdom had spoken decisively in favour of Irish disestablishment at the general election in late 1868. As Gladstone said when introducing the bill, Parliament must now 'recognize the judgement which has been pronounced at the tribunal of the nation'.[41] The Liberal MP for County Galway, W. H. Gregory, insisted that the Church of Ireland must accept the 'inevitable' and stop 'gazing idly up into Heaven'.[42]

Arguments against Irish Disestablishment

Many defenders of the Irish Church establishment, especially high Anglicans and Evangelicals, emphasised the 'sacred union' of church and state. For them, Irish disestablishment fundamentally threatened the divinely ordained political order in the United Kingdom. It would be nothing less than a sacrilege, an act of national apostasy, a collective rejection of the divine foundations of the state. Church defenders insisted it was the state's duty under God to maintain an established church to provide religious instruction, observances, and pastoral care for its people. The United Church of England and Ireland was a single established church, the mother church of the world Anglican Communion; the United Church was inseparable from the idea of the United Kingdom as a Christian state and of its Empire as serving a providential purpose. Disestablishing the Irish portion of the United Church would begin a process that would eventually abolish established churches throughout the United Kingdom. The Dissenters of the Liberation Society would not be satisfied with ending the established Church in Ireland; Wales would be next, then Scotland, and finally England. 'Let no one indulge in the illusion', insisted *Blackwood's Magazine*, 'that disestablishment, as raised by Mr Gladstone, is a purely Irish affair'.[43]

If an established church was admitted to be an unjust infringement on religious equality in Ireland, it was no less so in Britain.[44] The cause before them in Ireland, asserted A. C. Tait, the Broad Church archbishop of Canterbury, at a public meeting in May 1868 in London, was the principle of national religion, and 'as soon as our State shall, in an evil day, repudiate that which was its strength – the national religion – it will be weighed in the balance and be found wanting, and glory will depart from it'.[45] The bill, insisted Robert Bickersteth, Evangelical bishop of Ripon, in June 1869 in the House of Lords, 'involves the assumption that it is no part of the duty of a Christian State to connect itself with the maintenance of Christian truth'.[46]

Disestablishment, its opponents further argued, would seriously weaken the Union of Britain and Ireland. The United Church of England and Ireland had been formed 'forever' by the fifth clause of the Act of Union. It was a fundamental article of that Union: according to one commentator, it 'not merely united the two Churches into one, but makes their union an essential part of the Union between the two Kingdoms'.[47] To disestablish the United Church in Ireland, and leave Ireland without an established church, was to say that Ireland was no longer an integral part of the United Kingdom, but was rather a separate country, a colony perhaps.[48] 'You are endeavouring', insisted the Conservative MP, Gathorne Hardy, in the Commons in March 1869, 'to put Ireland on a different footing from England'.[49] Some opponents of disestablishment challenged the idea that the Church in Ireland could not be a national church because it was the church of a minority. An established church, they argued, existed to elevate the nation with religious truth, and religious truth was not determined by majorities; indeed, the true Church was often a minority Church in the world.[50] Others noted that while the United Church was a minority Church in Ireland, it was the majority Church in the United Kingdom as a whole.

For opponents, the Government's plans to disendow the Irish Church were a sacrilegious confiscation, a robbery of God. They rejected any idea that the endowments were the property of the state. 'That property', Gathorne Hardy told his fellow MPs, 'does not belong to you now, it never did.'[51] They also rejected the argument that the Crown had taken the endowments and property from the Catholic Church at the Reformation and given them to the Protestants; rather, they insisted, the ancient Irish Church of St Patrick had reformed itself at the Reformation. But even if Catholics believed that the Protestant Church should not have received endowments at the Reformation, was it justifiable for the state now to confiscate those endowments, which had been in the possession of the Protestant Church for over 300 years? Would not such a precedent also put at risk all the landed property owned by Protestants in Ireland?[52] 'You cannot', insisted the Liberal, Sir Roundell Palmer, in March 1869 in the Commons, 'take from those who have had a valid legal title for centuries that which they have done nothing to forfeit'.[53] It was an act of sacrilege for the state to seize property from the Church and use it for secular purposes, even for such a worthy purpose as care for the poor.

The Church of Ireland, moreover, needed its endowments, which were modest, in order to continue to provide a national ministry. Protestantism would not long survive in much of Ireland, especially in rural areas in the south and west of the country, without endowed parish churches. Many of those parishes had small, widely scattered, and often poor Protestant populations, with Protestant landlords who were absentee; it was the duty of a Protestant state to ensure those people received pastoral care and religious instruction. Without endowments, rural Protestant churches in the south and west would gradually close, and their Protestant populations would either leave the area or be absorbed into the surrounding Catholic community. Protestantism would be forced, as a result of state action, to withdraw into larger towns and to the north of Ireland.[54] Some defenders of the Irish establishment argued that its endowments enabled the establishment to maintain a resident gentleman and his family in parishes across Ireland, who, even if they did not minister directly to all the residents of the parish, did distribute charity, visit the sick, spread cultivation and provide examples of ethical behaviour. 'From every one of its parsonage-houses', insisted Bishop Wilberforce, 'in which a man of God and a holy family are living are daily diffused a thousand influences which are modifying the superstition around them, correcting its evil teaching, and tending to raise men to the true liberty of the Son of God.'[55]

The debates in Parliament, public meetings, and the press were carried on with great fervour and public opinion was divided. The Church of England was also divided on the issue. Most High Church Anglicans and Evangelicals opposed Irish disestablishment, believing the alliance of church and state was vital to a Christian United Kingdom, though High Anglicans placed more emphasis on the 'sacred union' while Evangelicals gave more emphasis to the practical pastoral benefits of a parochial establishment. However, Anglo-Catholics, including E. B. Pusey, H. P. Liddon and C. J. Vaughan, remained aloof, believing that the Irish Church might be elevated as a church by ceasing to be established.[56] With the notable exception of Archbishop Tait, Broad Church Anglicans tended to support Gladstone on Irish disestablishment. The debates over the Irish Church involved questions of profound importance. Did the United Kingdom state have a sacred duty to provide religious instruction and pastoral care to its people, or were its responsibilities primarily secular in nature? Was there a sacred union between church and state, or should the state be religiously neutral and all religious bodies be treated equally under the law? Was Ireland an integral part of the United Kingdom, as reflected by the United Church of England and Ireland enshrined in the Union, or was Ireland a separate country with a fundamentally different social, political and religious order? 'We are invited', observed Spencer Walpole in the House of Commons, 'for the first time in English history – and ... I might say for the first time in the history of Christendom – to do away with the religion of the country as a national religion, and thus to make ... a legislative revolution in our fundamental laws.'[57]

The End of the Irish Establishment

With passions running high, Gladstone moved to get his bill quickly through Parliament. It was in no one's interest, he stated in March 1869 when introducing the bill in the Commons, that 'the Irish Establishment should be subjected to the pains of a lingering death'.[58] His bill passed through the House of Commons by the end of May. It was an extreme measure. The Irish Church would be permitted to retain its church buildings, and the property gifted to it by pious donors after 1660, but the other properties and endowments would be taken from it. The existing clergy, including permanent curates, would continue to receive their incomes, in the form of an annuity, for the rest of their lives, provided they did some work for the Church. But otherwise the Church would have to support itself through voluntary means, and it would have to purchase back from the state the residence houses for its clergy. Landowners would continue to pay their tithe-rents, with the money now going to the state, though they were allowed to commute their tithe-rents into a lump sum payment and were offered generous loans to enable them to pay off the lump sum. Disestablishment and disendowment would go into effect on 1 January 1871, which meant the Irish Church would have little time to prepare for its new circumstances. Support for Maynooth College and the payment of the *regium donum* would also cease.

Supporters of the Irish establishment looked to the House of Lords to block the bill. Nearly all the Anglican bishops in the Lords opposed it, as did most lay peers, who saw the bill as a threat to property rights as well as to the Protestant constitution. On 8 June, a meeting of 150 peers pledged to oppose the bill at all costs. Open conflict between the Commons and the Lords, and a full constitutional crisis, now loomed. The Queen appealed to the recently appointed archbishop of Canterbury, the Oxford-educated Scot, A. C. Tait, to help find a compromise. Although he opposed Irish disestablishment, Tait helped convince the Lords not to resist the popular will, as expressed in the election of 1868, and instead to modify the bill in order to minimise the damage to the Irish Church.[59] Gladstone agreed to some of the Lords' modifications, which gave the Church a slightly improved financial settlement, and the Irish Church disestablishment Act passed in late July 1869.[60] With that Act, lamented E. H. Browne, the High Church bishop of Ely, 'a principle has been enunciated, never before accepted in Christendom, that a nation can with all the solemnity of law and equity throw off the Church and the faith handed down from its fathers'.[61] According to the historian Gabriel Daly, members of the Irish Church were forced to watch with 'helpless dismay' as their fate was sealed by 'one the smoothest operations ever carried through the British Parliament'.[62] As the Act went into effect in January 1871, the mood within the Church of Ireland was sombre. 'Dimly dawns the New Year', observed the Church of Ireland hymnwriter and poet, Cecil Frances Alexander, 'on a churchless nation'.[63]

Yet there was also a new beginning for the Church of Ireland. The Catholic archbishop, Paul Cullen, was certain the Protestants would make 'a sad mess' of their new status.[64] This was not the case. Although badly shaken, the Church of Ireland proved remarkably successful over the following years in adapting to disestablishment and disendowment. During the course of late 1869 and 1870, guided by some gifted lawyers among its membership, the Church prepared a new constitution – including a Representative Church Body to oversee property and revenues, a general synod and diocesan synods – which proved effective for the self-governing Church. Contrary to expectations, the large majority of existing clergy agreed to commute their state annuities into lump sum payments, which they deposited, at considerable personal risk, with the Church. Careful investments ensured that the resulting capital both paid the salaries of the existing clergy and generated a surplus to help support the work of the Church. The Church also successfully maintained its unity in doctrine and liturgy.[65]

The disestablishment and disendowment of the Irish established church was a momentous event, dissolving the 'sacred union' of church and state in one of the three historic kingdoms forming the United Kingdom. Parliament had broken up the United Church of England and Ireland, which had been defined in the Act of Union of 1801 as a church union made 'forever'. In the early 1870s, Nonconformists began major popular campaigns for disestablishment in England, Wales and Scotland, and the British established churches were thrown on the defensive. In Ireland, religion was now voluntary and the state now secular. With Irish disestablishment, Parliament confirmed that Ireland was different from the rest of the United Kingdom and should have its own constitutional arrangements. The treatment of the Irish Church, including the lack of consultation with the Church over its fate, had left many Irish Protestants feeling abandoned. 'I object to this change altogether', stated the Irish Protestant, William Magee, now bishop of Peterborough, in the Lords in June 1869, 'but if it was to be made, there could have been a more statesmanlike and generous mode of making it'.[66]

While it represented a serious political effort to deal with Irish problems in their Irish context, disestablishment did not ease the social unrest in Ireland. The endowments of the established church proved much smaller than had been expected, and the modest sums made available by disestablishment became largely an 'emergency reservoir' that the state used to supplement spending on such matters as roads and fisheries. The Irish poor did not benefit much. Irish disaffection with the Union continued, and less than a year after Irish disestablishment was passed, the Irish Home Rule Association was formed in Dublin.[67] Irish disestablishment had no doubt been necessary given the circumstances in Ireland; for the overwhelming majority in Ireland, the minority Irish establishment was unacceptable, and a symbol of injustice and inequality. Because of the effective response by Irish Protestants to their new circumstances, disestablishment also benefited the Irish Church in the long run. Yet, while Irish disestablishment had been necessary, the underlying religious conceptions of the United Kingdom political order, including the idea of the semi-confessional state, were profoundly impacted by this severing of the 'sacred union' between church and state in one of the three historic kingdoms making up the United Kingdom.

Notes

1 William Maziere Brady, 'Prospects of the Disestablished Church in Ireland', *Contemporary Review*, 12 (September 1869), 1.
2 'Mr Gladstone and Disestablishment', *Blackwood's Edinburgh Magazine* (February 1869), 238.
3 Benjamin Disraeli to Lord Cairns, March 1868, in W. F. Monypenny and G. E. Buckle (eds), *The Life of Benjamin Disraeli, Earl of Beaconsfield*, 2 vols (London: John Murray, 1929), vol. 1, p. 360.
4 E. R. Norman, *The Catholic Church and Ireland in the Age of Rebellion, 1859–1873* (London: Longmans, 1965), pp. 282–385; P. M. H. Bell, *Disestablishment in Ireland and Wales* (London: SPCK, 1969), pp. 1–225; Kevin B. Nowlan, 'Disestablishment, 1800–1869', in Michael Hurley (ed.), *Irish Anglicanism, 1869–1969* (Dublin: Allen Figgis, 1970), pp. 1–22; Kenneth Milne, 'Disestablishment and the Lay Response', in R. Gillespie and W. G. Neely (eds), *The Laity and the Church of Ireland, 1000–2000* (Dublin: Four Courts Press, 2002), pp. 226–49.
5 Peter B. Nockles, *The Oxford Movement in Context: Anglican High Churchmanship 1760–1857* (Cambridge: Cambridge University Press, 1994), pp. 44–103.
6 Stewart J. Brown, *The National Churches of England, Ireland and Scotland 1801–46* (Oxford: Oxford University Press, 2001).
7 Arthur Burns, *The Diocesan Revival in the Church of England, c. 1800–1870* (Oxford: Oxford University Press, 1999).
8 K. D. M. Snell, *Parish and Belonging: Community, Identity and Welfare in England and Wales, 1700–1950* (Cambridge: Cambridge University Press, 2006), p. 405; Chris Brooks

and Andrew Saint (eds), *The Victorian Church: Architecture and Society* (Manchester: Manchester University Press, 1995), p. 9.
9 Alan Haig, *The Victorian Clergy* (London: Croom Helm, 1984), p. 3.
10 *Parliamentary Papers*, 'Education Commission. Report of the Commissioners Appointed to Inquire into the State of Popular Education in England' (2794–I) (1861), vol. 1, pp. 592, 55.
11 Rowan Strong, *Anglicanism and the British Empire, c. 1700–1850* (Oxford: Oxford University Press, 2007), pp. 198–221; W. F. France, *The Overseas Episcopate: Centenary History of the Colonial Bishoprics Fund 1841–1941* (London: Colonial Bishoprics Fund, 1941).
12 William Smith, *Endowed Territorial Work* (Edinburgh: Blackwood, 1875), pp. 97–9.
13 Stewart J. Brown, 'After the Disruption: The Recovery of the National Church of Scotland, 1843–1874', *Scottish Church History*, 48:2 (2019), 103–25.
14 *Parliamentary Papers*, 'Report of Her Majesty's Commissioners on the Revenues and Condition of the Established Church (Ireland)' (4082) (1867–68), pp. vi, x, xxx–xxxi.
15 *Ibid.*, p. vii; Donald Harman Akenson, *The Church of Ireland: Ecclesiastical Reform and Revolution, 1800–1885* (New Haven, CT: Yale University Press, 1971), p. 220; *Hansard's Parliamentary Debates* (hereafter *Hansard*), 3rd series, vol. 194 (23 March 1869), cols 2015–16.
16 Peter Nockles, 'Church or Protestant Sect? The Church of Ireland, High Churchmanship, and the Oxford Movement', *Historical Journal*, 41:2 (1998), 457–93.
17 *Hansard*, 3rd series, vol. 194 (23 March 1869), cols 2015–16.
18 Desmond Bowen, *Souperism: Myth or Reality* (Cork: Mercier Press, 1970), pp. 183–212.
19 R. V. Comerford, 'Gladstone's First Irish Enterprise, 1864–70', in W. E. Vaughan (ed.), *A New History of Ireland, Volume 5: Ireland under the Union, I: 1801–70* (Oxford: Oxford University Press, 1989), pp. 434–9, quotation on p. 439; R. V. Comerford, *The Fenians in Context: Irish Politics and Society, 1848–1882* (Dublin: Wolfhound, 1985).
20 Emmet Larkin, 'The Devotional Revolution in Ireland, 1850–75', *American Historical Review*, 77:3 (1972), 625–52; Emmet Larkin, *The Making of the Roman Catholic Church in Ireland, 1850–1860* (Chapel Hill: University of North Carolina Press, 1980); Emmet Larkin, *The Consolidation of the Roman Catholic Church in Ireland, 1860–1870* (Dublin: Gill & Macmillan, 1987).
21 Norman, *Catholic Church and Ireland*, pp. 135–89; Larkin, *Consolidation of the Roman Catholic Church*, pp. 341–93.
22 Quoted in Norman, *Catholic Church and Ireland*, p. 147
23 W. E. Gladstone, *A Chapter of Autobiography* (London: John Murray, 1868).
24 W. E. Gladstone to J. Bright, 10 December 1867, in *Correspondence on Church and Religion of William Ewart Gladstone*, 2 vols, ed. D. C. Lathbury (London: John Murray, 1910), vol. 1, p. 154.
25 Nowlan, 'Disestablishment, 1800–1869', p. 13.
26 John Morley, *The Life of William Ewart Gladstone*, 3 vols (London: Macmillan, 1905), vol. 1, pp. 880–1.
27 *Hansard*, 3rd series, vol. 191 (3 April 1868), cols 916, 918. For Disraeli, Young England and the Church, see Brown, *National Churches*, pp. 335–7.

28 'The Irish Church', *Christian Remembrancer*, 56 (July 1868), 113.
29 J. P. Parry, *Democracy and Religion: Gladstone and the Liberal Party 1867–1875* (Cambridge: Cambridge University Press, 1986), p. 276.
30 Oxford, Bodleian Library, Wilberforce Papers, c.6/2, Richard Chenevix Trench to Samuel Wilberforce, 21 November 1868, fos 202–7.
31 *Ibid.*, Richard Chenevix Trench to Samuel Wilberforce, 5 January 1869, fos 227–32.
32 William Ewart Gladstone to Richard Chenevix Trench, 14 January 1869, and Richard Chenevix Trench to M. G. Beresford, 15 January 1869, in Richard Chenevix Trench, *Richard Chenevix Trench, Archbishop, Letters and Memorials*, 2 vols, ed. M. Wilson (London: Kegan Paul, 1888), vol. 2, pp. 73–4; Akenson, *The Church of Ireland*, pp. 241–2.
33 Oxford, Bodleian Library, Wilberforce Papers, d.37, William Ewart Gladstone to Samuel Wilberforce, 21 January 1869, fos 159–60.
34 London, Lambeth Palace Library, Tait Papers, Tait 87, J. W. Blakesley to A. C. Tait, 11 February 1869, fos 60–3.
35 Quoted in Gabriel Daly, 'Church Renewal: 1869–1877', in Hurley (ed.), *Irish Anglicanism*, p. 24.
36 George Anthony Denison, *The Churches of England and Ireland One Church by Identity of Divine Trust* (London: Rivingtons, 1868), p. 7.
37 *Hansard*, 3rd series, vol. 197 (18 June 1869), cols 164, 166.
38 *Ibid.* (18 June 1869), cols 210, 213.
39 W. E. Gladstone, *The Irish Church: A Speech delivered in the House of Commons on March 1, 1869* (London: John Murray, 1869), p. 5.
40 *Hansard*, 3rd series, vol. 194 (19 March 1869), col. 1881.
41 *Ibid.* (1 March 1869), col. 418.
42 *Ibid.* (18 March 1869). col. 1702.
43 'Mr Gladstone and Disestablishment', p. 238.
44 James Thomas O'Brien, *The Disestablishment and Disendowment of the Irish Branch of the United Church, Considered, Part I: Effects, Immediate and Remote* (London: Rivingtons, 1869), p. 45.
45 *The Great Church and State Meeting at St. James Hall . . . May 6th, 1868* (London: Church Institution, 1868), pp. 5, 6.
46 *Hansard*, 3rd series, vol. 197 (17 June 1869), col. 54.
47 O'Brien, *The Disestablishment and Disendowment*, p. 31.
48 *Ibid.*
49 *Hansard*, 3rd series, vol. 194 (23 March 1869), col. 2071.
50 John Deacon Massingham, *The Church of Ireland Defended* (London: William MacIntosh, 1868), p. 14.
51 *Hansard*, 3rd series, vol. 194 (23 March 1869), col. 2080.
52 'The Case of the Established Church in Ireland', *Quarterly Review* (April 1868), 553; O'Brien, *Disestablishment and Disendowment*, pp. 16–17.
53 *Hansard*, 3rd series, vol. 194 (22 March 1869), col. 1935.
54 O'Brien, *Disestablishment and Disendowment*, pp. 24–8.
55 *Great Church and State Meeting at St. James Hall*, pp. 9–10.

56 Owen Chadwick, *The Victorian Church, Part Two, 1860-1901*, 2nd edn (London: A. C. Black, 1972), pp. 429-30.
57 *Hansard*, 3rd series, vol. 194 (23 March 1869), col. 2004.
58 Gladstone, *The Irish Church*, p. 8.
59 Randall Thomas Davidson and William Benham, *Life of Archibald Campbell Tait*, 2 vols (London: Macmillan, 1891), vol. 2, pp. 1–43.
60 'The Irish Church Act, 1869, 32 & 33 Victoria Cap. 42': www.legislation.gov.uk/ukpga/1869/42/enacted (accessed 9 April 2020).
61 Edward Harold Browne, *A Charge delivered to the Clergy and Churchwardens of the Diocese of Ely* (London: Longman, Green and Co., 1869), p. 33.
62 Daly, 'Church Renewal: 1869–1877', p. 23.
63 Quoted in *ibid*.
64 Larkin, *Consolidation of the Roman Catholic Church*, p. 639.
65 Daly, 'Church Renewal: 1869–1877', pp. 23–38; Bell, *Disestablishment in Ireland and Wales*, pp. 158–212.
66 *Hansard*, 3rd series, vol. 196 (15 June 1869), col. 1874.
67 Bell, *Disestablishment in Ireland and Wales*, pp. 214–19; Stewart J. Brown, *Providence and Empire: Religion, Politics and Society in the United Kingdom, 1815–1914* (Harlow: Longman/Pearson, 2008), pp. 256–8.

Continuity and Development: Looking for Typological Treasure with William Jones of Nayland and E. B. Pusey

GEORGE WESTHAVER, PUSEY HOUSE, OXFORD

Abstract
This article compares the typological exegesis promoted by E. B. Pusey (1800–82) and his colleagues John Henry Newman and John Keble with that of their eighteenth-century Hutchinsonian predecessor William Jones of Nayland (1726–1800). Building on Peter Nockles's argument that Jones's emphasis on the figurative character of biblical language foreshadows the Tractarian application of the sacramental principle to exegesis, this article shows how this common approach differs from the more cautious one displayed by the High Church luminaries William Van Mildert and Herbert Marsh. At the same time, both Pusey's criticism of the mainstream apologetics of his day and his more explicit application of the doctrine of the Incarnation to exegesis resulted in bolder interpretations and a greater emphasis on the necessity of figurative readings (of both the Bible and the natural world) than Jones generally proposed. A shared appreciation of the principle of reserve may explain both these differences and the Tractarian emphasis on a patristic, rather than a Hutchinsonian, inspiration for their approach.

Keywords: figurative language; Oxford Movement; Hutchinsonianism; Incarnation; E. B. Pusey; William Jones of Nayland

Figurative Interpretation in Context

The prodigious contributions that Peter Nockles has made to the scholarship of the Oxford Movement include his detailed and illuminating examinations of both the continuities and discontinuities between the Tractarians and their High Church predecessors. The Tractarians' assessment of the religious life of the previous century as one characterised by cold formalism is well known. E. B. Pusey (1800–82) called it 'the last dreary century'.[1] H. P. Liddon, Canon of St Paul's Cathedral and Pusey's biographer, commented that the Oxford Movement 'was provoked by the prevalence of a latitudinarian theology in the last century, and by a dry and cold preaching of morality'.[2] In his *Oxford Movement in Context* (1994) Nockles discussed what is true in such characterisations while arguing also that the Tractarians often exaggerated both the unspiritual or moralistic elements of eighteenth-century theology and Church life.[3] Returning to the same theme in his 'Survivals or New Arrivals' (2003), Nockles drew on the work of Brian Young to argue that at least some characterisations of their High Church predecessors by the protagonists of the Oxford Movement amounted to 'an exercise in "present centred" history' with the intention, explicit or implicit, 'to further the cause of the Catholic revival'.[4] While the sense of crisis and decline was genuine and common among churchmen of different traditions in the early part of the nineteenth century, it is nonetheless helpful to ask what the particular character of these assessments reveal about the priorities of the Tractarians.[5] This article builds on Nockles's examination of one aspect of continuity and change by considering both the Tractarians' typological or sacramental approach to reading the Bible, and how they understood this approach in relation to the High Church tradition of their day.

According to Nockles, the advocacy of a 'typological or sacramental principle' in theology and biblical exegesis was a key part of the Tractarians' response to what they saw as an eighteenth-century overconfidence in the capacity of human reason to perceive 'religious truth'.[6] J. H. Newman in his *Apologia* described this 'mystical or sacramental principle' as an expression of 'the Sacramental system; that is, the doctrine that material phenomena are both the types and the instruments of real things unseen'.[7] As examples of a sacramental or typological approach to reading the Bible, interpreting the natural world or appreciating liturgical symbolism, Nockles pointed to Pusey's unpublished 'Lectures on Types and Prophecies of the Old Testament' (1836) and to John Keble's Tract 89, *On the Mysticism Attributed to the Early Fathers of the Church* (1841).[8] Newman's consideration of the allegorical exegesis of the Fathers in *Arians of the Fourth Century* (1833) and Isaac Williams's *Thoughts on the Study of the Holy Gospels* were also part of this project.[9] A recovery and advocacy of the sacramental or typological principle, particularly as it is shaped by the biblical exegesis of the Church Fathers, served as the fertile soil from which many of the better-known Tractarians ideas germinated and grew, even if the Tractarian emphasis on biblical interpretation is often neglected in contemporary scholarship.[10]

Nockles argued that in their advocacy of the figurative or typological exegesis of the Fathers, and their sacramental approach to theology more generally, 'the Tractarians overlooked the valuable witness of other eighteenth-century High Churchmen'.[11] He pointed out that the sacramental principle was not only 'expounded in the Fathers', but also 'part of the High Church spiritual inheritance'.[12] In particular, Nockles briefly examined the way in which the 'patristic theory of sacramental symbolism' was given expression fifty years before Pusey delivered his 'Lectures on Types' in another series of lectures by the influential eighteenth-century High Churchman and theologian William Jones of Nayland (1726–1800), *A Course of Lectures on the Figurative Language of Holy Scripture* (1786).[13] Specifically, Nockles asserted that in these lectures, 'the argument of Pusey's *Lectures on Types* of half a century later was strikingly prefigured'.[14] Geoffrey Rowell echoed Nockles's assessment, arguing that Jones anticipated the ideas of both Pusey and Keble about 'the symbolic character of the natural world'.[15]

This article argues that in order to assess the significance of the mystical or sacramental principle for the Tractarians, it is helpful to attend to the discontinuities as well as the continuities that one sees between the lectures offered by Jones and those of Pusey. To do this, the article attempts to supplement the arguments of Nockles and Rowell in three ways. First, this examination shows that while Pusey was especially critical of the way in which some near-contemporary representatives of the High Church tradition interpreted the Bible, he was willing to acknowledge some important continuities with this tradition, while overlooking or, perhaps intentionally, not mentioning others. Second, the article shows in greater depth the similarities between Jones's lectures, *Figurative Language*, and Pusey's 'Lectures on Types', with some reference to Keble, Newman and Isaac Williams. Third, it examines the discontinuities between these two courses of lectures, arguing that the differences reflect how Pusey saw the typological or sacramental principle as an expression of the doctrine of the Incarnation. Part of this involves showing how Pusey's insistence on the importance of typological interpretation also involved a trenchant criticism of a certain kind of apologetic theological writing common in his day.

Common Cause

While the Tractarians could be disparaging of their High Church predecessors, they were ready to acknowledge common cause with Jones of Nayland and those associated with him. In his *Apologia*, Newman referred to 'the admirable work of Jones of Nayland' as one of those who guided him in making 'a collection of Scripture texts' on the doctrine of the Holy Trinity.[16] H. P. Liddon declared that Pusey esteemed Jones highly as one of those 'holy men, who taught a generation of Latitudinarians and Methodists how the great men of the Caroline age in the Church of England had believed and lived and died'. Among this company Liddon included also, 'at a somewhat later period', 'Mr. Norris of Hackney and Mr. Joshua Watson'.[17] This 'Mr. Norris of Hackney' is the Revd Henry Handley Norris, who Liddon described as 'the chief figure of 'the Hackney School'.[18] The 'Hackney School', or Hackney Phalanx, was a High Church group linked by common ideas, friendship, family and patronage with the merchant Joshua Watson (1771–1855) and his brother Archdeacon John Watson (1767–1839), the rector of the village of Hackney in northeast London. H. H. Norris began his ministry as the curate to Archdeacon Watson, who was also his brother-in-law. William Stevens, another associate of the Hackney school, was Jones of Nayland's biographer, and a lifelong friend of Joshua Watson. Pusey himself, in a letter to Joshua Watson after visiting him in Brighton in September 1839, described his appreciation of the sense of common purpose with the Hackney school: 'I cannot say how cheering it was to be recognised by you as carrying on the same torch which we had received from yourself and from those of your generation, who had remained faithful to the old teaching.' In particular, Pusey characterised Watson and his associates as forming a kind of bridge to 'the old times and old paths, to which we wished to lead people back'.[19] Speaking of the Hackney school again, Liddon commented further, 'As Pusey said shortly before his own death, these men "must have prepared the ground for the Tracts".'[20] Pusey's assessment is supported by the recent studies of the Hackney Phalanx offered by Robert Andrews and Clive Dewey.[21] Alongside these affirmations of a common cause, we will see that Pusey was also highly critical of some associates of the Hackney school whose ideas were less in tune with the Tractarian approach to reading the Bible alongside the Fathers.

Jones of Nayland and Figurative Language

Jones delivered his course of lectures, *The Figurative Language of Holy Scripture*, in 1786 at the parish church in Nayland, Suffolk, where he had become the perpetual curate in 1777. In them, Jones argued that 'Scripture is found to have a language of its own, which doth not consist of words, but of signs or figures taken from visible things'. Because the Bible reveals or teaches 'such things as are above natural reason', 'It must abound with figurative expressions; it cannot proceed without them'. According to Jones, the 'materials of that figurative language' include things from 'the natural creation', 'the institutions of the law', 'the persons of the prophets and holy men', 'the history of the church', and 'the actions of inspired men'. These things serve as signs which carry 'an instructive signification' pointing 'to something greater than themselves', some 'spiritual truth'.[22]

Jones argued that his presentation of figurative language expressed the character of scripture itself and was guided by the expositions of the Church Fathers. He described the Apostles who wrote the New Testament as those who apprehended 'a deeper sense' which is also 'called the spirit' and which is beyond 'a literal sense of the words'. He also anticipated those who would criticise him for placing the Fathers above the Bible by arguing that the figurative and spiritual interpretations of the primitive Church are fundamentally scriptural: 'the apostles of Jesus Christ succeeded in their labours by being ministers of the spirit; that is, by interpreting and reasoning according to an inward or figurative sense in the law, the prophets, and the psalms. All the fathers of the Christian church followed their example: particularly *Origen*, one of the most useful and powerful of primitive expositors'.[23]

By emphasising that his argument was both scriptural and patristic, Jones also addressed the possible objection that his presentation of figurative language was partisan, and more specifically that it was a form of Hutchinsonianism. Jones had been introduced to the ideas of the naturalist and theologian John Hutchinson (1674–1737) while a student at University College, Oxford, from 1745 to 1749.[24] Hutchinson was a land surveyor, amateur geologist and scholar of Hebrew. He wrote his best-known work *Moses Principia* (1724, 1727) in response to Isaac Newton's *Principia Mathematica* (1687). Hutchinson rejected Newton's theory of gravity as a kind of materialism inspired by the corruptions of philosophy disconnected from scriptural revelation. He believed that one could discern the secrets of the created order through a careful study of Genesis and in particular by discovering the code which God provided in the Hebrew language and the revelation given to Moses.[25] It is beyond the scope of this article to offer a detailed consideration of Hutchinson's work, his understanding of God's Trinitarian action in the world, or how his ideas and followers helped to shape High Church reaction to latitudinarian tendencies in the theology of his day.[26] For the purpose of this argument, it is enough to see how Jones's Hutchinsonianism could have influenced and amplified his interest in the figurative interpretation of the Bible.

Jones himself acknowledged the connection between Hutchinsonianism and figurative interpretation in his biography of George Horne (1730–92). Horne had also been attracted to Hutchinsonian ideas while an undergraduate contemporary of Jones at University College, before becoming president of Magdalen College, Oxford, dean of Canterbury and, briefly, bishop of Norwich. Horne wrote *A Commentary on the Book of the Psalms* (1776), describing the types and figures by which the Psalms prophesy and reveal Christ and the Church. In his biography of Horne, Jones argued that Hutchinsonians, in company with 'the old Christian Fathers, and the Divines of the Reformation', 'take great delight' in 'the types and figures of the Scripture'.[27] Referring to another key element of his treatment of figurative language, Jones argued that according to the principles of Hutchinsonianism, 'divine things are explained ... by allusions to the natural creation', and by displaying analogies 'between the sensible and spiritual world'.[28]

At the same time as acknowledging these emphases of Hutchinsonianism, in his *Discourse on the Use and Intention of Some Remarkable Passages of the Scripture*, with which his lectures were published, Jones criticised those 'who ought to know better', for 'ascribing things to *Hutchinson*, which were borrowed from *Origen*'. The idea, argued Jones, that 'the visible world is a school, in which God teaches us by earthly things the nature of heavenly' is not specifically Hutchinsonian, but rather 'exactly what Christians knew and taught above a thousand years ago'.[29] This was not simply a matter of rhetorical flourish. While his interest in Hutchinsonian ideas would certainly have encouraged the exploration of figurative language, examining Jones's lectures alongside, for example, John Keble's detailed consideration of figurative or mystical interpretation in the Fathers emphasises the patristic and biblical character of Jones's work rather than anything uniquely Hutchinsonian.[30] In the words of his biographer, Jones 'has been particularly careful to have the sanction of Scripture itself for every explanation he has adopted'.[31]

Pusey's Lectures on Types

In his 'Lectures on Types and Prophecies of the Old Testament', delivered during the 1836–37 academic year in the course of his duties as Regius Professor of Hebrew at Christ Church, Oxford, Pusey investigated prophecy and the prophetic character of the Old Testament.[32] In them, Pusey compares the way in which the Church Fathers understood the Old Testament to be prophetic with the evidentialist or 'apologetic character which our theology has so largely assumed'.[33] He examines especially the principles of 'typical' prophecy which he sees to be characteristic of the 'antient Church'. Like Jones, he argued that he does not privilege the Fathers over the Bible, but over modern interpreters.

Pusey summed up this argument most succinctly in the preface to his translation of Augustine's *Confessions*, which serves as a general introduction to the Library of the Fathers: 'The contrast, then, in point of authority, is not between Holy Scripture and the Fathers, but between the Fathers and us ... between ancient Catholic truth and modern private opinions.'[34] The Fathers who interpreted in the 'Apostolic mode', argued Pusey, did not seek to identify isolated prophecies or types, but rather 'They had Christ always in their thoughts, and so with the full persuasion that the whole of the Old Testament, the Law, the Prophets and the Psalms, shewed before of Him, they read and understood of Christ therein, whatever naturally harmonized with His dispensation, whether it would approve itself to a more rigid understanding or no.'

A type is commonly understood to be an event, person or ceremony in the Old Testament that corresponds to, or prefigures, similar events, people or things in the New Testament, often referred to as the antitype. Pusey broadened this notion of type in significant ways, arguing that the language of the whole of the Old Testament is 'mainly typical'. To stress this point Pusey did not generally use the standard term 'antitype' to refer to a fulfilment which can be clearly connected to a specific Old Testament prophecy. Rather, he referred to the different degrees by which all types approach the one eternal Archetype, the Word and Son of God, in whom all types are fulfilled. Every type speaks more or less clearly of this one type, or contains more or less of 'the substance' of the 'one Archetype'.[35]

Figures and Types: The Theological Framework

For both Jones and Pusey, the figurative or typical character of scriptural language is grounded in a doctrine of creation and the figurative character of all created things. For Pusey, '"every thing is a type", if we could see it'.[36] For Jones, 'the visible world throughout is a pattern of the invisible, the figures of the sacred language built upon the images of nature, are as extensive as the world itself'. Jones argued that 'the world which we now see becomes a sort of commentary on the mind of God, and explains the world in which we believe'.[37] In a strikingly similar way, Pusey argued that 'the book of Nature' offers a 'commentary to revelation', which is also a commentary on the mind of God: 'The book of God's works thus, and the book of His word correspond, because they both are emanations of His Word ... Both reveal the unseen God being spoken in Him.'[38] Likewise Keble described the visible world as 'an index or token of the invisible', and 'the works of God in creation' as visible words, '*Verba visibilia*'.[39] For Newman both the world and the Bible offer types of 'an unseen world, truer and higher than themselves'.[40] Here Jones and the Tractarians speak with one voice.

Both Jones and Pusey emphasise that the elusive or indefinite character of communication by figures and types expresses the obscurity which is intrinsic to religious or spiritual knowledge. According to Jones, the 'hidden wisdom of the Scripture is to be considered as treasure hid in the earth, for which men must search with that same zeal and labour with which they penetrate into a mine of gold'.[41] For Pusey, God's wisdom is also both revealed and concealed, or veiled, in scripture; the Old Testament is 'one vast prophetic system, veiling, but full of the New Testament'. Like Jones's 'mine of gold', Pusey described what is veiled as 'a treasure which God had deposited in Scripture below the surface'.[42]

The emphasis on 'mystery' and the 'mystical' character of types, on what is revealed while remaining beyond the grasp of certainty or rational demonstration, is not an isolated matter of biblical exegesis.[43] Rather, this approach to reading the Bible is part of a way of conceiving theology which takes seriously the limitations of natural reason and 'sensible' knowledge while arguing that truths 'above natural reason' are nonetheless communicated through scripture. For Jones, 'divine wisdom' includes the knowledge of 'God, who is a spirit ... and of a spiritual world which no words can describe'.[44] For Pusey, 'God and His ways and His Nature we can, of course, know but in part; and our highest knowledge must be our indistinctness ... it belongs to another sphere, and just touches, as it were, upon that wherein we dwell'. This spiritual knowledge 'touches' the human sphere through types and figures: 'Being men, invested with an earthly body, which hath a sense of nothing but material things, we cannot see truth and reason ... we are obliged to conceive them as they are reflected to us in the glass of the visible forms.'[45] Pusey explained the necessity of mediation, why 'our eyes still need the mitigated light', in similar terms: 'Throughout hath God reference to our compound nature; there is an outward form allied to our material nature, an inward spiritual meaning, addressed to our spirit.'[46] The argument that types cannot be replaced by abstractions is a common Tractarian theme. In Newman's words, 'Instead of explaining, Scripture does but continue to answer us in the language of the type; even to the last it veils His deed under the ancient figure.'[47]

Pusey's Criticism of High Church Apologetics

For the Tractarians in general and Pusey in particular, emphasising the centrality of biblical types and figures was a necessary part of correcting fundamental theological errors. The Tractarians were not simply bringing forward discreet examples of figurative interpretation as isolated curiosities. Rather, they offered an alternative epistemology to the one they believed to be implicit in what they called the 'apologetic' theology of their day.[48] Seeing this helps to explain why the Tractarian advocacy of types was greeted in many quarters with both incomprehension and criticism, and how their approach was different in significant ways to that proposed by Jones. There was discontinuity, something genuinely new in the Tractarian approach, as well as continuity. Seen from a modern perspective where typological habits of mind are more unusual, different examples of biblical types may look the same.

Forty years ago George Landow investigated the prevalence of biblical typology in Victorian culture, a significance not relegated to the interpretation of the Bible, but which influenced literature, the visual arts, and even the interpretation of politics.[49] Landow considers examples of typical interpretations from Keble and Newman alongside the more mainstream definitions of the widely read Thomas Hartwell Horne and his *Introduction to the Critical Study and Knowledge of the Holy Scriptures* (1818). However, for Pusey, Horne represented an approach which undermined a proper appreciation of types, and Horne's definitions would relegate many of the interpretations offered by Pusey, Keble and Newman to the category of 'extravagant *typifications*', not genuine types.[50] Both in the context of the day and in relation to Jones, the approach promoted by Pusey and his colleagues was distinct and more radical from that generally accepted.

One can see more clearly both the significance and newness of the Tractarian approach, as well as differences between Jones's exposition of figurative language and that of Pusey, by first considering Pusey's criticisms of two illustrious associates of the Hackney school, William Van Mildert (1765–1836) and Herbert Marsh (1757–1839).

Thomas Hartwell Horne quotes both Marsh and Van Mildert in his description of types.[51] Van Mildert was appointed Regius Professor of Divinity at Oxford in 1813 before becoming bishop of Llandaff in 1819. After his translation to Durham in 1826 he helped to found the University of Durham. Marsh was Lady Margaret Professor of Divinity in Cambridge from 1807 until his death. He preceded Van Mildert as bishop of Llandaff, and was translated to Peterborough in 1819. In the manuscript of the 'Lectures', Pusey generally did not refer to living or recently deceased divines. However, the notebook of one of the students who attended the lectures, Edward Marshall, reveals that Pusey departed from his notes to criticise contemporary writers during his lectures. As we have seen, Pusey argued for an expansive view of types and figurative language; the types which, in the New Testament, 'the Apostles took and authorized [which] were not isolated phenomena but specimens ... guides to direct where and how to seek, not guards to withhold us from prying beyond what it has authoritatively disclosed'.[52] Marshall's notes show that Pusey criticised Van Mildert and Marsh directly as representatives of the apologetic approach which treated New Testament fulfilments not as 'guides' but very much as 'guards' or limits. Before turning to his near contemporaries, Pusey faulted Daniel Waterland (1683–1740), who wrote *Scripture Vindicated* (1730–32) in response to the deist Matthew Tindal's *Christianity as Old as Creation* (1730). Marshall noted:

> Fearful of unskilful application, they draw the line as to admit only what are types in the New Testament, but leave the rest in abeyance. To this school Waterland belonged (Preface to *Sacred Scripture Vindicated* p. 18). He will only allow as types those which Sacred Scripture has directly or indirectly Typified. This is corrected in a degree by Bishop van Mildert though he too in part admits it (Bampton Lecture vii). Bishop Marsh carries it still further than even Waterland. This is dangerous like all timid policy. It endeavours to get rid of all typology and to make us suspicious of them, it draws also an arbitrary line.[53]

In the Bampton lectures to which Pusey referred, Van Mildert argued that 'It is, indeed, essential to a Type ... that there should be competent evidence of the Divine *intention* in the correspondence between it and the Antitype ... resting on some solid proof from Scripture itself, that this was really the case.'[54] Marsh's influential *Lectures on Biblical Criticism and Interpretation* (1809–16) stressed the same cautionary principle. We can only know that a person or thing 'was designed to pre-figure *another* person or thing', argued Marsh, 'if this 'pre-figuration has been declared by *divine authority*' in the New Testament.[55]

According to Pusey's framework, both Van Mildert and Marsh exemplify the apologetic approach which both narrows 'our whole creed' and misrepresents biblical revelation.[56] Keble's censure of 'modern prejudices' which make mystical interpretations seem 'far-fetched and extravagant' pertains equally well to these important associates of the Hackney Phalanx.[57] The Tractarian view may seem unfair. Marsh sought to present the insights of new forms of German historical criticism to an English audience in a way that was compatible with orthodox faith.[58] Waterland had been a champion against the threats posed by deism. However, Pusey's extensive study of German theology – his knowledge of new forms of German higher criticism was virtually unparalleled among English theologians in the 1820s to the 1840s – led him to the view that in seeking to defend supernatural revelation, the opponents of both the deists and the new German critics often accepted principles and approaches which undermined their attempts to buttress orthodoxy. In the same way, he thought that an apologetic or evidentialist approach to typological interpretation was not compatible with a theological appreciation of religious knowledge or of the Bible. For Pusey, the emphasis on using the Bible as a kind of evidence undermined whatever elements of Christian doctrine, however important, could not be proved apart from a standpoint of faith.[59] On the one hand, this assessment demonstrates continuity between Jones and Pusey, between the Oxford Movement and their High Church predecessors. Peter Nockles argues that 'Hutchinsonian High Church rhetoric against the contemporary cult of human reason strikingly prefigured that of the Tractarians'.[60] Jones's approach to figurative interpretation was part of his reaction to rationalism in theology. In a similar way, the Tractarian criticism of the genre of 'evidence writing' and their advocacy of a patristic mysticism (i.e. typology) was not merely a form of antiquarianism or pietism, but a theological response to what Pusey's former colleague Mark Pattison described as 'the assumption of the supremacy of reason in matters of religion', and the idea that 'Christianity appeared made for nothing else but to be *proved*'.[61]

For both Jones and the Tractarians, the necessary obscurity of figurative and typological language illustrates that certainty comes at the expense of proper apprehension of the highest kind of knowledge; the kind of certainty which evidence writing secures undermines rather than promotes theological understanding.[62] Part of what distinguished the Tractarian approach from that of Jones, and what made their use of figurative, typological or sacramental interpretations more radical, was their trenchant criticism of rationalism not only in those who attacked Christian orthodoxy explicitly, but also of the rationalism the Tractarians found in those defenders of the faith who they believed had adopted principles and ideas which were corrosive to orthodoxy even as they sought to defend or advance it. Pusey's criticisms of the apologetic school, which for him was represented by Marsh and Van Mildert, were not so much a form of 'present centred' history, but rather a criticism of what he saw as contemporary theological rationalism and utilitarianism.[63]

In the approach of both Jones and Pusey, the rejection of a mechanistic view of reason is closely connected with the idea that the kind of knowledge which types communicate is a moral knowledge. Divine wisdom is not data analysable by sufficiently sharp intellectual tools, but the knowledge of a living divine person in whom truth and holiness are one. This means that being able to read types and figures is both an exercise in sanctification, and an expression of a holy life. Jones described reading the Bible as a moral trial: 'For it pleased God, for wise ends, to exercise the faith and devotion of his people with a system of forms and ceremonies, which had no value but from their signification.'[64] Similarly, Pusey argued that the types of the Old Testament offer a sort of trial; they 'were so many tests whereby to distinguish this true Messiah: tokens, given to as many as looked and longed for

Him'.[65] Like Pusey, Jones insisted that unbelief is a moral problem which the appeal to evidence cannot solve; the 'word of God' is a seed which 'must find something congenial with itself in the soil into which it falls'.[66] Pusey described the necessity of this holy correspondence between the knower and the known in his account of reading the types and figures of the 'book of Nature': 'To the worldly or sensual it is a sealed book. What is Divine in it can be read only by what is Divine in man.'[67] Both Jones and Pusey criticised the idea that belief could be secured primarily by rational conviction, and saw a sanctifying virtue in the uncertainty which many of their contemporaries saw as a principal weakness of figurative interpretations.

Jones's Reserve and the Tractarian Difference

Returning to Jones after Van Mildert and Marsh helps one to see both how Jones's approach is organically related to that of Pusey and his colleagues, while, at the same time, that it is more cautious and less bold. On the one hand, Jones's open-ended presentation of figurative language is much closer to Pusey's comprehensive view of type than the evidentialist principles of Van Mildert and Marsh would allow. Both Pusey and Jones root their expansive view of the figurative or typical language of the Bible in the broader canvas of a symbolic or sacramental view of the created order. That '"every thing is a type", if we could see it', is an expression equally at home in the lectures of Pusey and Jones, but not in those of Van Mildert or Marsh. Jones's argument that the 'hidden wisdom' of scripture is a kind of buried treasure fits well with Pusey's argument that the fulfilments disclosed in the New Testament are 'guides to direct where and how to seek'. However, having emphasised the importance of the hunt for hidden treasure in his first lecture, Jones for the most part limits his discussion to types which are, in the language of Marsh, 'declared by *divine authority*' in the New Testament.[68]

One can see both instructive differences and similarities in how Jones and Pusey treat the story of the patriarch Joseph as a figure or type of Christ. With the '*divine authority*' to see Joseph in relation to Christ provided by St Stephen's words, 'the patriarchs, moved with envy, sold Joseph into Egypt' (Acts 7:9), Jones examines Joseph's dreams (Gen. 37:5–11). As Joseph's brothers hated him 'for his dreams and for his words', so, Jones argues, 'when Christ asserted his own dignity, his brethren took up stones to cast at him for making himself the Son of God'. However, after remarking that 'Much more might be said to shew how exact the parallel is between the history of Joseph and the history of Christ', Jones did not carry further his suggestion.[69] Pusey, on the other hand, does describe something of this 'much more' to which Jones alludes. Drawing on St Ambrose's *On Joseph*, for example, Pusey argued that the explanation of Joseph's brothers about the money they found in their sacks exposed their reliance on their own merits and their failure to accept salvation as a free gift: 'He gave you money in your sacks – Christ is the joyous gift; He is your silver, He your price.'[70] This kind of more speculative interpretation is common in Pusey and rare in Jones – as has been pointed out already, Jones is 'careful to have the sanction of Scripture itself for every explanation he has adopted'.[71] On the other hand, Jones's approach is not open to the kind of censures which Pusey makes against Van Mildert and Marsh. Jones was willing to speculate, like Pusey and unlike Marsh and Van Mildert, that: 'The church that went from Egypt to Canaan gives us an example of every thing that can happen to the Christian Church, from the beginning of it even to the end of the world.'[72] However, if Jones did not insist on New Testament authorisation in principle, his expositions tend to stay closer to authorised types than those of Pusey. Jones opened the door to possibilities which Pusey explores, a door which Van Mildert and Marsh insisted should remain shut, but Jones did not generally walk through it himself.

While both Jones and Pusey argue that figures and types have a sacramental character, Pusey makes this sacramental principle both more comprehensive and more controversial by linking it more directly with the doctrine of the Incarnation. Jones argues that the figures of the Bible are like sacraments, 'outward signs with an inward and spiritual meaning', signs which confer something of the life which they reveal: 'the spirit of those figures under which the bible delivers to us the things of God, has a power of raising and glorifying, even in this life, the spirit of man'.[73] In a similar way, Pusey argues that the typical language by which the Psalms speak of Christ, both of 'the Head' and of 'His members', gives to them 'a *Sacramental force* as being used in Him, and being His words in us'. In other words, for Pusey as well as for Jones, reading the types of the Old Testament offers a means of communion or participation in the divine life. However, Pusey took this idea further than Jones by linking this sacramental understanding of types closely to the Incarnation. Pusey described the union of the type or figure with the truth which it reveals as analogous to the union of the divine and human in Christ: 'God has appointed, as it were, a sort of sacramental union between the type and the archetype ... God has joined them together, and man may not and can not put them asunder.' For Pusey, Christ took on flesh not only in the Incarnation, but in the Bible, which he described as 'a living and true Body, which it hath pleased God to take, in order to be accessible to us'.[74] These descriptions give Pusey's advocacy of typical or figurative prophecy a greater theological significance than those of Jones, even if Jones's ideas gesture towards the incarnational analogy which Pusey develops. Unlike Jones, Pusey suggested that one does not really understand the doctrine of the Incarnation if one does not accept the comprehensive approach to figurative language and typical prophecy which he offers. Newman's argument, that 'it may almost be laid down as a historical fact, that the mystical interpretation and orthodoxy will stand or fall together', gives succinct expression to Pusey's approach, while it would seem forced in Jones's lectures.[75]

Present-Centred Reserve

One particularly bold interpretation which Jones offers, when read alongside Nockles's description of the way in which Jones anticipated the Tractarians, highlights the similarities between Jones and Pusey, and suggests why Pusey did not evoke Jones's authority for his typical exegesis. In the *Discourse* which Jones wrote to supplement his lectures, he considered the account of the borrowed axe-head lost in the river Jordan when the 'sons of the prophets' built a dwelling for their master Elisha (2 Kgs 6:1–6). Jones examined the significance of the story: how 'the head of the axe, being the better part' corresponds to 'the soul or spirit of man, the better part of him', and how the 'borrowed' axe-head symbolises the soul which belongs first to God. The iron on the bottom of the river is like 'the soul of man ... under the dominion of death', which is then raised up by the power of Christ's resurrection after this 'branch of the stem of Jesse' was first 'cut down, and cast with us into the waters of death'. This passage would not be out of place in Pusey's 'Lectures', and is also one of the few places where Jones refers explicitly to a patristic source, Irenaeus and his *Against Heresies*.[76] Jones did not simply parrot Irenaeus, but built on his exposition. Why does Jones offer this creative exposition, having avoided suchlike in his extensive lectures? Here we are assisted by Nockles's consideration of the Tractarian 'Doctrine of Reserve', the principle of 'restraint and self-effacement that ... became a distinctive element of the Tractarian spiritual *ethos*'.[77] In Nockles's account, Jones exemplifies 'Reserve': '"those whose minds were wont to find a centre of action at Nayland parsonage looked not for earthly applause" but rested content with a "humble, secret unaffected, unaspiring practice of piety"'.[78] In the most extensive Tractarian presentation of reserve, Isaac Williams discerned a kind of reserve in God's restrained revelation of himself: 'there appears in God's manifestations of Himself to mankind, in conjunction with an exceeding desire to communicate that knowledge, a tendency to conceal, and throw a veil over it, as if it were injurious to us, unless we were of a certain disposition to receive it'.[79]

According to the Tractarians, if God is careful to avoid injury by an overly bright manifestation of divine light, so should the teacher exercise a similar caution. If Jones of Nayland exemplified this Tractarian *ethos*, one would expect that he would only offer the kind of expositions that his listeners or readers would be disposed to receive. This is indeed what Jones's biographer suggests, describing how Jones, knowing that he 'might seem to be "bringing many strange things to the ears of some people"', kept the supplemental *Discourse* 'in reserve', printing it for 'those only, who were prepared, by what they had already seen in the other Lectures, to give it due consideration'.[80] Jones's praise of Origen, who for Marsh represented a kind of 'indefensible' and ahistorical allegorical interpretation, also highlights Jones's nearness to Pusey, albeit without the explicit incarnational analogy.[81] The similarity between Jones's *Discourse* and Pusey's lectures, coupled with the likelihood that Jones in his lectures exercised a cautious reserve, intimates an even greater correspondence between Jones's approach and that of the Tractarians than Jones's lectures taken by themselves would prove.

The principle of reserve may also suggest why Pusey and his colleagues did not point to Jones's example in their presentation of the sacramental or typological principle. Pusey's decision not to publish his lectures was almost certainly, at least in part, the result of a similar cautious reserve.[82] Pusey and his colleagues were aware that in advocating patristic exegesis they were opposing, in Pusey's words, 'Laws of Interpretation' more in accordance with the empiricist and utilitarian 'Spirit of the Age'.[83] The sharp criticism of both Keble's Tract 89 on patristic mysticism, and of Isaac Williams's Tracts 80 and 87 on reserve, even by the friend and historian of the Oxford Movement, Richard Church, as 'hardly what the practical needs of the time required', shows that they were correct in their assessment.[84] If an appeal to the Fathers who were evoked by the English Reformers as well as the Caroline divines was not enough to win over even close friends and supporters, then claiming the support of a divine like Jones who was associated with the more esoteric school of Hutchinsonianism was unlikely to seem like a good way to make typological exegesis more palatable to a generation fed on evidence writing. Jones himself acknowledged this problem when he emphasised that his approach was biblical and traditional rather than Hutchinsonian. Given the high regard Pusey had for Jones, a debt that Newman was also willing to acknowledge, the goal of making the advocacy of patristic exegesis as attractive as possible could explain the absence of any reference to Jones's lectures by Pusey. If this proposal is correct, then the overlooking of Jones described by Nockles would indeed be a kind of 'present centred' history, but a present-centredness expressing a concern for the spiritual capacities of the expected audience which was entirely consistent with the principles of both Jones and Pusey and his colleagues. This suggestion about why Pusey did not refer to Jones is inevitably speculative. It is more certain that following in the path suggested by Nockles, and investigating the continuities and differences between Jones's lectures and those of Pusey, offers an example of the ongoing and rich fruitfulness of Peter Nockles's extensive and nuanced study of the Oxford Movement.

Notes

1 E. B. Pusey, *Parochial Sermons*, vol. 1, 3rd edn (Oxford: John Henry Parker, 1852), p. vii.
2 Henry Parry Liddon, *Life of Edward Bouverie Pusey*, 4 vols, ed. J. O. Johnston and Robert J. Wilson (London: Longmans, 1893), vol. 1, p. 254.
3 Peter B. Nockles, *The Oxford Movement in Context: Anglican High Churchmanship, 1760–1857* (Cambridge: Cambridge University Press, 1994). See, for example, pp. 109–11, 148, 201–3. 'Part I' of Stewart J. Brown, Peter B. Nockles and James Pereiro (eds), *The Oxford Handbook of the Oxford Movement* (Oxford: Oxford University Press, 2017) [henceforth *OHOM*], pp. 9–93, offers a summary of recent scholarship considering the background to the Oxford Movement and the dynamic of continuity and change.
4 Peter B. Nockles, 'Survivals or New Arrivals: The Oxford Movement and the Nineteenth Century Historical Construction on Anglicanism', in Stephen Platten (ed.), *Anglicanism and the Western Christian Tradition: Continuity, Change and the Search for Communion* (Norwich: Canterbury Press, 2003), pp. 144–5.
5 On this general sense of crisis, see James Pereiro, *Ethos and the Oxford Movement* (Oxford: Oxford University Press, 2007), pp. 49–52.
6 Nockles, *Oxford Movement*, p. 206.

7 John Henry Cardinal Newman, *Apologia Pro Vita Sua*, ed. F. M. Turner (New Haven, CT: Yale University Press, 2008), pp. 148, 154.
8 Pusey House, Oxford, (MS) E. B. Pusey, 'Lectures on Types and Prophecies of the Old Testament', [1836] and J. Keble, *On the Mysticism attributed to the Early Fathers of the Church*, Tract 89, *Tracts for the Times*, 5 vols (London: Rivington, 1841), vol. 5.
9 John Henry Newman, *The Arians of the Fourth Century* (London: Rivington, 1833); and Isaac Williams, *Thoughts on the Study of the Holy Gospels* (London, Rivington, 1870 [1842]).
10 On the neglect of the Tractarians as biblical scholars, see Timothy Larsen, 'Scripture and Biblical Interpretation', in *OHOM*, esp. pp. 231, 237–8, 240. On the centrality of mystical exegesis for the Tractarians, see George Westhaver, 'Mysticism and Sacramentalism in the Oxford Movement', in *OHOM*, pp. 262–4.
11 Nockles, *Oxford Movement*, p. 207.
12 *Ibid.*, p. 206.
13 William Jones, *A Course of Lectures on the Figurative Language of the Holy Scripture* [1786], in *The Theological and Miscellaneous Works*, new edn in 6 vols (London: Rivington, 1826), vol. 3.
14 Nockles, *Oxford Movement*, p. 207.
15 Geoffrey Rowell, '"Church Principles" and "Protestant Kempism"', in Paul Vaiss (ed.), *From Oxford to the People* (Leominster: Gracewing, 1996), pp. 24–5.
16 Newman, *Apologia*, p. 135, probably referring to Jones's *The Catholic Doctrine of a Trinity* (1756).
17 Liddon, *Life*, vol. 1, p. 256.
18 *Ibid.*, p. 258.
19 Edward Churton (ed.), *Memoir of Joshua Watson*, 2nd edn (Oxford: John Henry and James Parker, 1863), pp. 236–7. See also Liddon, *Life*, vol. 1, p. 260. For Watson's understanding of a common cause with Pusey and his colleagues, and of Watson's concerns with Tractarianism post-1841, see A. B. Webster, *Joshua Watson* (London: SPCK, 1954), pp. 95–8, 105–13.
20 Liddon, *Life*, vol. 1, p. 259.
21 *Ibid.* For a nuanced treatment of the contribution of the Hackney school throughout the nineteenth century, and of both shared ideas and differences between High Church and Oxford Movement approaches and emphases, see Robert M. Andrews, 'High Church Anglicanism', in Rowan Strong (ed.), *The Oxford History of Anglicanism*, 5 vols (Oxford: Oxford University Press, 2017), vol. 3, pp. 141–64. Andrews's monograph, *Lay Activism and the High Church Movement of the Late Eighteenth Century* (Leiden: Brill, 2015), considers this milieu through a study of Jones of Nayland's biographer. Clive Dewey, in *The Passing of Barchester* (London: Hambledon Press, 1991), pp. 125–41, helpfully describes the social and political networks which the Phalanx nurtured and argues that this group 'preserved Laudian doctrines and practices', putting in place the necessary components for 'the Anglican revival' of the 1830s (p. 138). For Nockles's consideration of the Hackney Phalanx, see his *Oxford Movement*, pp. 14–15, 63–7, 119–22, 205.
22 Jones, *Lectures*, pp. 5, 6, 20, 23, 20.
23 *Ibid.*, pp. 16, 18.

24 See Nigel Aston, 'Hutchinsonians', *Oxford Dictionary of National Biography*, and Derya Gurses Tarbuck, *Enlightenment Reformation: Hutchinsonianism and Religion in Eighteenth-Century Britain* (Abingdon and New York: Routledge, 2017), pp. 131–2.
25 See Nigel Aston, 'From Personality to Party: The Creation and Transmission of Hutchinsonianism, c. 1725–1750', *Studies in History and Philosophy of Science*, 35:3 (2004), 627.
26 See B. W. Young, *Religion and Enlightenment in Eighteenth-Century England: Theological Debate from Locke to Burke* (Oxford: Clarendon Press, 1998), pp. 136–63, and Nockles, *Oxford Movement*, pp. 200–11.
27 W. Jones, 'Preface to the Second Edition', *Works*, vol. 6, p. 16, pp. 13–18, cf. Rowell, '"Church Principles"', pp. 21–4.
28 Jones, 'Preface', p. 14. Jones's interest in 'the Book of Nature' and in fossils as a record of the flood, another characteristic of Hutchinsonianism, may lay behind his lifelong interest in natural science. See G. M. Ditchfield, 'William Jones of Nayland', *Oxford Dictionary of National Biography*.
29 Jones, *Lectures*, p. 194.
30 Keble, *Mysticism*, pp. 137–62.
31 William Stevens, 'Life of the Author', in Jones, *Works*, vol. 1, pp. xxi.
32 See George Derrick Westhaver, 'The Living Body of the Lord: E. B. Pusey's "Types and Prophecies of the Old Testament"' (PhD thesis, Durham University, 2012). When referring to Pusey's lectures, page numbers of the manuscript and of the thesis, which is available online, are given. 'L1/W39' refers to p. 1 of Pusey's manuscript as quoted on p. 39 of the thesis.
33 Pusey, 'Lectures', L1/W39.
34 Augustine, *The Confessions*, Library of the Fathers, tr. E. B. Pusey (Oxford: John Henry Parker, 1838), vol. 1, p. iii.
35 Pusey, 'Lectures', L10/W46; L13/W142; L123/W168. For the Tractarians, the terms 'allegorical', 'typical', 'typological', 'spiritual', 'mystical', 'figurative', and 'sacramental', as describing a way of reading the Bible, are generally interchangeable. See Westhaver, 'The Living Body', pp. 193–202.
36 Pusey, 'Lectures', L14/W214.
37 Jones, *Lectures*, pp. 20, 6.
38 Pusey, 'Lectures', L17/W226; Pusey, 'Book of God's Works' (MS), in Westhaver, 'Living Body', p. 226.
39 Keble, *Mysticism*, pp. 148, 152.
40 John Henry Cardinal Newman, 'Milman's View of Christianity', in *Essays Critical and Historical*, 2 vols (London: Pickering, 5th edn, 1881 [1841]), vol. 2, p. 193.
41 Jones, *Lectures*, p. 15.
42 Pusey, 'Lectures', L8/W45; L39/W63.
43 Jones, *Lectures*, p. 13; Pusey, 'Lectures', L136/W140.
44 Jones, *Lectures*, pp. 5, 182, 5–6.
45 Pusey, 'Lectures', L2/W8; Jones, *Lectures*, p. 169.
46 Pusey, 'Emblematic Language' (MS), in Westhaver, 'Living Body', p. 186.

47 John Henry Newman, 'Mysteries in Religion', *Parochial and Plain Sermons* (San Francisco: Ignatius Press, 1997 [1835]), p. 361.
48 For a detailed description of Pusey's assessment of some forms of apologetic or evidence writing as forms of rationalism, and for how this assessment guides his account of typological interpretation, see Westhaver, 'Living Body', pp. 27–80.
49 George P. Landow, *Victorian Types, Victorian Shadows* (London: Routledge & Kegan Paul, 1980), pp. 3–12.
50 *Ibid.*, p. 37. See also pp. 22–46 for a general discussion illustrated by examples from Keble and Newman, as well as T. H. Horne's definitions. For a detailed examination of differences between Horne's approach and that of Pusey, see Westhaver, 'Living Body', pp. 144–8.
51 Thomas Hartwell Horne, *An Introduction to the Critical Study and Knowledge of the Holy Scriptures*, 3 vols (London: T. Cadell and W. Davies, 1818), vol. 1, p. 614.
52 Pusey, 'Lectures', L8/W148.
53 Edward Marshall, 'Notes on Pusey's Lectures' (MS), in Westhaver 'Living Body', p. 146.
54 William Van Mildert, *An Inquiry into the General Principles of Scripture-Interpretation*, 2nd edn (Oxford: University Press, 1815), p. 239. For Van Mildert's debt to Hutchinsonian ideas, with reference to W. Jones and G. Horne, see C. D. A. Leighton '"Knowledge of Divine Things": A Study of Hutchinsonianism', *History of European Ideas*, 26:3–4 (2000), 159–75.
55 Herbert Marsh, *Lectures on the Criticism and Interpretation of the Bible* (Cambridge: Rivington, 1828), p. 373, cf. p. 378.
56 Pusey, 'Lectures', L2/W52.
57 Keble, *Mysticism*, p. 6.
58 Robert K. Forrest, 'Marsh, Herbert (1757–1839)', *Oxford Dictionary of National Biography*.
59 See Westhaver, 'Living Body', pp. 55–61.
60 Jones, *Lectures*, p. 179. Nockles, *Oxford Movement*, p. 203. For Jones's anti-rationalism, see also Young, *Religion and Enlightenment*, p. 162, and Jones, 'The Life and Writings of Dr Horne', in Jones, *Works*, vol. 6, pp. 38–9.
61 M. Pattison, 'Tendencies of Religious Thought in England, 1688–1750', in *Essays and Reviews*, 8th edn (London: Longmans, 1861 [1860]), pp. 257, 259.
62 *Ibid.*, p. 297 for Pattison's concurrence in this assessment of the 'evidential school'. For the Tractarian emphasis on figurative interpretation as a response to rationalism and evidence theology, see Nockles, *Oxford Movement*, pp. 190–206, and Westhaver, 'Mysticism and Sacramentalism', pp. 264–7, and 'Living Body', pp. 39–80. Pusey's understanding of rationalism and its causes, rather than the youthful liberalism sometimes ascribed to him, also explains the difference between Pusey's assessment of German theology (and the dangers of 'orthodoxism', a dry speculative faith), and the assessment offered by another ally of the Hackney school, Hugh James Rose. On Rose, see Jonathan Sheehan, *The Enlightenment Bible: Translation, Scholarship, Culture* (Princeton: Princeton University Press, 2005), pp. 248–50. The way in which Pusey both criticises S. T. Coleridge for specific 'liberal' interpretations of the Bible, while at the same time adopting Coleridge's theological framework for understanding religious knowledge and communication by

symbols (types), suggests some weaknesses in Sheehan's account of both Coleridge and Pusey. See Larsen, 'Scripture and Biblical Interpretation', for a description of Tractarian biblical conservatism, and Westhaver, 'Living Body', pp. 75–80 and 117–33, for the importance of Coleridge and Schleiermacher in shaping the Romantic epistemology, which guided Pusey's consideration of types.
63 For Pusey's assessment of the dangers of theological rationalism and utilitarianism, see Westhaver, 'Mysticism and Sacramentalism', pp. 264–7.
64 Jones, *Lectures*, p. 8.
65 Pusey, 'Lectures', L4/W90.
66 Jones, *Lectures*, p. 12. This was a common patristic theme reaffirmed by Joseph Butler in *The Analogy of Religion* (Oxford: Clarendon Press, 1874), p. 234 (II.6.8).
67 Pusey, 'Book of Nature' (MS), in Westhaver, 'Living Body', p. 238.
68 Jones, *Lectures*, pp. 94–117, 88, on the journey through the wilderness as offering types of Christian life and Noah's flood as a type of baptism.
69 *Ibid.*, p. 129, also pp. 126–32.
70 Ambrose, *On Joseph*, 9.47–8, 50; Pusey, 'Lectures', L75A/W278, Gen. 43:19–23.
71 Stevens, 'Life', p. xxi.
72 Jones, *Lectures*, p. 112.
73 *Ibid.*, pp. 14, 175.
74 Pusey, 'Lectures', L133/W192; L23/W182; L24/W188.
75 John Henry Newman, *An Essay Concerning the Development of Christian Doctrine* (London: James Toovey, 1845), p. 324.
76 Jones, *Lectures*, p. 204; Irenaeus, *Against Heresies*, 5.17.4.
77 Nockles, *Oxford Movement*, p. 198.
78 *Ibid.*, pp. 199–200, quoting J. Freeman, in his *Life* of the Hutchinsonian William Kirby.
79 Isaac Williams, *On Reserve in Communicating Religious Knowledge*, Tract 80, *Tracts for the Times*, 5 vols, 2nd edn (London: Rivington, 1840), vol. 4, p. 3.
80 Stevens, 'Life', p. xxii.
81 Jones, *Lectures*, p. 18; Marsh, *Lectures*, pp. 361, 358–64.
82 *Ibid.*, p. xxi.
83 Marshall, 'Notes', in Westhaver, 'Living Body' p. 27, cf. Keble, *Mysticism*, p. 3.
84 R. W. Church, *The Oxford Movement* (London: MacMillan, 1897), pp. 264–5. On opposition to mystical exegesis by allies of the Tractarians, see Westhaver, 'Living Body', pp. 279–85 and Larsen, 'Scripture and Biblical Interpretation', p. 240.

Henry Manning's Journey to Roman Catholicism

KENNETH PARKER, DUQUESNE UNIVERSITY

Abstract

Henry Manning's (1808–92) transition from Anglican to Roman Catholic convert has not received the extensive attention that John Henry Newman's journey to Roman Catholicism has received. Though more than a half dozen treatments have appeared in recent decades, newly acquired archival resources received by the Westminster Diocesan Archives in 2014 warrant a new appraisal of the events leading to his conversion. How could a committed adherent of the Oxford Movement, who did not initially follow Newman's example in 1845, make the decision to leave the Church of his birth in 1851? What interior process enabled Archdeacon Henry Manning to preside over the assembly of Chichester clergy that condemned 'papal aggression' in 1850, and announce at the conclusion of the vote that he would be received into the Roman communion? This article outlines undercurrents in Manning's thought, traces of which can be found in his undergraduate years, and considers concepts that culminated in the decision that changed his life, and guided his Roman Catholic ecclesial outlook. His role in shaping the agenda of Vatican I and the post-conciliar era heightens the significance of this background.

Keywords: Henry Manning; Oxford Movement; papal aggression; conversion; Church of England; Roman Catholicism

In 1825, at age 17, Henry Manning (1808–92) wrote an essay for his Oxford tutor entitled 'Use and Abuse of Theory'. The essay reveals a fine and agile undergraduate mind, keenly aware of the rapidly evolving intellectual life of nineteenth-century Europe. It also reflects a very precise vision of truth and a conviction that modern forms of enquiry had clear limits. After examining the ways natural sciences test and verify theories proposed, he turned to contemporary moral theories. Here he observed, 'all is contingent, intangible and abstract'.[1] Manning explained that the evidence collected is not subject to experimentation or the rules of observation used by scientists.

The young Manning recognised that in all areas of knowledge, including 'religious contemplation', theorists are tempted to 'suffer their reason to be out-stripped by their desires and to acquiesce in the adoption of crude and fanciful conceits'.[2] While all sciences, natural and moral, are temporal, mutable and subject to change, Manning posed the burning question of his, and perhaps any era: Where is eternal, immutable, and changeless truth to be found? Manning concluded: 'It is to moral truths in their revealed shape we assign these qualities. They are the Eternal and immutable subjects of contemplation. In comparison with these Science is as nothing and the most admirable developments of abstract truth but unprofitable and bootless speculation.'[3] Over the course of the next twenty-five years, Manning continued to ponder this ultimate question, and came to two important conclusions: the need for an earthly locus of absolute, unchanging and eternal truth, and the role of the

Holy Spirit in making that truth manifest in the Church. These convictions proved decisive in his conversion to Roman Catholicism.

Yet Rome was not the obvious destination of his spiritual journey. This article examines Manning's quest to establish a sure ground for his Christian faith, and the confidence he ultimately placed in an infallible papal office as the safest foundation on which to establish his certainty. A close examination of his early Anglican years reveals that the contours of his belief system long pre-dated his conversion to Roman Catholicism. The analysis of his later Anglican thought demonstrates his belief that irreconcilable tensions existed between modern historical scholarship and the ideals he cherished. Chief among these was his conviction that scholastic deductive logic – based on divinely revealed truth – was superior to the contingent truths asserted by the inductive practices of modern scholarship.

Manning was the youngest of eight children, whose early life reflected that of a wealthy middle-class Englishman. During Manning's childhood his father enjoyed major successes in the West Indian sugar trade and in Tory politics, though by age 21 the family fortunes had collapsed. While Manning's youthful ambition had been to enter politics, the collapse of his family's fortune dashed these hopes, and he found himself reluctantly drawn into holy orders.[4] Though connected by blood and friendship to William Wilberforce's Evangelical family, Manning's own upbringing tended towards high and dry Anglicanism.[5] When he set about learning theology before his ordination in 1832, he focused on the English Reformation, Caroline divines and the early Church Fathers.[6] He fell under the spell of Newman's first 'Tract for the Times' in 1833, and a mutual friend reported to Newman, 'Manning has reviewed his opinions and adopts Apostolic Succession.'[7] It was a conversion which marked the rest of his life.[8]

Yet Manning's own theological priorities became evident, even as he embraced elements of the Oxford Movement. By 1834, Manning noted that Newman's doctrine did not take sufficient account of the Holy Spirit's agency, 'as a person continually present, helping, teaching, strengthening, guiding, and enabling us to use God's appointed means of renewal'.[9] This theme perdured and intensified over time. Manning's 1835 sermon, *The English Church, Its Succession, and Witness for Christ*, emphasised the Holy Spirit's enabling work, 'whose presence and support was invoked upon us at our ordination, and for the establishment and comfort of our minds in the discharge of our ministerial commission'.[10] Inextricably linked to Manning's focus on the Holy Spirit were his affirmations of the foundation of the Church by Christ and the succession of those set aside to teach and minister. Manning explained that 'the Lord went forth in His representatives, and by His Spirit; beginning from Jerusalem unto the uttermost parts of the earth, preaching the Gospel of the Kingdom'.[11] Drawing a line of succession from Christ to his own day, Manning made clear to the clergy addressed in the sermon that they were 'propagators of a doctrinal scheme, and upholders of a time-honoured fabric ... and the authority we exercise is a valid commission derived to us from Himself [Christ]'.[12] Yet he cautioned that the validity of their priestly authority rested on an unbroken succession.[13] Manning affirmed that the bishops of the Church of England were the lineal descendants of the 'first witnesses', and asserted that about this there had been no dispute for fifteen hundred years.[14] Continuity of doctrinal truth and valid sacramental ministry rested on episcopal succession and the work of the Holy Spirit through these successors of the apostles. Manning's doctrine during the 1830s focused on the working of the Holy Spirit in the Church and found its grounding in scripture as interpreted by the consensus of the ancient fathers.[15] The Holy Spirit's agency at Pentecost as well as the truth received and preserved through apostolic succession remained fundamental principles for Manning's theological reasoning in the decades that followed.[16]

In the latter half of the 1830s Manning's understanding of apostolic truth received through the succession of bishops was challenged by Roman Catholics and Evangelical Anglicans. Manning seemed particularly stung by Nicholas Wiseman's *Lectures on the Principal Doctrines and Practices of the Catholic Church*, which asserted a contradiction in the Thirty-nine Articles. Comparing Articles 6 and 20, Wiseman noted that 'in the first place ... the Church has authority in matters of faith; and then, that the Church cannot prescribe anything contrary to Scripture'.[17] Wiseman seemed to rhetorically ask: who is the judge of this? '[I]s each person thus constituted judge over the decisions of his Church?'[18] This question plagued Manning for the next fifteen years. In his sermon before Bishop William Otter of Chichester, on 13 June 1838, Manning clearly rejected claims made for ecclesiastical authority by Roman Catholics and for private judgment by Protestants, which suggested immediate inspiration of the Holy Spirit and went beyond the truths received from antiquity and continuous apostolic tradition.[19] In response to Evangelical reactions against his sermon – which focused on misperceptions that he attributed infallible authority to the Church – Manning added an appendix to his sermon, *The Rule of Faith*. In the appendix, Manning examined Anglican adherence to the Canon of St Vincent of Lérins: *quod semper, quod ubique, quod ab omnibus creditum est*.[20] In 1838 Manning had no problem agreeing with William Palmer that the truth belonging to the universal tradition could be determined by critical historical methods. Using Palmer's words he affirmed that the 'existence of such a tradition from the beginning is a matter of fact, which is to be established on the same sort of evidence as proves any other historical fact'.[21] He had already affirmed in his sermon that, '[a]lthough it is always both the right, as men speak, and the privilege of Christians to labour out their belief by analysis and induction, by evidence and history, it can never be their necessary duty until the Church has failed of hers'.[22] The Church was not infallible, but rather its truth claims bore the marks of *universitas, antiquitas, et consensio*.

Manning maintained that 'Christians cannot possibly admit that any doctrine, established by universal tradition, can be otherwise than *divinely, infallibly, true*.'[23] He employed this argument to critique the reliance of both Protestantism and 'Romanism' on 'living interpreters' of scripture over the consensus of ancient universal tradition. After quoting William Chillingworth's refutation of the Roman theory of papal infallibility, Manning stated, 'although this investing of the pope with infallibility is the *Italian* doctrine, the *Gallican* and *British* Romanists placing it in the Church assembled in council ... the *infallibility of the living judge*, whether *pope* or *Church*, is turned against the very ground on which Chillingworth stood . . . *i.e. primitive and universal tradition*'.[24] He used lengthy quotes from Newman's *Lectures on the Prophetical Office of the Church* to illustrate this point.[25] While Romanists had introduced corruptions in the name of magisterial authority, and Protestants had promoted innovations while invoking *sola scriptura*, it was the catholic charism of Anglicanism to maintain and preserve apostolic truth which stood the test of the Vincentian Canon. Knowledge of, and fidelity to, apostolic truth was Manning's passionate quest. In the summer of 1841, Manning stated in a letter to Archdeacon Julius Hare, 'I find myself a member of a branch of the Catholic Church, which has *personal* identity with the Church of the Apostles. The properties of this personal identity are a knowledge of the pure truth: and a power to do in Christ's name the same acts for the reconciling of man to God.'[26]

The years 1838–42 witnessed a sharp reaction against Oxford Movement ideals, as events, public opinion, and episcopal and university censure marginalised those who asserted the catholic character of the Church of England. Prior to this period, Manning's views hewed closely to High Church understandings that looked very much like Anglican orthodoxy. Yet Manning pressed forward to clarify his understanding of apostolic succession, which had taken such deep root in his theological imagination since 1833. In 1845, he published a substantial volume entitled *The Unity of the Church*. Apostolic truth mediated through episcopal succession was the theme of this work.[27] James Pereiro noted that it is here that Manning made an original contribution; for Manning argued that the Church's unity is twofold: 'one kind of Unity being objective, consisting in the faith, sacraments, and organised polity; the other subjective, in the peace and brotherly love of the several members'. Objective, organic unity is 'the identity of the Church of any age with the church of the Apostles in the faith and sacraments, and in the commission received from Christ, and transmitted by lawful succession'. Subjective unity consisted in submission to the lawful pastor of the local church and charity in relations with the Churches dispersed throughout the world.[28]

Yet during 1841 and 1842, Manning detailed in a manuscript entitled '*Religio Anglo-Catholici*' his antipathy for notions of 'national churches' and 'the empty theory of the church as a development or organization of the national life'. He stated, 'My allegiance to the Church *in* England . . . is on the hypothesis of its agreement and unity with the Church universal.' He called himself an Anglo-Catholic, as a member of the universal Church, 'born and dwelling in this Realm of England'. His adherence to the Church of England rested on its apostolic character and its embrace of truths affirmed to be universal.[29] This shift marked a departure from his earlier High Church views.

However, Manning's sympathies were still far from Rome. In a sermon preached at St Mary's Church, Oxford, on Guy Fawkes Day 1843, he rejected papal claims to supreme jurisdiction over the spiritual and temporal realms. Instead, he argued that in Britain, 'both the Spiritualty [*sic*] and Temporalty [*sic*] of this Church and Realm severally possess full authority and jurisdiction derived to them by succession and devolution; and that both, under Christ alone, are within their respective spheres perfect and complete'. Manning stated emphatically that '[t]here does not exist any fountain of jurisdiction below Christ the Head of all, on whose will and authority the acts of either for right or for validity depend.' Moreover, he stressed that the 'Church is to be found in the independent action of the "Episcopatus unus concordi numerositate diffusus"'.[30]

In a passage which harked back to his undergraduate essay, Manning stated in *Unity of the Church* that revealed truth which had been received by the apostles from Christ, and preserved intact by the Holy Spirit since the day of Pentecost through the succession of bishops, continued to be available to humanity. 'This [truth] is directly encountered by the delivery of a dogmatic faith embodied in creeds and Catholic traditions; and the probation of the moral reason is brought to a point by the subjection of men as learners to an order of men who are divinely commissioned to teach.' Manning stressed that 'the objective Unity of the Church tries man in the two points of moral duty least akin to his fallen nature – forbearance and submission'.[31]

As one looks back over Manning's line of argument during this period, fissures appear. He had articulated his understanding of the rule of faith for Anglicanism in 1838; however, his means of judging that rule of faith – when disputes arose – departed from Roman Catholic and Protestant resolutions. Instead, he argued that disputes over apostolic truth could be resolved by the intellectual and critical labours of theologians and historians. Yet a statement in his *Unity of the Church* (1845) seemed to suggest problems with this solution. While he called the believer to submit to those who held legitimate apostolic authority, he rejected theories of infallibility, and asserted that when Church leaders lost their way, individual believers must engage in the hard labour of sorting through competing truth claims. He asserted that his Church was a branch of the Church catholic; yet he had difficulty resolving the national character of the Church into which he had been born. After Newman's 1845 conversion, Manning confronted these anomalies, and struggled to work out these pressing problems; for he longed for certainty in his appeal to apostolic truth that bore the marks of *universitas, antiquitas, et consensio*.

Just two days before Newman's reception into the Roman Catholic Church (8 October 1845), Manning lamented that Anglican theology 'is a chaos [with] ... no principles, no form, no order, or structure, or science'. He looked to the deductive precision of scholastic theology, grounded in revealed truth, to provide 'proof as exact as the inductive sciences'.[32] While Manning declared that '[n]o living man has so powerfully affected me: and there is no mind I have so reverenced',[33] after reading Newman's *An Essay on the Development of Christian Doctrine* he wrote to William Ewart Gladstone on 26 December 1845 that he remained where he was before.[34] Yet Newman's book motivated him to take up the subject of first principles – the 'necessity of decisions open to no review' – and do his best to resolve these for himself and others disturbed by Newman's theory. He confessed to Gladstone that Newman's book demanded a 'higher theology', and acknowledged that 'I cannot do things for the nonce, or patch an inconsistent theory.'

While he admitted his sense of inadequacy, Manning did hope to 'find ultimate positions in which I can stand and work for life, in my poor way'.[35] Four days later, in a letter to Robert Wilberforce, he declared development the destitute refuge of Protestants and Romanists. The faith had been perfected at Pentecost and the only developments were logical and verbal, 'not ideal or *conceptual*'.[36] On 6 March 1846 Manning wrote to Gladstone that he had 'launched out to try what I can do on the science of proof in Theology'. Yet he stated clearly that 'I am a long way off from Development.' He doubted the viability of Newman's theory of development, and speculated that its impact would not be seen soon, 'Certainly not for a long time'.[37] Just four days later he observed to another correspondent that 'the Tridentine Doctors would have severely censured the modern theories of development, or gradual rise as false, and dangerous – and I hold their principle.'[38] This appeal to the council fathers of Trent signalled a shift for Manning – a transition that had wider implications.

By the spring of 1846 Manning raised questions that cast doubt on his critique of the Roman Catholic doctrine of the infallibility of the Church. In May 1846, after his sister-in-law Sophie Ryder and her family converted to Roman Catholicism, Manning confided to his journal, 'I am conscious to myself of an extensively changed feeling towards the Church of Rome. It seems to me nearer to the truth and the Church of England in greater peril.' In July 1846, he articulated his concern over the apostolic character of the Anglican episcopate: 'I have felt that the Episcopate of the English Church is secularised and bound down beyond hope ... I feel as if a light had fallen on me.' Manning acknowledged, 'I am further from the English Church and nearer Rome than I ever was – How do I know where I may be two years hence? Where was Newman five years ago?'[39] His health declined, and a nervous facial tic began.[40]

Early in 1847, Manning fell seriously ill and by February he feared that it might be life-threatening. The malady baffled physicians. While Robert Gray hinted that the root cause was psychosomatic, what can be said with certainty is that he spent three months confined to his home convalescing.[41] During this period, Manning read works by Pope Leo the Great, Pope Gregory the Great, Augustine and Optatus.[42] He also studied Melchior Cano's treatment of the infallibility of the Church and the pope in his *De locis theologicis* (1563). As he worked through these theological texts, he also drafted volume four of his *Sermons* (published 1850)[43] and came to an overt understanding of a principle he had invoked since 1834. He stated in later autobiographical notes, 'I began to find and to express the truth which afterwards brought me into the Church: and has filled my mind with increasing light to this day: I mean the Personal coming, abiding and office of the Holy Ghost.' He attributed this insight to Cano.[44] Yet evidence presented earlier demonstrates that this theological premise had been central for Manning since 1834. Melchior Cano's more probable influence centred on Manning's shifting disposition towards the infallibility of the Church, and whether the pope – as head of the Church – was infallible. On 20 April 1847, Manning noted in his diary two questions that vexed him: '1. Is it the will of our Lord Jesus Christ that His flock should be subject to Saint Peter and his successors? 2. Is it part of the mystery of Pentecost that the Church should be infallible?' The notes that followed indicate that Manning leaned towards admitting, '1. The Infallibility of the Church, 2. The Church of Rome that Church'.[45]

In July 1847, Manning embarked on a Roman holiday. While physical recuperation provided the pretext, he remained focused on his interior turmoil. On 5 July 1847 Manning recorded in his diary, 'To-morrow by the will of God I go forth, it may be for a year, it may be for ever. I feel to be in His hands. I know not what is good for myself.'[46] While his progress to Rome is recounted in detail elsewhere, diary entries provide an inventory of religious practice on the Continent – Catholics always cast in a positive light, and Protestant deficiencies recorded in detail.[47] He finally arrived in Rome on 28 November 1847, and seemed enthralled by his five months there.[48] Though Manning and Newman met on three consecutive days, neither recorded the substance of their discussions, and Newman left for England in early December.[49] It is not surprising that, in January 1848, Manning reported to Robert Wilberforce, 'Things seem to me clearer, plainer, shapelier and more harmonious; things which were only in the head have got down into the heart.'[50] A month later he wrote:

> There are truths so primary and despotic that I cannot elude them ... Such is the Infallibility of the Mystical Body of Christ on Earth, through the Indwelling of the Holy Spirit. I could as soon disbelieve the Canon of Scripture, or the perpetuity of the Church. Infallibility is not an accident; it is a property as inseparable by the Divine Will as perpetuity. This is evident to me from Holy Scripture, from Catholic Tradition, from internal and necessary relations of Divine Truth and Divine acts, as well as from reasons which alone would prove nothing.[51]

While Manning sojourned in Rome, Prime Minister John Russell nominated Oxford's Regius Professor of Divinity, Renn Dickson Hampden, to the bishopric of Hereford in December 1847. Despairing, Manning confided to Robert Wilberforce in February 1848 the personal angst Hampden's case generated in him. Shedding forever the appeal to universal ancient consensus in tradition, he stated: 'It is useless to offer me antiquity for my foundation. What do I know of antiquity? At my next birthday, if I live, I shall be forty. I must rest [on] something which itself rests continuously on antiquity, whose consciousness is therefore continuous, running down from the Day of Pentecost to this hour.' He concluded, 'God knows that I would rather stand in the lowest place within the Truth, than in the highest without it. Nay outside the Truth the higher the worst ... If I could but know *one* great truth, all would be clear.'[52]

Although Manning had a lengthy private audience with Pius IX on 8 May 1848, three days before his return to England, he made no record in his diary beyond, 'Audience to-day at the Vatican'. Decades later he explained, 'I remember the pain I felt at seeing how unknown we were to the Vicar of Jesus Christ. It made me feel our isolation.'[53]

If Manning was Romeward bound, his resolve seemed to dissipate on his return to England. Gladstone recalled Manning stating firmly 'that the English Church ... is a living portion of the Church of Christ'.[54] Indeed, John Keble reported to Edward Bouverie Pusey that same month that Manning had returned from Rome a stalwart Anglican.[55] Even more striking was his *Charge* – published July 1848 – as archdeacon of Chichester. In this sixty-two page document, Manning defended the

Church of England in the wake of Hampden's consecration as bishop of Hereford. Because Hampden had not been convicted of heresy by a Church tribunal and had subscribed to the Thirty-nine Articles, Manning argued, the Church of England stood vindicated.[56] Yet when he sent a copy of the *Charge* to his former tutor, friend and confidant, George Moberly, he explained: "'My opinions are what they were when I wrote to you from Rome. My Charge is the case for the Church of England'".[57] No conclusive judgment can be made of his interior motives.[58] Manning's resolve and sense of duty seemed intact during Holy Week 1849, when he wrote to Mary Wilberforce, 'My deep belief is that He wills me to be where I am; and all those whom He has submitted to me.'[59] Yet by Advent of the same year, he admitted to her, 'I have felt and do feel an overwhelming fear lest I should be under an illusion.'[60]

Manning had spent much of 1849 consumed by the Gorham Case. George Gorham, an Evangelical cleric whom the bishop of Exeter had refused to install in a living because he rejected baptismal regeneration, had taken the bishop to court. Despite a series of lost court cases, Gorham continued to appeal until he reached the ultimate British court, the Judicial Committee of the Privy Council.[61] Manning pored over Anglican canon law and applied it 'like arguments from pure mathematics'.[62] If the Church was infallible, the Gorham case seemed to argue against the Church of England being that Church. In a letter to Samuel Wilberforce, dated 24 January 1850, Manning explained that 'The Appeal removes the final decision of a question involving both doctrine and discipline out of the Church to another centre and that a Civil Court.'[63]

As he struggled with the current events of 1849, Manning revised the fourth volume of his sermons, drafted during his 1847 illness,[64] and saw them through to their final proofs in the latter months of that year. The overt subject of the collection was the nature of the Church, its sacraments, and their impact on individual Christians. Yet in his private correspondence, the driving issue was the infallibility of the Church. He explained to Mary Wilberforce on 2 July 1849 that he intended 'to publish as full a book on the subject of infallibility as I have a light to make. And by that book to take my path.'[65] In this collection Manning articulated the dramatic alteration in his ideas about the nature of truth, the Church and the working of the Holy Spirit.[66] In *The Analogy of Nature*, Manning posed a question which echoed the problem explored in his undergraduate essay: 'What is the proper faculty or instrument by which the truth is to be apprehended?' The answer to this rhetorical homiletic question was simple in its directness: 'By faith'. In a starkly bifurcated analysis, Manning stated unambiguously that we either know truth 'by discovery or reception ... by reasoning or by faith'. To underline this conclusion he stated emphatically, 'there is no third way'.[67] Truth had been given 'to the prophets, by the inspiration of God; to the Apostles, by the descent of the Holy Ghost, by the presence and guidance of Christ'.[68] That gift had been received by faith and was perpetuated by faith. 'It was not first *given*, then left to be *discovered*; first consigned to faith, then to be proved by reason'.[69] For Manning, the ultimate proof rested in his understanding of apostolic succession, the human agency through which the Holy Spirit preserved and perpetuated revealed truth.[70]

After attacking Butlerian appeals to the analogy of nature and to discerning truth through reasoning, Manning stated, 'faith means trust in divine authority ... But faith is an infused grace of God'.[71] In *The Intuition of Faith*, Manning clarified that 'Faith is a spiritual consciousness of the world unseen, infused into us, in our regeneration, by the supernatural gift of God.'[72] Tying the infallibility of God to the infallibility of the Church, he presented his reader with a striking dilemma:

> The infallibility of the Church is made up of these two elements; perfect certainty in the object revealed, and spiritual illumination in the subject which perceives it, that is, the Church itself. Shake this foundation, and faith becomes uncertainty; and what is uncertainty, as a rule of life or as a principle of action? ... What gives to faith its confidence of trust, its enduring strength in action, its intense insight in contemplation? Certainty founded on revelation. And what is the very first idea of revelation, but a clear and infallible knowledge of the truth given direct from God?[73]

Manning assured his reader that preservation and perpetuation of truth was an office of the Holy Spirit, always present in the mystical body of Christ.[74] While not explicitly stated in his sermons, Manning's line of reasoning pointed towards conclusions that he had communicated only to his journal: that the bishop of Rome was the infallible judge of doctrine by virtue of his role as Peter's apostolic successor, and the ultimate expression of the unity of the episcopate.[75]

Despite refining the theological case for leaving the Church of England and becoming a Roman Catholic, Manning continued in his Anglican affiliation through 1850 and into 1851. On 19 March 1850, two days after the positive outcome of Gorham's appeal, Manning led a group of clergy in drafting a repudiation of the Gorham decision, which appeared in *The Times* of London on 20 March. The Gorham decision severed the final tie binding him to the Church of England.[76] On 30 June 1850, Manning confided to his sister, Caroline Austen, his struggles with '"whether the Church of England be a Divine or a human society"'.[77] On 5 August 1850, Manning admitted to a female disciple that the Gorham case had taken its toll. He explained, 'I always felt that the Low Church had no objective Truths, and the High Church little subjective religion. Now I see that in the Catholic System the objective and subjective are the concave and the convex ... God and man are one by Incarnation. A Theology of 300 years is in conflict with a Faith of 1,800 years. I was born in the 300. My mature thoughts transplant me into the 1,800.'[78]

Though his reception into the Roman Catholic Church did not occur until months later, the final trajectory was evident.[79] On 8 September 1850, Gladstone wrote to Samuel Wilberforce and observed that if Manning converted, 'he will do it upon the broad grounds reaching far back into history as well as forward into the future'.[80] On 14 September 1850, Samuel Wilberforce affirmed this judgment: 'It is, as you say, the broad ground of historical inquiry where our paths part.' He described a frame of mind that focused on ancient practices, and ignored subsequent corruptions, 'until a system which wants them seems to him incomplete and uncatholic and one which has them is the wiser and holier and more catholic for having them'.[81]

In the end, external events forced Manning to act. On 29 September 1850, Pius IX created twelve episcopal jurisdictions in England. The following day Nicholas Wiseman, newly appointed archbishop of Westminster, was made a cardinal. In an exuberant act of indiscretion, Wiseman issued on 7 October a pastoral letter commonly called *Out of the Flaminian Gate of Rome*. The decorous language of the pastoral, though standard for Roman Catholic documents of the period, conjured up the worst anti-papal prejudices of the English people. It concluded with a call for the faithful to pray for the Pope's long life, 'and that consolations, temporal and spiritual, may be poured out upon him abundantly, in compensation for past sorrows and past ingratitude'.[82] Reaction against *The Papal Aggression*, as it became known, not only resulted in the pelting of Catholic priests in the streets and the smashing of Catholic chapel windows, but also turned iconoclastic ire on the 'mummeries of superstition' in the Church of England. Tractarian-inspired liturgies were disturbed, and anti-ritual riots occurred.[83] After denouncing the papal actions in a public letter dated 4 November 1850, Prime Minister John Russell went on to highlight a danger he found more alarming than aggression by a 'foreign sovereign'. He denounced '[c]lergymen of our own Church, who ... have been most forward in leading their flocks "step by step to the very verge of the precipice"'.[84] Russell decried the veneration of saints, 'the muttering of the liturgy', use of the sign of the cross, encouragement of auricular confession and promotion of 'the claim of infallibility for the Church'.[85] Queen Victoria shared Russell's views – especially concerning Tractarian clergy – though she lamented the demonstrations of intolerance and acts of violence.[86]

On 7 November 1850, Manning described in detail to Robert Wilberforce the dilemma he faced. The clergy of Chichester were pressuring him to 'convene this archdeaconry against the act of the Pope'.[87] On 15 November 1850 he wrote to Wilberforce again and described his meeting with the bishop. Manning had told the bishop that the Royal Supremacy violated Christ's law, that it severed the Church of England from the Church universal, and that the Pope acted legitimately, because the English episcopate stood outside the universal Church. He had proposed to resign at once, or convene the clergy, express his dissent, and then resign. The bishop endorsed the latter proposal.[88] Manning related these events to James Hope on 23 November 1850, explaining that the clerical 'anti-Popery cry' had 'driven me to a decision'.[89] Manning fulfilled his last duty as archdeacon of Chichester. He opened the meeting without an address and presided over the passage of resolutions against the 'Papal Aggression'. In response to their vote of thanks to him, Manning explained to the assembled clergy that he 'had been separated in conviction and action from them'. Amid tears and great emotions, he announced his resignation as archdeacon and left the meeting. On 8 December 1850 (Feast of the Immaculate Conception), Manning left Lavington – his long-time parish and home – and returned only once, after his conversion, to pack his books.[90]

While Manning's withdrawal from Anglican responsibilities became the object of intense reaction from concerned friends – Gladstone foremost among them – it was his eldest brother, Frederick Manning, who touched a most sensitive nerve. His brother could not understand how his Anglican brother of 1835 could have become the papist brother of 1850. On 5 December 1850, Henry responded that a 'perfect identity of principle' had governed his actions since 1835, and that what appeared to be inconsistency was in truth 'expansion'. In a complicated analogy, he asserted that what had changed was his awareness of 'facts'. As he explained, 'I mistook this and that proof; I was ignorant of this and that evidence. I did not perceive this or that error in my own statement. I did my sum *wrong* . . . The fault is mine, but the sum bears proof now.' In conclusion he quoted Romans 3:4 and observed, '"Let God be true and every man a liar," much more let me be scourged as inconsistent. But His Truth is not mine but His.'[91] Manning's defiant reaction to fraternal chastisement has the ring of truth. Over that period Manning had worked out the logical implications of his trajectory of thought. If apostolic succession was true and the basis of the Church's continuous tradition, then one's quest for Christian truth stretched back to the day of Pentecost, when the Church was founded. The Holy Spirit, who endowed the apostles with that truth, must have preserved it from corruption and would not have abandoned the faithful and forced them to rediscover saving knowledge through human ratiocination. Thus, the truth could not be subject to change or development through the passage of time.[92] As he reached the end of his Anglican life, Manning determined that his first principles were incomplete without a living judge to adjudicate disputes over the rule of faith (scripture and tradition). Only a living judge, endowed with spiritual authority by the Holy Spirit, could discern and proclaim the truth of the day of Pentecost to each successive generation. With this theory fully formed and shaped into a deeply held conviction, Henry Manning converted to Roman Catholicism with an apodictic certainty that shaped his worldview for the rest of his life. While prior scholarship has in one way or another acknowledged Manning's mistrust of the 'scientific' endeavours of his age, Manning's quest for a 'living judge' who could 'discern and proclaim the truth of the day of Pentecost' helps explain his Roman Catholic quest for a definition of papal infallibility. It is crucial for understanding how he could declare, in the wake of Vatican I, that the dogma of papal infallibility was 'the triumph of dogma over history'.[93]

Notes

1. Oxford, Bodleian Library, MS. Eng. Misc. d. 1278, 'English Essay No. 11', fo. 22.
2. *Ibid.*, fo. 42.
3. *Ibid.*, fos 44–5.
4. For an account of his early years, see Robert Gray, *Cardinal Manning: A Biography* (London: Weidenfeld & Nicolson, 1985), chs. 1–2.
5. Limitations of space do not permit a deeper analysis of this very important dimension of Manning's formation. The influence of his Quaker friend, Favell Bevan, is notable; and his wife's Evangelical background no doubt influenced his understanding of the affective experience of faith. Peter Nockles has written on this subject and distilled the complex co-mingling of his High Church instincts with the Evangelical fervour he encountered in early adulthood. Peter B. Nockles, 'The Oxford Movement and Evangelicalism: Parallels

and Contrasts in Two Nineteenth-Century Movements of Religious Renewal', in Robert Webster (ed.), *Perfecting Perfection: Essays in Honor of Henry D. Rack* (Eugene, OR: Pickwick Publications, 2015), pp. 233–59, esp. pp. 244–8. See also James Pereiro, *Cardinal Manning: An Intellectual Biography* (Oxford: Oxford University Press, 1998), p. 14. For more on the complex role of Evangelicals, some of whom became Tractarians, see Gareth Atkins, 'Evangelicals', in Frederick D. Aquino and Benjamin J. King (eds), *The Oxford Handbook of John Henry Newman* (Oxford: Oxford University Press, 2018), pp. 173–95.

6 David Newsome, *The Convert Cardinals: John Henry Newman and Henry Edward Manning* (London: John Murray, 1993), p. 47; Christopher O'Gorman, 'A History of Henry Manning's Religious Opinions, 1808–1832', *Recusant History*, 21:2 (October 1992), 161.

7 John Henry Newman, *The Letters and Diaries of John Henry Newman*, 32 vols, ed. C. S. Dessain et al., (London: Thomas Nelson; Oxford: Oxford University Press, 1961–2008), vol. 4, p. 92.

8 O'Gorman, 'Religious Opinions', 163.

9 David Newsome, *The Wilberforces and Henry Manning: The Parting of Friends* (Cambridge, MA: The Belknap Press of Harvard University Press, 1966), p. 202. Pereiro identified 1847 as the year Manning came to this insight; yet evidence suggests a continuity of theological reflection that expanded over time. James Pereiro, 'The Mystical Body of Christ: Manning's Ecclesiology in His Late Anglican Period', in V. Alan McClelland (ed.), *By Whose Authority? Newman, Manning, and the Magisterium* (Bath: Downside Abbey, 1996), p. 169.

10 Henry Manning, *The English Church, Its Succession, and Witness for Christ* (London: Rivington, 1835), p. 5.

11 *Ibid.*, p. 7.

12 *Ibid.*, p. 8.

13 *Ibid.*, p. 9.

14 *Ibid.*, pp. 9–10.

15 *Letters and Diaries of Newman*, vol. 5, p. 237, n. 3. The italics are found in the original text.

16 See Pereiro, 'The Mystical Body of Christ', p. 168.

17 Nicholas Wiseman, *Lectures on the Principal Doctrines and Practices of the Catholic Church*, vol. 1, 2nd edn (London: Charles Dolman, 1836), pp. 29–30.

18 *Ibid.*, vol. 1, p. 30.

19 Henry Manning, *The Rule of Faith: A Sermon* (London: Rivington, 1838), pp. 41–2.

20 Manning, *The Rule of Faith: Appendix* (London: Rivington, 1838), p. 62.

21 *Ibid.*, p. 112.

22 Manning, *The Rule of Faith: A Sermon*, p. 44.

23 Manning, *The Rule of Faith: Appendix*, p. 112. The italics are found in the original text.

24 *Ibid.*, p. 87. The italics are found in the original text.

25 *Ibid.*, pp. 100–1.

26 Oxford, Bodleian Library, MS Eng. Lett. c. 653, Manning to Julius Hare, 21 July 1841, fo. 136.

27 Henry Manning, *The Unity of the Church* (London: John Murray, 1845), pp. 280–1.

28 *Ibid.*, pp. 86, 162. See Pereiro's examination of this matter in *Manning*, p. 42.

29 V. Alan McClelland, '"A Stranger and Dark unto Himself": Manning's Second "Conversion", 1844–1847', in McClelland (ed.), *By Whose Authority?*, p. 195. Emphasis mine. For references to the *Religio Anglo-Catholici*, see Revd Alphonse Chapeau, 'Manning the Anglican', in John Fitzsimons (ed.), *Manning: Anglican and Catholic* (London: Burns and Oates, 1951), p. 13; Albert Schmitt, 'Kardinal Manning', *Erbe und Auftrag*, 39 (1963), 106. The most extensive treatment of the *Religio Anglo-Catholici* can be found in Alphonse Chapeau, 'La vie anglicaine de Manning' (PhD thesis, Université de Paris, 1955), pp. 425–30. This manuscript may now be found in London, Westminster Diocesan Archives, among the Manning-Chapeau Papers.
30 Henry Manning, *Sermons Preached before the University of Oxford* (Oxford: John Henry Parker, 1844), p. 92.
31 Manning, *Unity*, pp. 268–9.
32 Edmund Sheridan Purcell, *Life of Cardinal Manning, Archbishop of Westminster*, 2 vols (London: Macmillan, 1896), vol. 1, pp. 504–5.
33 Atlanta, Georgia, Emory University, Pitts Library Archives, Manning Collection, Box 1, Folder 22, Manning to Gladstone, 29 October 1845.
34 Shane Leslie, *Henry Edward Manning: His Life and Labours* (New York: P. J. Kenedy and Sons, 1921), pp. 66–7.
35 Henry Manning, 'Letters of Manning to Gladstone: 1837–1851', in Chapeau, 'La Vie Anglicaine de Manning', pp. 188–9. The full text can also be found in: [Shane Leslie], 'Manning and Gladstone: The "Destroyed" Letters', *Dublin Review*, 138 (1906), 52–4.
36 Oxford, Bodleian Library, MS. Eng. Lett. c. 655, Manning to Robert Wilberforce, 30 December 1845, fo. 34r. Italicised text is underlined in the original.
37 Atlanta, Georgia, Emory University, Pitts Library, Manning Collection, Box 1, Folder 22, Manning to Gladstone, 6 March 1846.
38 Oxford, Bodleian Library, MS. Eng. Lett. c. 662, Manning to unknown correspondent, 10 March 1846, fo. 68r.
39 Purcell, *Manning*, vol. 1, pp. 484–7. Chapeau, 'Manning the Anglican', p. 20.
40 R. J. Gasquet, *Cardinal Manning* (London: Catholic Truth Society, 1895), p. 46.
41 Gray, *Cardinal Manning*, p. 115.
42 Chapeau, 'Manning the Anglican', p. 23. Optatus's singular work, 'Against Parmenian the Donatist', provided the starting point for Augustine's work against the Donatists. His argument attacked their 'catholicity' and claims to holiness. For an extended study, see José Luis Gutiérrez-Martín, *Iglesia y Liturgía en el Africa Romana del Siglo IV: Bautismo y Eucaristía en Los Libros de Optato, Obispo de Milevi* (Roma, CLV, 2001).
43 Pereiro, *Manning*, p. 78.
44 Chapeau, 'Manning the Anglican', p. 23. See also Robert Ornsby, *Memoirs of James Robert Hope-Scott*, 2 vols (London: John Murray, 1884), vol. 2, p. 91; Oxford, Bodleian Library, MS Eng. Lett. c. 656, Manning to Robert Wilberforce, 22 January 1851, fo. 108.
45 Purcell, *Manning*, vol. 1, p. 487.
46 *Ibid.*, vol. 1, p. 342.
47 *Ibid.*, vol. 1, pp. 343–61.
48 *Ibid.*, vol. 1, pp. 362–417.
49 Gray, *Cardinal Manning*, p. 121; *Letters and Diaries of Newman*, vol. 12, p. 154.

50 Oxford, Bodleian Library, MS. Eng. Lett. c. 655, fo. 62.
51 *Ibid.*, fo. 63v.
52 *Ibid.*, fos 63v–64v. Printed text found in Purcell, *Manning*, vol. 1, pp. 512–13. Emphasis in the original.
53 *Ibid.*, vol. 1, p. 416.
54 *Ibid.*, vol. 1, p. 570.
55 Georgina Battiscombe, *John Keble: A Study in Limitations* (New York: Alfred A. Knopf, 1964), p. 304.
56 Henry Manning, *A Charge Delivered at the Ordinary Visitation of the Archdeaconry of Chichester, July 1848* (London: John Murray, 1848).
57 John Bodley, *Cardinal Manning. The Decay of Idealism in France. The Institute of France* (London: Longmans, Green, and Co., 1912), p. 27.
58 Perry Butler, *Gladstone: Church, State, and Tractarianism* (Oxford: Clarendon Press, 1982), pp. 200–1; Purcell, *Manning*, vol. 1, pp. 569–70; Bodley, *Cardinal Manning*, pp. 27–8. Pereiro, *Manning*, p. 108.
59 Oxford, Bodleian Library, MS. Eng. Lett. c. 655, fo. 110r. Printed text available in Newsome, *The Parting of Friends*, p. 326.
60 Oxford, Bodleian Library, MS. Eng. Lett. c. 655, fo. 138r.
61 Gray, *Cardinal Manning*, pp. 131–2.
62 *Guardian*, 17 July 1850, as quoted in Arthur Wollaston Hutton, *Cardinal Manning* (London: Methuen & Co., 1894), p. 66.
63 Newsome, *The Parting of Friends*, p. 350. Manning worked out elements of this argument in his 12 and 18 January 1850 letters to Robert Wilberforce. See Oxford, Bodleian Library, MS. Eng. Lett. c. 655, fos 150r–158v.
64 *Ibid.*, fos 131r–132v.
65 *Ibid.*, fo. 136v.
66 See Pereiro, *Manning*, pp. 80–104; Pereiro, 'The Mystical Body of Christ', pp. 168–86.
67 Henry Manning, 'The Analogy of Nature', published in Henry Manning, *Sermons* (London: William Pickering, 1850), vol. 4, p. 168.
68 *Ibid.*, pp. 168–9.
69 *Ibid.*, p. 169.
70 *Ibid.*, pp. 169–70.
71 *Ibid.*, p. 171. For more on Manning's critique of Butler's appeal to probability, see Pereiro, *Manning*, pp. 100–3.
72 Henry Manning, 'The Intuition of Faith', published in Henry Manning, *Sermons*, vol. 4, p. 377.
73 *Ibid.*, p. 171.
74 *Ibid.*, p. 172.
75 For examples of this in the Manning diaries, see Purcell, *Manning*, vol. 1, pp. 482–8.
76 Gray, *Cardinal Manning*, p. 133.
77 Purcell, *Manning*, vol. 1. p. 548.
78 Leslie, *Manning*, p. 91.
79 See his letters to Robert Wilberforce: Oxford, Bodleian Library, MS. Eng. Lett. c. 656, fos 33r–179v; see esp. fos 33r–40v. Gray, *Cardinal Manning*, p. 135.

80 Oxford, Bodleian Library, MS. Eng. Lett. c. 193, 8 September 1850.
81 London, British Library, Add. MS. 44343, Samuel Wilberforce to William Gladstone, 14 September 1850, fos 120r–v.
82 *English Historical Documents: 1833–1874*, 12 vols, ed. by G. M. Young and W. D. Handcock (Oxford: Oxford University Press, 1956), vol. 9, pp. 365–7.
83 E. R. Norman, *Anti-Catholicism in Victorian England* (New York: Barnes & Noble, Inc., 1968), p. 62. Also see Dennis Gwynn, *A Hundred Years of Catholic Emancipation 1829–1929* (London: Longmans, Green and Co., 1929), pp. 96–7.
84 *English Historical Documents: 1833–1874*, vol. 9, p. 368. The quote is from Bishop Blomfield's 'Charge' to the London Diocese, published 2 November 1850. Blomfield was a High Churchman who distanced himself from 'Puseyites'. Walter Walsh, *The History of the Romeward Movement in the Church of England: 1833–1864* (London: James Nisbet and Co., 1900), pp. 315–16.
85 *English Historical Documents: 1833–1874*, vol. 1, p. 368.
86 *The Letters of Queen Victoria*, 3 vols., ed. by Arthur C. Benson and Viscount Esher (London: John Murray, 1907), vol. 2, pp. 331, 336, 337. In a letter to her uncle, the King of Belgium, Victoria observed, 'this *unfortunate* "Papal Aggression" business' had resulted in one good effect: 'that of directing people's serious attention to the very alarming tendency of the *Tractarians*, which was doing *immense* harm'. *Ibid.*, p. 334.
87 Oxford, Bodleian Library, MS. Eng. Lett. c. 656, fos 77r–80v.
88 *Ibid.*, fos 87r–88v.
89 Ornsby, *Memoirs*, vol. 2, p. 69.
90 Purcell, *Manning*, vol. 1, pp. 579–80.
91 *Ibid.*, pp. 586–7.
92 Henry Manning's embrace of scholastic principles brought with it an ahistorical, static understanding of the preservation of truth received through the Holy Spirit on the day of Pentecost. When Newman converted to Roman Catholicism and published his *Essay on the Development of Christian Doctrine* (1845), Manning wrote that he considered 'development' the destitute refuge of Protestants and Roman Catholics. The truth had been perfected on the day of Pentecost, and any developments were logical and verbal, 'not ideal or conceptual'. Oxford, Bodleian Library, MS. Eng. Lett. c. 655, fo. 34r, Manning to Robert Wilberforce, 30 December 1845. For a more detailed treatment of this matter, see Kenneth L. Parker, 'Historical Consciousness and the First Vatican Council: Manning, Döllinger, Newman, and Acton's Uses of "History" in the Papal Infallibility Debates', in Kenneth L. Parker and Erick H. Moser (eds), *The Rise of Historical Consciousness Among the Christian Churches* (New York: University Press of America, 2013), pp. 89–113, esp. pp. 91–4.
93 Henry Manning, *Religio Viatoris*, 4th edn (London: Burns and Oates, n.d.), p. 79. He went on to observe, 'The scientific historian reads the history of the Catholic Church in one sense, the Catholic Church reads its own history in another. Choose which you will believe.' *Ibid.*, p. 80.

'Am I my brother's keeper?' Cardinal Manning and the Jewish People

JAMES PEREIRO, UNIVERSITY OF NAVARRA

Abstract

Henry Edward Manning (1808–92) was involved in some of the most pressing social issues of his time, from the defence of workers and trade unionism to finding a solution for the dock strike and the education of the poor. English Catholic social conscience, as a whole and with some singular exceptions, was somewhat slow in following the leadership of the cardinal in some of these matters. This article studies a barely known aspect of Manning's social activity: his involvement in the British response to the Russian pogroms of 1881–82 and in other contemporary Jewish issues.

Keywords: Cardinal Henry Edward Manning; Jews; Catholic Church; Mortara; Russia; pogroms; Blood Libel

Henry Edward Manning's engagement with many contemporary social questions is well known to historians. His work in favour of the Jewish people, however, has not received the same attention.[1] Manning's concern with the London poor and his awareness of their needs led him to admire Jewish care for the disadvantaged in their community; indeed, he held it as an example for Catholics to imitate. It was not, however, until the early 1880s that he became directly involved in Jewish issues; the occasion being the Russian pogroms of 1881–82 and the British appeal to the Tsar in favour of the Jews.

There are few references to Jewish questions in Manning's early writings and correspondence. Perhaps one of the first instances of his touching on the subject was in 1848. Catholic emancipation (1829) had opened the door for Catholics to participate more fully in the social life of the country after centuries of legal and political discrimination, if not always of open persecution. English Jews considered that this was a propitious time to ask for the removal of Jewish political disabilities, such as those that prevented them from being elected to Parliament. The question came to public attention after the election of Lionel de Rothschild for the City of London in the June 1847 election. He was unable to take his seat because of the requirement that those elected take the oath of allegiance 'on the faith of a Christian' in order to sit. The House of Commons hurriedly passed a bill proposing an oath that could be taken by those who were not Christian; the bill, however, was thrown out by the House of Lords.

William Ewart Gladstone was among those who had supported the bill.[2] Manning wrote to him a few days later and commented, among other things, on Gladstone's speech on the subject. Manning did so from the point of view of Richard Hooker's theory of the relationship of church and state in England. Within that perspective, Parliament was effectively the lay synod of the Church of England, with powers to control worship, doctrine and the appointment of bishops. The admission of Dissenters and Catholics to Parliament had already disturbed that notion; now, the admission of Jews would further imply abandonment of any idea of Parliament as a Christian assembly:

> As to the Jews I have doubts. It is a final abandonment of Christianity as a nation, which with you may perhaps weigh somewhat more than with me. A nation is represented by its organization. Denizens and sojourners unless they partake of that organization are in a nation but not of it. This is a distinction, however, which I feel to be of little worth in this case as a Socinian is to me less of a Christian than a Jew, if possible ... The Jews were in it but not of it – and ill enough they fared – now we have inverted the order and are thrusting away the Christianity which formed us, first by the civil equality of all Christian sects, and now by the Equality of Christian and Jew.[3]

The Jews Relief Act, allowing Jews to sit in Parliament, was finally approved in 1858 after several attempts were frustrated by the House of Lords. All Catholic MPs voted for the measure. Manning, a Catholic since 1851, had by now given up his previous ideas of the nature of the relationship of the state and the Church of England. He did not, however, give up altogether his idea that Parliament had a moral role to play in the life of the nation, one it could hardly perform without the guidance of Judeo-Christian moral principles. It was on those bases that he would later oppose the admission of atheists like Charles Bradlaugh to Parliament.

The Mortara Case

The Mortara case caused a sensation in 1858. Edgardo Mortara, a 7-year-old Jewish boy from Bologna, then within the Papal States, had been taken from his parents on the allegation of a Catholic servant girl, who affirmed that she had baptised the boy during an illness which threatened his life. As a result, Edgardo was removed from the family home and transferred to Rome to be educated as a Catholic. Public opinion across Europe was soon mobilised to demand the return of the boy to his parents. In Great Britain, dignitaries political and ecclesiastical signed a letter addressed to the French ambassador, asking for France to exert pressure on the Pope to achieve that objective. The letter was signed by twenty-seven dukes (including the Duke of Wellington) and other peers, twenty-two archbishops and bishops (including the Anglican archbishops of Canterbury, York and Dublin), and thirty-six MPs.[4]

The Catholic reaction in England did not focus its attention on the merits of the Mortara case but on presenting what had happened in the Papal States as happening in reverse, and on a much larger scale, in this country. Thousands of Catholic children in workhouses and district poor schools were prevented from being educated in the religion of their parents. Catholic newspapers and periodicals pointed out that, ironically, the anti-Catholic cry had been specially taken up by the ultra-Protestants – among them the Evangelical Alliance – who, when the occasion arose, resisted the Poor Law Board's aim that children in care should be educated in the religion of their parents. The *Dublin Review*, in a lengthy article, also presented cases in which English and Irish courts had pronounced against the right of Catholic parents to have their children educated in their faith, ordering that they should be brought up as Protestants.[5] Dr Barnardo and his homes, later in the century, were particularly reluctant to surrender Catholic children to be educated in Catholic institutions, even when the courts had pronounced in favour of returning a Catholic child to the custody of his or her natural parents.

There do not seem to be any extant records of Manning's opinion on the Mortara case. However, his concern for the education of poor Catholic children was to be the cause of his association with it. In two of his first pastoral letters he dealt with the subject of education, and the topic would be the theme of many of his later pastorals. Manning considered that providing Catholic education for thousands of Catholic children left without proper instruction or training should be his first pastoral concern, and his intention was to delay the building of a Westminster Cathedral until provision had been made for them. In his Pastoral Letter of 8 June 1866 he complained that as many as a thousand Catholic children were detained in workhouses and workhouse schools, where the education was exclusively Protestant.[6] The word 'detained' was not an overstatement, given that the Guardians of Poor Law Schools objected to transferring Catholic children to Catholic institutions when these were provided, even when the Reformatory and Industrial Schools Acts established that parents, step-parents, or close relatives could apply for a child to be sent to a school where he or she could be educated in the Catholic faith.[7]

In 1869, Manning published his pastoral *Denominational Education*, defending the right of parents to educate their children. The pastoral affirmed: 'Every father and mother has by natural and Divine law the moral right and the moral duty to educate their children, and to determine the nature of that education ... The state has no rights, therefore no duties, higher than those of the parents. Sacerdotalism claims no such rights against the natural rights of parents.'[8] The *Jewish Chronicle* did not let Manning's pastoral pass without comment. Under the title 'Roman Catholics Liberal when not dominant', the *Chronicle* quoted Manning's words, focusing its attention on the last sentence: 'Sacerdotalism claims no such rights against the natural rights of parents.' The paper felt that this principle 'may need to be appealed to where the same church is in the ascendant'.[9] The *Chronicle* returned to the subject in a later issue, arguing that the principle enunciated by Manning should have been applied in the Mortara case. It was ironic, the paper added, that Manning had claimed there was no greater wrong than to rob an unconscious child of its religion: how could he excuse his own church tearing young Mortara from his parents?[10]

Roles were reversed in 1876 when the ultra-Protestant Committee for General Purposes of the Guardians of the City of London refused to hand over to the Jewish Board of Guardians a 7-year-old foundling, Samuel Fountain, who had been baptised and educated as a Christian, although he was a Jew. The Committee's reasoning was that Fountain was now a Christian and they were bound to take care of him until he was of an age to decide for himself. The *Jewish Chronicle* argued that this was the same reasoning adduced in the Mortara case, adding: 'The prince of the

Roman Catholic Church (Cardinal Antonelli) and the Ultra-Protestant Committee for General Purposes [are] at one when a Jewish child is to be kidnapped! How Cardinal Manning will chuckle.'[11]

The subordination of parental rights to the overriding consideration of the welfare of the child, which was at the heart of the arguments in the Mortara case and in the British case, were partially acknowledged in the Custody of Children Act of 1891 which established that the courts, having regard for the welfare of the child, should be satisfied that the parent was a fit person to be entrusted with his or her custody. The Act added that the courts would, however, have power to make orders in order to secure that the child be brought up in the religion in which the parent had a legal right to require such upbringing. There was, however, a further clause establishing that the courts would also have the power to consult the desires of the children and respect their freedom to decide.[12]

The Russian Pogroms

As mentioned, Manning became directly involved in Jewish concerns with occasion of the Russian Pogroms of 1881–82 and the British appeal to the Tsar in favour of the Jews. Russia, towards the end of the eighteenth century and at the beginning of the nineteenth, had considerably expanded its frontiers westwards from the Baltic to the Black Sea, absorbing a great part of what is now Lithuania, Poland and the Ukraine. In so doing Russia had annexed some territories in which the Jews made up 12–18 per cent of the total population. The subsequent policy of Russification – cultural and religious – of these territories and populations followed by successive tsars encountered opposition in just about all of them. In particular, the Jewish resistance to assimilation, or to conversion to the Orthodox Church, was as determined as it had been in other Christian lands all over Europe. In Russia, the failure of the policy of 'integration' gave place to one aimed at minimising what was considered the harmful influence of the Jews on the rest of society.[13]

The Jewish Pale of Settlement, established at the end of the eighteenth century in the new territories, restricted Jewish permanent right of residence and work outside the Pale, and, among other things, limited their right to buy farm land. There were some exceptions to this general rule. Jews practising certain professions, students, and some others were allowed to live outside the Pale. Their status, however, was precarious and subject to sudden reversals, leading to expulsion from the cities where they had settled. That was the fate, in 1891, of the Jews then living in Moscow.[14]

The assassination of Tsar Alexander II on 3 March 1881 marked a worsening in the situation of the Jewish people in Russia. One of those implicated in the murder was of Jewish origin and rumour added other Jews to the plot. This provided the pretext for anti-Jewish riots, particularly in the southern part of the Jewish Pale of Settlement. The loss of property, destroyed or stolen, was considerable, and thousands were left homeless. There were also numerous reports of violence, including the killing of some forty people during the riots. Different causes contributed to the spread of the disturbances, or prevented their effective control: economic depression and crop failures, traditional anti-Semitism and prejudice, rumours of an imperial ukase (or edict) favouring the anti-Jewish riots, accusations against Jews enriching themselves by usury ('Jewish exploitation'), the desire to gain possession of Jewish property or get rid of possible competitors in particular trades, the connivance or weakness of the authorities in some cases and, in others, their fear of intervening decisively in case the rioting might be turned into wider social disturbances. All these elements, in different degrees, according to time and place, played their part in the initiation and subsequent violence of the pogroms.[15] The report published by *The Times* suggested that the violence would never have reached the levels it had if there had been an official declaration against the existence of an imperial ukase or a more decisive military intervention to quell the riots.[16]

In view of the situation, the Board of Deputies and the Anglo-Jewish Alliance decided to intervene in support of their Russian brethren. On 25 May 1881 representatives of the Board met Earl Granville to ask the Foreign Office to make representations to the Russian government, seeking protection for Russian Jews from further outrage. Earl Granville 'stated in reply that this country would not be justified in making any kind of protests or representation to the Russian Government as the Great Powers were jealous of interference in their domestic concerns', adding that such intervention might actually make matters worse.[17] The Board and the Anglo-Jewish Association continued looking for ways to help Russian Jews and, in November of the same year, a Russo-Jewish Committee was constituted to consider measures to provide relief. The representatives of British Jews considered that the most effective way of presenting their case was to call on Christian leaders to convene meetings of protest against events in Russia. In those meetings, as recorded in the minutes of the Anglo-Jewish Association, the 'Jewish speakers should confine themselves to proposing and seconding votes', leaving speech-making to the Christian leaders.[18]

In the first week of 1882, before the publication in *The Times* of the long report on Russian events, Cardinal Manning had been approached by Sergeant-at-Law John Simon MP (later Sir John Simon) and his son Oswald, who briefed him about the sufferings of Russian Jews and asked him to support the call for a public meeting to address the issue.[19] Manning asked for, and was provided with, further information on recent events in Russia. He agreed with the suggestion that the Lord Mayor convene a meeting at the Mansion House, and he was indeed the first to sign the request, suggesting that the Archbishop of Canterbury should also be invited to do so. Manning further suggested several names as other possible signatories to the request; among them, that of the Duke of Norfolk.[20] The request was signed by some three dozen well-known clergy, academics, authors and a few politicians. The list was headed by the Archbishop of Canterbury, Cardinal Manning and Lord Shaftesbury.[21] The Lord Mayor of London convened the meeting on 1 February, in the Egyptian Hall at Mansion House.[22] Shaftesbury and Manning agreed to address it and to propose two of the four resolutions to be passed at it: Manning was to propose the second, the first being allocated to the Earl of Shaftesbury.

Manning's resolution read: 'That this meeting, while disclaiming any right or desire to interfere in the internal affairs of another country ... feels it its duty to express its opinion that the laws of Russia relating to Jews tend to degrade them in the eyes of the Christian population, and to expose Jewish subjects to the outbreaks of fanatical ignorance.'[23] His speech proposing the resolution was wide-ranging. Manning disclaimed any intention of interfering or dictating in the internal affairs of another country. However, he added, 'there are laws larger than any country's: the laws of humanity and of God'. And 'if in any legislation they be violated all the nations of Christian Europe, the whole commonwealth of civilized and Christian men would instantly acquire a right to speak out aloud'.[24] The Russian Jews, he added, were being degraded by having closed to them honourable careers of public life; they were restricted to living in certain places; and so on. Manning also made a reference to the anti-Semitic movement in Germany and the influence it might have had on Russian recent events.

According to the report in *The Times*, Manning thought that the atrocities against Jewish subjects of the Tsar had been given a certain degree of justification by General Nikolay Pavlovich Ignatyev, Russian Minister of the Interior, who had suggested that the riots had been a spontaneous outburst of popular anger against Jewish exploitation. After several months of pogroms, Ignatyev had issued a rescript containing not a word of censure for the atrocities. It did, however, appoint a Commission of Enquiry to study the poor condition of the southern provinces, which trades carried out by the Jews were injurious to inhabitants, and how to prevent Jews evading the laws that limited their right to buy and farm land. One of the measures taken at the time was a more stringent application of legal restrictions on Jewish right of domicile, which had been relaxed for some time. *The Times* account of the Egyptian Hall meeting included that:

> Manning, to loud cheers, went on to show his appreciation of the Jewish people, the eldest people upon earth. Russia, Austria and England are of yesterday compared with the imperishable people, which with an inextinguishable life, and immutable traditions and faith in God and in the laws of God, scattered as it is all over the world, passing through the fires unscathed, trampled into the dust and yet never combining with the dust into which it is trampled, lives still a witness and a warning to us. We are in the bonds of brotherhood with it. The New Testament rests upon the Old.[25]

He went on to praise the Jews in France and Germany, and particularly those in England: 'for uprightness, for refinement, for generosity, for charity, for all graces and virtues that adorn humanity where will be found examples brighter or more true of human excellence than in this Hebrew race.'[26] *The Times*, in its editorial of the following day, would comment that 'among many admirable speeches made yesterday that of CARDINAL MANNING is the most remarkable.'[27]

The fourth proposition approved at the Mansion House meeting established a fund to help the many Jews leaving Russia in search of a freer and better life. Manning was appointed a member of the Committee set up to administer what was to be known as the Mansion House Russian Relief Fund. The subscriptions collected on occasion of the meeting at Mansion House amounted to some £25,000. The first list of subscribers published by the *Observer* was headed by Messrs N. M. Rothschild and Sons from London and Messrs de Rothschild Brothers from Paris, each branch of the family donating £5,000.[28] The fund reached £100,000 in the next few months. Manning took an active part in the Committee's weekly meetings, presiding at them on many occasions, and that at a time when the influx of Russian refugees was as its height.[29] Among his suggestions was the creation of a subcommittee to consider and report on immediate steps to relieve the distress of the Russian Jews and of the refugees from that country, studying among other proposals the formation of Jewish colonies in America, a subject Manning discussed with the visionary Laurence Oliphant and with Sir Julian Goldsmith.[30]

The meetings and protests had little influence on developments in Russia. General Ignatyev's Commission of Enquiry concluded that the pogroms had been the result of Jewish oppression of the native agricultural population. Results of the enquiry included the May Laws of 1882, promulgated as 'a temporary measure, and until a general revision is made of their [the Jews'] legal status'. The May Laws reinforced the Pale of Settlement regime, restricting movements from towns to villages within the Pale, limiting the right to acquisition of property by Jews (particularly farms), and banning Sunday trading. Another of the provisions established that families not appearing in the local registry before May 1882 were to be deported. Given the condition or non-existence of local registries in many places, this lead to numerous deportations. The May Laws did not apply, however, in the Polish part of the Pale of Settlement.[31]

In March 1882 Manning's attention was directed by the Minister of the Great Synagogue Chambers at Manchester, Berendt Salomon, to the dangers threatening the Polish Jews. He asked Manning to petition for a Pastoral Letter from the Pope, to be read from pulpits, to prevent attacks on them. Manning responded by assuring Salomon that he was willing to do whatever possible to help, although he felt he could do little. Three weeks after receiving Manning's letter, Salomon learnt that a papal encyclical, along the lines he had suggested to the Cardinal, had been read in all the pulpits of the Catholic churches in Poland. He attributed this to Manning's intervention.[32] There were few and limited clashes between Jewish and Christian populations in Poland in 1881–82. According to Markowski, that these did not develop 'along pogroms lines, [was] owing to the actions of the administrative, police, and ecclesiastical authorities'.[33] The Polish Catholic clergy had expressed strong opposition to any violence against the Jews, and the Catholic press had joined in their condemnation.

The Blood Libel

Anti-Semitism would, however, continue to raise its ugly head in different parts of Europe, bringing up old and new charges against Jews. Among the old ones was the so-called 'Blood Libel', the accusation that the Jews kidnapped Christian children and used their blood for baking unleavened paschal bread. The accusation seems to have been first put into circulation in England by Thomas of Monmouth, in his *Life and Miracles of St William of Norwich* written in 1173.[34] The libel was to have momentous consequences, fuelling a fire of anti-Jewish suspicion and persecution all over Europe, where similar cases of child sacrifices were claimed to have taken place. It had become a common weapon in the panoply of anti-Semitism and was to surface in varied places well into the twentieth century, when it also played a role in Nazi propaganda.[35] The majority of the heads of church and state rejected the accusation from the first and opposed the circulation of the libel, beginning with Pope Innocent IV in 1247; his declaration being subsequently renewed by other popes. Perhaps the best known rejection of the libel is that of Cardinal Lorenzo Ganganelli, later Pope Clement XIV, in a report prepared for the Holy Office in 1758 at the request of Benedict XIV, to whom an appeal had been made by the Jews in Poland.[36]

Manning was also involved in efforts to prevent the spread of the Blood Libel. In 1889 Hermann Adler, at the time Acting Chief Rabbi of the British Empire, wrote to him bringing to the Cardinal's attention the publication in France of a book reviving the libel. It was not the only publication to do so at the time but, in this case, the author claimed that the book had been commended by Rome.[37] Manning responded by return of post, telling Adler that he was sending his letter to Rome without delay and assuring him that he had 'neither sympathy nor credulity for such horrors'. The response from Cardinal Mariano Rampolla was a disclaimer, saying that a formal letter of acknowledgement was sent to everyone who sent a book to the Pope before the book was examined and even before it was seen; it did not mean approval of the book as the author pretended and 'that nothing could be farther from the mind of the Pope than to wound gratuitously the susceptibilities of the Jewish people'.[38] Some thought at the time that there was a need for a clearer denunciation of the Blood Libel, as had been done by some of Leo XIII's predecessors, given that the libel continued to be spread around.

Manning's Jubilee and Renewed Troubles for Russian Jews

In 1890 Manning celebrated the silver jubilee of his episcopacy. The Council of the Anglo-Jewish Association noticed the occasion and, in its meeting of 6 July, decided to present him with a congratulatory address.[39] The *Jewish Chronicle*, reporting the decision, added a comment by Mr F. D. Mocatta to the effect that, 'if Cardinal Manning had been Chief Rabbi he could not have acted more energetically in favour of the Jews than he did on the occasion of the Russian persecution'.[40] The presentation took place on 30 October 1890, at Archbishop's House, Westminster.[41] Dr Adler, the Acting Chief Rabbi, prefaced the presentation with some personal remarks, saying that the Jewish representatives were there as Britons, to thank Manning for his labours on behalf of all in need, and as Jews, grateful for his intervention on their behalf. He then read the address. It made reference to Cardinal Manning's 'wide sympathy and the steadfast devotion to the interests of all sections of society' which had distinguished his life, mentioning some of the social concerns he had championed. The address, naturally, focused its attention on Manning's intervention at the Mansion House meeting in support of the persecuted Jewish people in Russia and his later participation in the Committee set up to provide for them. It ended by affirming that the memory of the Cardinal's 'words and actions in that season of affliction will not depart from us and our children'.[42]

The address, on richly decorated parchment, was enclosed in an ebony cabinet – seven feet high and four feet broad – with the monogram of the Cardinal and the date of Manning's jubilee engraved on it.[43] He later used to show the cabinet to some of his visitors, pointing out that this gift was 'the one incident in my life of which I am most proud'.[44] The Lord Mayor, Sir Julian Goldsmid, Sebag Montefiore, and Sir John Simon also pronounced words of congratulation, thanking Manning for his work in favour of the Jewish people. The Cardinal responded by saying that in his forty years of work in London all sorts of suffering, poverty, and vice had come before him. Manning declared that he could bear witness to the generosity and efficiency of 'my Jewish fellow-countrymen' in taking care of their children, the poor and the sick. 'Sometimes perhaps we have wronged one another', he added. 'For all are not Christians who are called Christians; and all are not of Israel who are called Israelites.'[45] He ended by saying that what he had done in 1882 he was ready to do again, if the occasion were ever to arise.

The occasion did arise soon enough; 1890 saw a worsening of the conditions experienced by Jews in Russia. Since 1882, their circumstances had been made harsher by the regulations introduced by the May Laws. Manning, again, signed a request asking the Lord Mayor for a meeting to complain on behalf of the Russian Jews. It was called for 10 December 1890, to take place at the Guildhall.[46] The Cardinal expressed his intention of addressing the meeting but, in the end, he was unable to attend.[47] He wrote to Sir John Simon, regretting the fact that he was too weak to be present. The long letter contained what he had intended to say, had he been at the Guildhall. In it, he supported the resolution exonerating the Tsar from condoning or being aware of the harshness endured by his Jewish subjects, and calling on him to order an enquiry into their sufferings. Manning, as he had done in 1882, also rejected the objection of those who maintained that this demand violated the convention of non-interference in the internal affairs of another nation. He answered that serious violations of the great and primary laws of humanity, whether in Russia or in Central Africa, 'not only justified, but called on, to intervene'. The public moral sense of all nations, he added, 'rests on this universal common law, when this is anywhere broken, or wounded, it is not sympathy but civilisation that has the privilege of respectful remonstrance'. How much more on 'behalf of a race who, in their past and their present and their future, demand of us an exceptional reverence: a race with a sacred history of nearly four thousand years; a present without parallel[,] dispersed in all lands, with an imperishable personal identity, isolated and changeless, greatly afflicted, without home or fatherland; visibly reserved for a future of signal mercy'.[48]

Manning's active public life was coming to an end due to debilitating old age. He died on 14 January 1892. On the occasion of his death the *Jewish Chronicle* published a long article recognising in him 'one of the most disinterested friends of the Jewish community ... His sympathies were never bounded by a Creed. They were in the highest sense Catholic ... He was essentially human, and was a splendid illustration of the moral worth which different forms of religious training are capable of constructing.'[49] The presidents of the Board of Deputies and of the Anglo-Jewish Alliance sent their joint condolences to the Provost and Chapter of Westminster. It was a brief text but it gave an unintended answer to a question Manning had asked himself in his address at the Mansion House meeting in 1882: 'Am I my brother's keeper?' They said of the Cardinal:

> By the broad and unsectarian charity which he preached, and the large-hearted benevolence which he practised; by the eloquent denunciation of religious persecution and intolerance; by his devoted work on the Committee of the Mansion House Fund for the Relief of the Russo-Jewish Refugees; by his assiduous labours in the interest of the toiling masses of the metropolis; by his noble life and the uniform kindliness and courteousness of his manner, the lamented Cardinal earned for himself the esteem and admiration of all classes and the sincere and enduring gratitude of the Anglo-Jewish Community.[50]

Manning's death did not mark an end to the involvement of the archbishops of Westminster in Jewish issues. His successor, Cardinal Herbert Vaughan (1832–1903), who had been a member of the Emigration Committee of the Mansion House Relief Fund set up in 1882, continued having an active interest in the welfare of the Jewish people and was later instrumental in obtaining from the Archbishop of Malta the removal of the latter's imprimatur from a publication renewing the Blood Libel.[51]

Notes

1 There are only passing references in the standard biographies to Manning's involvement in Jewish issues. Purcell's two-volume biography dedicates a short paragraph to the subject (Edmund Sheridan Purcell, *Life of Cardinal Manning, Archbishop of Westminster*, 2 vols [London: Macmillan, 1896], vol. 2, pp. 652–3); see also Shane Leslie, *Cardinal Manning: His Life and Labours* (London: Burns Oates & Washbourne, 1921), pp. 485–6; Arthur W. Hutton, *Cardinal Manning* (London: Methuen, 1892), p. 246; Robert Gray, *Cardinal Manning: A Biography* (London: Weidenfeld & Nicolson, 1985) does not mention Manning's interventions in favour of the Jews.

2 *Hansard's Parliamentary Debates*, 3rd series (1830–91), vol. 95, cols 1282–1314.

3 H. E. Manning to W. E. Gladstone, Rome, 20 January 1848, in *The Correspondence of Henry Edward Manning and William Ewart Gladstone*, 4 vols, ed. Peter Erb (Oxford: Oxford University Press, 2013), vol. 2, pp. 260–1. Many years later – in an article under the title 'Is the Christianity of England worth preserving?' – Manning was still affirming the country's Christian character and defended the importance of preserving it through

the Christian education of its people. See Henry Edward Manning, *Miscellanies*, 3 vols (London: Burns and Oates, 1888), vol. 3, pp. 49–78.
4 *The Times*, 19 October 1859, p. 11. French troops were then protecting the last remnants of the Papal States.
5 'The Mortara Case and the Murphy Case', *Dublin Review*, 46 (1859), 19–42; Josef L. Altholz, 'A Note on the English Catholic Reaction to the Mortara Case', *Jewish Social Studies*, 23:2 (1961), 111–18. See also Charles Langsdale's letters to *The Times*, 26 October, p. 8, and 7 November 1858, p. 9.
6 Manning recognised that part of the problem was that there was not enough provision of Catholic schools for the education of poor Catholic children. This was to be the first priority of his episcopacy.
7 For the Catholic effort to found and fund schools for the poor, see Vincent Alan McClelland, *Cardinal Manning: His Public Life and Influence, 1865–1892* (London: Oxford University Press, 1962), pp. 26–87; also Eric G. Tenbus, *English Catholics and the Education of the Poor, 1847–1902* (Abingdon: Routledge, 2016). For the difficulties encountered by Manning in transferring Catholic children from non-Catholic workhouses and other institutions to Catholic schools or orphanages, when these were available, see Edward St John, *Manning's Work for Children* (London: Sheed and Ward, 1929), pp. 88ff.
8 Henry Edward Manning, *Denominational Education: A Pastoral Letter to the Clergy and Laity of the Diocese of London* (London: Burns, Oates & Co., 1869), p. 10.
9 *Jewish Chronicle*, 25 June 1869, p. 4.
10 *Ibid.*, 16 July 1869, p. 9.
11 *Ibid.*, 8 September 1876, p. 358.
12 Custody of Children Act, 1891, c. 3, sections 3 and 4.
13 Antony Polonsky, *The Jews in Poland and Russia, Vol. II, 1881 to 1914* (Oxford: Littman Library of Jewish Civilization, 2010).
14 For the political Anglo-Jewish reaction to the expulsion, see Daniel Gutwein, 'The Politics of Jewish Solidarity: Anglo-Jewish Diplomacy and the Moscow Expulsion of April 1891', *Jewish History*, 3:2 (1991), 23–45.
15 John Doyle Klier, *Russians, Jews, and the Pogroms of 1881–1882* (Cambridge: Cambridge University Press, 2011); I. Michael Aronson, *Troubled Waters: The Origins of the 1881 Anti-Jewish Pogroms in Russia* (Pittsburgh: University of Pittsburgh Press, 1990); and 'The Pogroms of 1881–84', in John D. Klier and Shlomo Lambroza (eds), *Pogroms: Anti-Jewish Violence in Modern Russian History* (Cambridge: Cambridge University Press, 1992), pp. 44–61. These studies conclude that the violence was not actually instigated by the government.
16 *The Times*, 11 January 1882, p. 4 and 13 January 1882, p. 4. The report was published afterwards in pamphlet form under the title: *Persecution of the Jews in Russia 1881* (London: Spottiswoode & Co., 1882).
17 London Metropolitan Archives, Board of Deputies of British Jews, Minutes Book 12 (April 1878 to February 1889), fol. 135. A later approach to Lord Salisbury in 1891 on the part of the Board of Deputies with occasion of renewed troubles for Russian Jews received a similar response (Board of Deputies of British Jews, Minutes Book 13 [March 1889 to October 1898], fos 82–3 and 95).

18 University of Southampton Special Collections, Anglo-Jewish Association, Council Minutes Book, vol. 2 (October 1881 to June 1895), fos 12–13. A special meeting was held on 24 January 1882 to discuss the Russian situation.
19 H. E. Manning to Sir John Simon, 8 December 1890, *The Times*, 10 December 1890, p. 3.
20 The list of signatories included few political figures or members of the aristocracy. Among those who signed the petition were Charles Darwin, Benjamin Jowett and Matthew Arnold. There is no record of whether Manning invited the Duke of Norfolk; his name is not among the signatories.
21 Lord Shaftesbury, the Evangelical social reformer, had been approached at the beginning of the campaign to promote the Mansion House Meeting. Shaftesbury shared contemporary Evangelical concerns for the welfare of the Jews, the Evangelical interest in the Jewish people's physical return to Palestine, and on the prophecies about their future restoration and conversion. See Donald M. Lewis, *The Origins of Christian Zionism* (Cambridge: Cambridge University Press, 2010).
22 *Observer*, 22 January 1882, p. 5.
23 The resolution was supported by Canon Farrar, who attended the meeting in representation of the Archbishop of Canterbury.
24 *The Times*, 2 February 1882, p. 4.
25 *Ibid.*
26 *Ibid.*
27 *Ibid.*, 3 February 1882, p. 7.
28 *Observer*, 5 February 1882, p. 1.
29 *Jewish Chronicle*, 10 January 1896, p. 15. For the activities of the Mansion House Committee (later known as the Russo-Jewish Committee), see Eugene C. Black, *The Social Policies of Anglo-Jewish Jewry, 1880–1920* (Oxford: Blackwell, 1988), p. 254. An idea of the complexity of the operation and numbers of people involved may be found in the pamphlet published by the Liverpool Commission of the Mansion House Relief Fund: between April and July 1882 they dealt with 6,274 Russian Jews in transit to the United States and Canada, at a cost of some £30,000 (*Persecution of the Jews in Russia: Mansion House Relief Fund. Liverpool Commission* [Liverpool: n.p., 1882]).
30 *Jewish Chronicle*, 17 February 1882, p. 14. The great numbers of poor Jewish refugees coming to England was a prospect unwelcomed by the *Chronicle*, which concurred with the policy of sending emigrants on to America. It also suggested at one time that those who were not real refugees should be sent back to their countries of origin. See David Cesarani, *The Jewish Chronicle and Anglo-Jewry, 1841–1991* (Cambridge: Cambridge University Press, 1994). Many Jews were economic migrants from areas where pogroms had not taken place. The Jews of Habsburg Galicia, for example, although enjoying toleration, had also joined the migratory current. The immigration question was also taken up by both houses of Parliament. The Jewish population in Britain in 1880 was about 60,000. It is estimated that from 1881 to 1914 between 120,000 and 150,000 Jews from Eastern Europe settled permanently in Britain; many others stayed for shorter periods en route to other countries, particularly the United States.
31 For further details, see the bibliography in note 15.

32 The exchange of letters, dated 25 and 26 March 1882, was published by Berendt Salomon in the *Jewish Chronicle*, 7 November 1890, p. 7.
33 Arthur Markowski, 'Anti-Jewish Pogroms in the Kingdom of Poland', in Glenn Dynner, Antony Polonsky and Marcin Wodziński (eds), *Jews in the Kingdom of Poland, 1815–1918* (Oxford: Littman Library of Jewish Civilization, 2015), pp. 235, 248, 252.
34 Thomas of Monmouth, *Life and Miracles of St William of Norwich*, ed. Augustus Jessop and M. R. James (Cambridge: Cambridge University Press, 1896, reprinted 2011). The first volume of the *Life* had appeared in 1150. See also E. M. Rose, *The Murder of William of Norwich: The Origins of the Blood Libel in Medieval Europe* (Oxford: Oxford University Press, 2015).
35 Darren O'Brien, *The Pinnacle of Hatred: The Blood Libel and the Jews* (Jerusalem: Hebrew University Press, 2011), pp. 9–55.
36 Lorenzo Ganganelli, *The Ritual Murder Libel and the Jews: The Report by Cardinal Lorenzo Ganganelli*, ed. Cecil Roth (London: Woburn Press, 1918). Appeal to Ganganelli's report was made in 1889 by Hermann Adler, in his letter to Manning, and in 1913 by Lord Rothschild, in a letter to the Vatican Segretario di Stato, asking for confirmation of its existence and content, as both had been disputed. Cardinal Merry del Val answered in the affirmative (*ibid.*, pp. 31–3). Besides the popes named here, others like Urban IV, Clement VI, Paul III and Gregory X had also published condemnations of the Blood Libel.
37 Letter of H. Adler to H. E. Manning, 11 December 1889, *The Times*, 7 February 1890, p. 3. The book was Henri Desportes, *Le Mystère de sang chez les juifs de tous les temps* (Paris: Savine, 1889). The author, a French priest, also produced other anti-Semitic works.
38 Letters of H. E. Manning to H. Adler, 13 December 1889 and 16 January 1890, *The Times*, 7 February 1890, p. 3.
39 University of Southampton Special Collections, Anglo-Jewish Association, Council Minutes Book, vol. 2, October 1881–June 1895. The Board of Deputies also decided to associate itself with the address.
40 *Jewish Chronicle*, 11 July 1890, p. 9.
41 *Jewish Chronicle Supplement*, 31 October 1890, had on its front cover Manning's portrait. It also included an engraving depicting the cabinet.
42 *Jewish Chronicle*, 31 October 1890, p. 18; see also *The Tablet*, 1 November 1890, p. 701. The list of signatories of the address included, among others, Dr Adler, Lord Rothschild, barons Henry de Worms and Ferdinand de Rothschild, Sir John Simon and representatives of the Committee of Deputies of British Jews and trustees of the Russo-Jewish Mansion House Fund. Some of the signatories, Lord Rothschild among them, sent their apologies for not being able to attend the presentation. The supplement of the *Jewish Chronicle* contained a report of the meeting and of the speeches of those who took part in it.
43 The cost of cabinet and testimonial was £105 18*s.*; the Board, the Anglo-Jewish Association and the Russo-Jewish Committee each contributing a third of the cost (London Metropolitan Archives, Board of Deputies of British Jews, Minutes Book 13 [20 March 1889 to 12 October 1898], fo. 84). It has not been possible to locate the present whereabouts of the cabinet and testimonial. Manning's will of 15 October 1890 left 'all the

residue of his state and effects whatsoever and wheresoever including all manuscripts, papers, books copyrights unto the Very Reverend Robert Butler' and other members of the Oblates of St Charles (London, Westminster Diocesan Archives, Manning Papers, AP 3/13).

44 Letter of Lewis Emmanuel, *Jewish Chronicle*, 25 March 1892, p. 16.
45 *The Tablet*, 1 November 1890, pp. 701–2; also in *Jewish Chronicle*, 31 October 1890, p. 19. Manning's address was subsequently published by *L'Osservatore Romano*.
46 A report on Russia was published at the time, in advance of the meeting: *The Persecution of the Jews in Russia. With an Appendix Containing a Summary of Special and Restrictive Laws* (London: Wethermeier, Lea & Co., 1890). A second edition containing a report of the Guildhall meeting and a text of the memorial to the Tsar was published in 1891. This latter pamphlet, like the previous one, was issued for free distribution and circulation by the Russo-Jewish Committee.
47 Virginia Crawford visited the Cardinal a few days before the Mansion Hall meeting. In her diary (6 December 1890), she recorded Manning's words on that occasion: 'Whereas Christ prayed for them in the last hour of His Life on earth, I feel we ought to treat them with all the justice of the old law, and all the charity of the new', and a great deal more to the same effect, and at the end he said with a laugh 'Now, if my Catholic subjects like to break their teeth against that file they are welcome' (quoted in Robin Gard, 'The Cardinal and the Penitent: Cardinal Manning and Virginia Crawford', in Sheridan Gilley (ed.), *Victorian Churches and Churchmen: Essays Presented to Vincent Alan McClelland* (Woodbridge: Catholic Record Society, 2005), p. 43.
48 H. E. Manning to Sir John Simon, 8 December 1890, *The Times*, 10 December 1890, p. 3. The American Cardinal James Gibbons, of Baltimore, joined Manning in protesting against the pogroms.
49 *Jewish Chronicle*, 15 January 1892, pp. 12–13.
50 *Ibid.*, 29 January 1892, p. 6.
51 *Ibid.*, 22 September 1899, p. 18.

EU authorised representative for GPSR:
Easy Access System Europe, Mustamäe tee 50,
10621 Tallinn, Estonia
gpsr.requests@easproject.com

www.ingramcontent.com/pod-product-compliance
Ingram Content Group UK Ltd.
Pitfield, Milton Keynes, MK11 3LW, UK
UKHW051848210426
5322IPUK00024B/609